THE AUTOBIOGRAPHY OF
Alec Stewart
playing for keeps

BBC
BOOKS

Patrick Murphy, who assisted Alec Stewart in writing this book, has reported on cricket and football for BBC Radio Sport for the past 25 years. He has covered twelve England cricket tours, most of them involving Alec Stewart. This is his 41st book; he has collaborated with, among others, Imran Khan, Wassim Akram, Allan Donald, Viv Richards and Graham Gooch. He has also written acclaimed biographies of Brian Clough and Ian Botham. He lives in Worcestershire and plays village cricket to a stunningly mediocre standard.

Statistics kindly provided by Wendy Wimbush.

Published by BBC Books, BBC Worldwide Ltd,
Woodlands, 80 Wood Lane, London W12 0TT

First published in hardback 2003. This paperback edition published 2004.
Copyright © Alec Stewart 2003 and 2004
The moral right of the author has been asserted.
ISBN 0 563 52143 0

Commissioning editor: Ben Dunn. Project editor: Sarah Lavelle
Copy editor: Steve Dobell. Designer: Annette Peppis. Picture research: David Cottingham. Production controller: Christopher Tinker

Set in Helvetica Neue and Minion
Printed and bound in Great Britain by Mackays of Chatham, Kent
Covers printed by Belmont Press Ltd, Northampton
Plate sections printed by Lawrence-Allen Ltd, Weston-super-Mare
Plate sections originated by Radstock Reproductions Ltd, Midsomer Norton

BBC Books would like to thank the following for providing photographs and for permission to reproduce copyright material. While every effort has been made to trace and acknowledge all copyright holders, we would like to apologize should there have been any errors or omissions.

Section 1 Courtesy the Author except: Empics page 5 (top left); Patrick Eagar pp. 5 (below), 7 (below); Getty Images pp. 6, 7 (above), 8.
Section 2 © BBC p. 5 (top right); Camera Press p. 7; Colorsport p. 2 (top left); Getty Images pp. 1, 2 (top right & below), 3, 4, 5 (top left, centre & below), 6 (below), 8 (top left, top right and below); Reuters/David Gray p. 6 (above).

If you require further information on any BBC Worldwide product call 08700 777 001 or visit our website on www.bbcshop.com

contents

acknowledgements

There are many people along the way who have helped me progress as a cricketer and person.

Micky Stewart, my father, has been the biggest influence on me from an early age, coaching, supporting, criticizing constructively and passing on his vast knowledge at every opportunity.

Geoff Arnold, the former Surrey and England great, has also played a huge part in my development, bowling to me for hours on end, and fine-tuning my technique.

Alan Knott, the greatest wicketkeeper ever and my boyhood hero, must also take credit for turning me from a batsman who kept a bit into a wicketkeeper who has kept for England in more than 70 Test matches – even though it meant my favoured opening-batting career was short-lived!

Midland-Guildford CC in Perth, Western Australia, where I spent eight fantastic winters playing 'A' grade cricket in the 1980s, and, in particular, Kevin Gartrell, who coached me throughout my time with the club. The experience I gained from my time 'down under' has been immeasurable.

Duncan Fletcher, the current England coach, has been able to take my game forward even at this stage of my career – a credit to his skills.

There have been many other people who have helped me fulfil my goals and ambitions and I thank you all.

In the course of putting this book together, thanks must go to Pat Murphy for his tireless work and continued enthusiasm. I would also like to thank Gerrard Tyrrell for his invaluable legal advice concerning my career, and for his help in drafting chapters 12 and 16. My thanks also to Ben Dunn, Sarah Lavelle, Steve Dobell and all at BBC Worldwide for doing such an excellent job of publishing my autobiography.

My largest thanks, though, on the cricket front are without doubt to Surrey CCC for everything that they have done for me from the moment I walked through the Hobbs Gates to begin my professional career. The support and help that they have provided throughout my career has been top class. Playing for the biggest and best club in the land has been an honour and a privilege. Success on the field was not always there to begin with, but in recent times the hard work that people have put in over the years has resulted in all the silverware that is being won now. To everyone associated with the club, I thank you for making my times at Surrey enjoyable ones, and I am sure there are many more to come.

My biggest and greatest 'thank you' has to be to my fantastic wife Lynn and our two wonderful children Andrew and Emily. Being married to, or children of, an international cricketer cannot be easy. Having to put up with months apart owing to the long tours overseas, and my varying moods depending on how the day's play has gone, is never straightforward. For Lynn to have been left to bring up the children on her own is far from ideal, and for the children to grow up with a daddy who isn't around as much as he or they would like is tough on us all. To have such an understanding family is a credit to them and I know how lucky I am.

CHAPTER ONE
sport in the blood

I was eight years old when I set my mind on being a professional sportsman and I'll never forget what crystallized that ambition. I was at Loftus Road, in West London, watching Queen's Park Rangers playing Chelsea. My Dad was with me, and there was a noisy crowd of about 25,000. Caught up in the atmosphere of a local derby, I told Dad that I'd love to be a footballer or a cricketer one day. As any father would, he tried to be realistic about it, and when the attendance figure was announced over the tannoy he said, 'Son, out of the 25,000 here today, only one person could possibly have a chance of playing sport for a living.' Apparently I wasn't thrown by those odds. I looked around at the crowd and said, 'All right – that one will be me then.'

Nothing Dad said about the hard work or the competition put me off at all. In fact, from that day on I was convinced that if hard work, ambition and dedication had anything to do with it, I'd be a sportsman. I was simply hooked on sport and accepted early on that nothing was going to deflect me from realizing that dream.

Luckily for me, we were a sports-mad family. My Dad, Micky Stewart, had played cricket for Surrey and England, and football in the old First Division for Charlton Athletic. Mum was a fine swimmer and hockey player. My sister Judy, who is three years younger than me, had played netball for Surrey and was also good at gymnastics and hockey. Neil, my elder brother, was good enough to have played cricket for Surrey seconds. As early as I can remember, Neil and I played cricket in the back garden, with Mum umpiring if Dad wasn't around. Mum would also drive us to football and cricket matches if Dad was working. She wasn't one of those long-suffering mothers who help out just because it's expected of them. Mum loved seeing us play sport and she gave as good as she got when we talked about sport at home – and that was almost every waking hour!

It was never a burden having a father who had played sport for his country. Sometimes it was hard for us all when he was away for long periods in the winter on overseas tours, and I remember the telephone calls he would put through to us. We missed him greatly, but Mum was terrific at filling the gaps. The street cred at school wasn't bad either – 'What does your Dad do, then?' 'Oh, he's the captain of Surrey and he used to open the batting for England.'

When Dad was still playing for Surrey, Neil and I used to love going up to the Oval in our school holidays. We would carry his gear into the dressing-room, meet the players and then, at lunchtime or when we were waiting for him to change at close of play, we'd bat and bowl on the outfield. We never wanted it to end. He finally retired from first-class cricket in 1972, and we were at the Oval when he walked out to play his last game, a Sunday League match. He was given a tremendous standing ovation and I remember thinking, 'He must have been pretty good.' He certainly was, as I found out later after researching his career: eight caps for England, 49 hundreds in first-class cricket, one of the best fielders ever close to the wicket, captain of Surrey for ten seasons and fit enough still to be playing at the age of 39. Must run in the family! Later, he would be my first coach, both with Surrey and England,

and he has been a huge influence on my career.

Because Dad was so good at both football and cricket, my brother and I used to get first-class coaching from him at an early age. Every Sunday morning, he would take us down to the Pearl Assurance Sports Ground at New Malden – five minutes' drive from home – and we'd practise with him, summer and winter. He'd show us how to tackle, to juggle a football and the proper technique for shooting. When we practised cricket in the nets, he would simulate a match situation. He'd shout out, 'Right – ten to win, and you've got six balls left.' If you played a good shot through extra cover, he'd tell you that was two runs knocked off the target, with so many deliveries left. If you got out, it was game over, even though there were as many as five balls left. He was never harsh on us, simply competitive. When I played football in matches, I would ask him to mark me out of ten, and although we'd often have disagreements over his assessments, it was fantastic to have someone of his expertise and knowledge to encourage and educate us.

We had no idea then about the need for mental strength in professional sport, but Dad drummed into us the importance of having confidence in your own ability and the necessity of doing all that you could to give yourself a chance of success. He'd go in goal at the Pearl Assurance Ground, telling us we had ten penalties each, and he'd dive around, doing his best to stop every one, making sure that we earned our goals. No self-indulgence from father to his two sons: it all had to be worked for. He had taken his FA coaching badge and had managed Corinthian Casuals, so he obviously knew what he was talking about. It made it even more effective that he could show us exactly the right way to do things.

One piece of cricketing advice from Dad stuck with me

all through my career. I had shown an aptitude for batting early on, and even though Neil was the more technically correct batsman, I could always time the ball well. Dad told me, 'Always look to dominate when you're batting. You're the boss, the guv'nor. Never stop wanting to hit the ball, but work out when's the right time to attack or defend – and defend positively; don't be tentative.' Dad obviously saw something in me when I batted as a youngster, and he saw his role as getting the best out of me while keeping that aggression. He was a different sort of batsman from me – more of a deflector, very patient – but, like me, he would happily play the hook and the cut to the short ball. He spent hours and hours stressing the importance of showing the full face of the bat to the ball, and hitting through the line. In my career I've been lucky with my natural sense of timing when playing well, but also that the man who coached me just happened to have played for England and knew what he was talking about.

All of my family were ultra-competitive in their attitude to sport and that's what fostered my huge desire to win. I used to get frustrated with Neil when I wanted to play cricket in the back garden and he was happy watching sport on the television. I'd go out to set up the stumps and stand around waiting for him. Neil was a lot more laid-back than me, and he probably didn't make the best use of his talent as a cricketer. He's a very good cricket coach now, and he is a help to me at times when I need some fine-tuning, but when we were kids, I was the one desperate to get out there and play. He had an amazing memory for sporting facts, and even at the age of six or seven he knew all about racing form and could recite the names of any touring cricket side from watching them on TV.

Once we started competing against each other after I'd managed to drag him away from the telly, the battles were ferocious. I still have the scar on my right forearm that I picked up at the age of seven when I went straight through the French windows from our back garden. We had decided to have a race, and instead of being sensible and running away from the windows, we ran towards them. I put my arm out to stop myself and you can guess the rest. I won the race, though – despite the three-year age difference.

At Christmas, the Stewart household was a hotbed of competitiveness with various games being played by the five of us. The Question of Sport board game was a nightmare for our parents. Mum would ask the questions, Dad would do his best to make sure none of the kids ever won, and I would contest every answer on the card that I hadn't got. 'That can't be right!' was the complaint from me at regular intervals. None of us knew how to take it easy if ever there was a competition.

We were so into sport that Neil and I used to conduct imaginary football interviews on a tape recorder. Colin Bell of Manchester City and England was one of my heroes at the time (although John Hollins of my beloved Chelsea Football Club was my all-time hero), while Neil would pretend to be Francis Lee or Mike Summerbee from the same City team. So Neil would be the interviewer and I'd be Colin Bell, reflecting on my hat-trick that day. Then he'd have a go as Mike Summerbee, talking about the way he had laid on the goals from the right wing. My parents still have those tapes, but thankfully I've never had to listen to them! And, of course, the brothers would try very hard to outdo each other in the interviews…

We also got to know genuine football heroes. Dad knew a lot of the Fulham players very well when we were kids, and the likes of Bobby Robson, George Cohen and Alan Mullery – all internationals – used to go out socially with my parents. Years later, when England played a one-day international up in Durham, I met up with Bobby Robson. Now Sir Bobby, and the manager of Newcastle United, he hadn't forgotten the times when we would play football or cricket in the sitting room. He loved his cricket and often played in Surrey benefit matches. I remember Alan Mullery giving me one of his England shirts when he was a regular in the national side.

Until I was about fifteen, I was hoping that my career in professional sport would be as a footballer. In my naivety I assumed that, as long as I worked as hard as I could at the game, listened to sound advice and concentrated a hundred per cent, then I'd be good enough to earn a living out of football. I didn't think that my confident forecast to Dad at Loftus Road a few years earlier would come back to haunt me. You don't when you're a youngster, fanatical about sport, and lucky enough to have some fantastic support from your parents. You just enjoy it all and expect to keep progressing.

My football had gone well by the time I was fifteen. I was a natural goalscorer – a hundred goals one season for Clarions FC, a Sunday side – and then I played for Mitcham Royals, a feeder club for Wimbledon and Chelsea. Scouts from Crystal Palace and Chelsea came to watch the games, and I also played a few matches for Wimbledon's Youth team. Glyn Hodges, who later played for Wimbledon, Sheffield United and Wales, was in the same team as me at Mitcham Royals and he didn't seem to be all that much better than me. So it seemed a logical progression to me that I'd eventually be offered a contract by one of the London clubs. When you're that young, and all you want to do is play sport, failure doesn't enter your thoughts. I soon got the wake-up call, however, and it was what I needed.

The coach at Mitcham Royals at the time was Dario Gradi. We knew we were lucky to have him at the club, because he had worked at Chelsea, Wimbledon and Derby County while still a young man. Later he went to Crewe, where he nurtured young players and coached them superbly before sending them on to the big clubs, to become internationals. Think of David Platt, Geoff Thomas, Rob Jones, Neil Lennon and Robbie Savage, to name just a few. So this bloke knew what he was talking about when it came to spotting talent and polishing up rough diamonds to shine as professionals. Unfortunately, Dario didn't think I had it in me to progress at football. He used to give me a lift home from training every Monday night, and we'd talk football, so of course he soon knew how ambitious I was. I was scoring goals for Mitcham Royals, and at the age of fifteen I thought I had a chance. Dario didn't agree. Knowing that I had another promising string to my bow in cricket, he thought I should opt for that. I never asked why he had that opinion about my footballing abilities, because I was too disappointed. Anyway, he knew far more than I did about spotting young talent, so who was I to argue?

Even though I never stopped loving the game of football – I was crazy about both sports – from that day on I dedicated myself to cricket. I'd played my first game of proper cricket at the age of seven – for the cub scouts at the Decca Sports Ground in Tolworth. Neil was playing for the cubs and I'd got into the habit of taking along my kit in my parents' car, just in case the team was a player short. As luck would have it, someone was ill and I played against boys who were all three years older than me. When I went in to bat, I was given a harsh reminder that you should always wear a box, even at that age, as I was hit in a rather sensitive area! At least the story has a happy ending: batting at number seven, I scored 41 not out to help win the match. I was presented with the Man of the Match award, a little wooden shield, by Graham Roope, who would eventually be a team-mate at Surrey. He never mentioned any of that when we used to change together in the same dressing-room, so presumably it was not as memorable to him as it was to me!

I got into club cricket early, being picked for the third team at Malden Wanderers when I was eleven, and it was great to play with and against adults. I remember scoring 40-odd for them in a close game that we won, early on in my time at the club, and helping the team win that match gave me a real buzz. Even then, it was apparent to me that producing the goods when it was really necessary was the hallmark of a sportsman. I'd been lucky to learn that from Dad earlier than most boys of the same age.

I was also fortunate to go to a grammar school that prided itself on its cricket teams. Tiffin School, at Kingston, was only ten minutes' drive from our home at New Malden. It was a rugby-playing school, which meant no football, but I still managed to play both codes in the winter – rugby for school and club football on Sundays. The standard of cricket at Tiffin was excellent. During my five years at the school we lost just three matches. Neil was captain of the first eleven and he had a better cricket brain than me as a schoolboy. Neil was a good enough all-rounder to go as captain on a National Schools' Association tour to Canada with the likes of Neil Foster and Raj Maru in the team. For fifteen years he ran the indoor cricket school at East Molesey and now he coaches Surrey's Under-14s and Under-15s, as well as being head cricket coach at the City of London Freeman's School in Ashtead. Both Ian Ward and Mark Butcher, team-mates of mine with Surrey and England, have worked with Neil.

So my cricket education in my early teens involved

playing during term-time for Tiffin School on Saturdays and Malden Wanderers on Sundays, and in the summer holidays for the Wanderers every weekend. I scored my first hundred at the age of twelve – 111 not out for Tiffin against Kingston Grammar. Dad gave me a pocket-money bonus of 50 pence as a 'well done' present. Funny how things like that stick in your mind. In that summer of 1975 I averaged 44 for my school, and in the handbook for that year our cricket master, Mr John Rice, wrote some very complimentary things about me, including this: 'Alec Stewart is one of the best cricketers I've seen at that age. Check the first-class averages in ten years' time.' Thanks very much, Mr Rice, and well called – exactly ten years later, I was awarded my county cap by Surrey.

Mr Rice's words were very nice to read, but I knew that hard work was necessary if I was to achieve my ambition of playing professional cricket. Dad never had to push me in that direction, because even as a boy I was always an avid practiser. I just loved all team sports and it seemed obvious to me that if you wanted to improve at your chosen sport then you needed to work at it. I never lacked advice from Dad, but he was very good at not pressurizing me. He knew I had something to build on as a cricketer, because he liked the way I performed under pressure from an early age. But I needed his support one day when I was just fifteen.

I'd just started to keep wicket at that time, graduating from the back garden to the school eleven. I found it relatively easy to catch the ball, and whenever we played in the garden, I'd put on the gloves and enjoy taking the throws and the catches. Dad encouraged me to work at my keeping, saying that it was another string to my bow, even though he saw me as a batsman first and foremost (and certainly not a bowler!).

So I was picked for various South of England sides, as I moved up through the age groups, occasionally keeping wicket and doing well. The regional tournament took place at Oakham School, with the English Schools' Cricket Association eleven to be chosen from all the under-15s competing in the games. This would be a big challenge for me, and a step up after I'd shown what I could do in my own region. I scored fifty in one match and kept wicket well throughout. All the other lads in our game said I was bound to get picked for the final eleven, especially as I ended up third-highest scorer in the whole tournament. All our parents were present at Oakham as the ESCA President and former England batsman Hubert Doggart read out the eleven names. Mine was not one of them. I was bitterly disappointed, as I really thought I had done enough to make it. Somehow I managed to bottle up my emotions – good training for later years with England! – but I didn't say a word to my parents on the journey home. Dad kept looking at me in the driving mirror, spotted that I had tears in my eyes and wisely left me alone with my thoughts. It was my first rejection in cricket, but it came not long after Dario Gradi had marked my card about my football prospects. I was a confused fifteen-year-old that day. Later Dad and I had a chat about it, and he told me not to worry. I was grateful for his continued support after that blow.

I found out years later what Dad had been told by Hubert Doggart about my omission from the eleven. Mr Doggart said, 'Oh, Micky, he's going on to greater things.' Not much of a consolation for the old man, or for me when I eventually discovered the reasoning. There was another interesting sting in that particular tail. The lad who displaced me as wicketkeeper was one R. C. Russell, from Stroud in Gloucestershire. That's right, Jack Russell, a brilliant wicket-keeper and true eccentric, who would later be a great friend and team-mate with England. Jack and I have never seen each other as rivals, even though we have replaced each other at times in the Test team. In those days he was already a legend on the schools circuit. I'd played against him for the South of England against the West, and he was clearly an absolute star with the gloves. He also had a moustache ridiculously early for one so young! So Jack understandably got the nod ahead of me for the ESCA eleven as wicketkeeper, but to this day I'll never understand why I wasn't picked as a batsman. After all, Hubert Doggart presumably thought Jack Russell was also destined for greater things...

At least I was improving as a cricketer, and handling the differing challenges you get when stepping up a grade or two. I played for Surrey Under-16s, then the Under-19s (at the age of sixteen), and for South of England Under-15s, then Under-19s. Strangely enough, I never played for the full England team at any age level, or even the 'A' side. The only England team I have represented was the senior team, and I was nearly 27 when that finally came about. The feeder system that's been in place for more than twenty years usually gets the talented young player into the mix fairly early, but that didn't happen in my case.

Yet the fire to succeed remained in me. I dedicated myself to doing all I could to make the professional grade. When I left school at the age of seventeen, in the summer of 1980, I had set my heart on getting a contract with my home county. By then Dad had returned to the Oval as cricket manager, but I expected no favours from him. I wanted to make my way on merit, although I was aware of the good fortune I'd already had in getting such a grounding at home. I played for Surrey Young Cricketers in the last half of the 1980 summer, against lads like Neil Williams, Alan Wells, Neil Foster and Chris Penn from the other southern counties, and I did well, scoring four centuries. My aim was a contract with Surrey, and if that meant working with my father, then I'd deal with it.

For a couple of years I had been gearing myself up for the challenge of being a professional cricketer. It wasn't something I'd have dreamt of talking about to friends and team-mates, but my family knew the extent of my ambition. I was sixteen when I blurted out my dream to my school careers master, Mr Reg Dodgson. He and I both knew I was no academic, and after the usual routine discussion about my prospects he asked me what I wanted to do with myself. Straight out I answered, 'I want to play professional cricket.' Mr Dodgson smiled, I suspect in some relief, and said, 'Yes, I think that's a good idea.' I doubt if he actually knew what it would take to make the grade in county cricket, but he seemed happy that I had a career calling. Quite simply, I'd set my heart on playing cricket for a living, and I wanted it to be with Surrey. If that was to happen, I had to sort out a satisfactory working relationship with the man I had made that rash forecast to at Loftus Road all those years ago: my Dad – and, if I was lucky, my future boss.

CHAPTER TWO

one ambition realized

In October 1980 I signed a professional contract with Surrey. I was seventeen and thrilled to bits. The contract was for two years which meant that, for six months from 1 April until 30 September each year, I would be paid £1,780, plus any bonuses that would be earned by success. Seventy pounds a week to play professional cricket! I could have done it for nothing. I had been earning £42 a week, helping out in a sports shop in Kingston, and to be paid so much more to play for Surrey was wonderful.

There was one slight complication about the contract. It was signed by me at home – no haggling over terms! – in front of my delighted father. That was the concern for both of us. Dad had returned to the Oval as Surrey's cricket manager the year before, and he had identified the need to enlist young talent as a priority. He had sent me down to Sussex for a week's trial in 1979, under the tutelage of three former Surrey colleagues, Geoff Arnold, Stewart Storey and Arnold Long. I had stayed a week at Stewart's house and had done well.

In fact I made my county second-eleven debut for Sussex, the year before I signed for Surrey. It was against Hampshire and I kept wicket. I had kept in my last year at school, and for Malden Wanderers, and enjoyed it – but nothing had prepared me for keeping to Tony Pigott for Sussex seconds. He was far and away the fastest I'd ever had to keep to, but I must have done well. Dad was given good reports by the cricketing fraternity in Sussex. He needed other opinions about me, because he wanted to be certain that I had the necessary qualities to be a professional player. He did not want to offer me a contract and then see me fail, or his own neck was on the block.

It was against Sussex that I made my second-team debut for Surrey, in 1980. I had sat my history 'O' level paper on the first morning of the three-day game, and I was still in my school blazer as Mum drove me down to Horsham. They stuck me in at first slip, instead of making me run around in the outfield or lumbering me with the usual young player's position – short leg. I didn't get a bat in the first innings and finally came in with 7 runs needed. I had to face the big South African, Garth le Roux, who had been so impressive in the Packer series over in Australia just a few months earlier. Le Roux was a tough, competitive character who gave nothing to anyone on the field, least of all a seventeen-year-old whipper-snapper wearing a cap instead of a helmet. I never thought to ask to borrow a helmet. I played and missed at the first one, and got behind the line for the other two before David Thomas smacked the winning runs in the next over after which I had to face the big guy again. It was exhilarating for me – from sitting history 'O' level to facing one of the world's fastest bowlers in a couple of days. And – amazingly – I passed the exam as well!

I played a few more second-team games for Surrey and did well. It was fantastic playing at the Oval, even if there was no crowd to watch us. I took no notice of the grimy flats, or the grim surroundings when the weather was bad. The famous gasometers were an inspiration to me. 'I'm playing on a Test match ground,' I'd say to myself. 'Those gasometers were here when Bradman played his last Test on this ground.' Just a few years earlier I'd been happily playing on the outfield with my brother, and now I was out there in a competitive match. I had become familiar with the home dressing-room at the Oval, knew all the senior players and respected them hugely. Some of them – like Pat Pocock, Graham Roope, Intikhab Alam and Robin Jackman – had played with Dad for Surrey, and then gone on to represent their countries. I was inspired by the chance of playing in the same side as them. The passionate desire to play for Surrey full-time burst out of me during that period. I'd set my heart on getting a contract with Surrey and I wouldn't be lacking in attitude, fitness or desire. Others would have to judge whether I had the necessary talent.

Fortunately for me, Dad thought I had enough of that. It must have been a difficult call for him, because he knew how it would go down in one of the toughest dressing-rooms on the county circuit if the manager's son took up a precious place on the staff and failed to come up to scratch. From the days when Surrey won the championship seven years in a row in the fifties – with Dad in the side – there had been a confidence and a swagger about Surrey that made them unpopular with other sides. I'm sure Dad was just as confident as his team-mates. He used to tell me when I was very young, 'It's up to you to boss the bowlers; let them worry about you,' and that you should walk on to a cricket pitch looking as if you deserve to be there. I suppose I've never lost that swagger – our detractors call it the Surrey Strut – and now that we have won the championship a few times in recent years, the 'strutting' is just as prevalent as it was in Dad's great days at the Oval.

That collective swagger among Surrey players also meant there would be no hiding place for the manager's son if he wasn't good enough – and they would not just be talking behind my back. Surrey has long had a reputation for plain speaking in the dressing-room. At the age of seventeen, with every day just seeming like an opportunity to play cricket for hour after hour, I was too naïve to appreciate such things. All I wanted to do was play cricket for Surrey. But Dad had to weigh up such matters, with harmony in the dressing-room a priority. I was now one of the best young cricketers available to Surrey, but would I be mentally strong enough to withstand potential suggestions that I only got on the staff because of my Dad?

So we sat down at home on that October day in 1980 and talked through all the pros and cons. Dad told me that Sussex, Nottinghamshire and Hampshire were all showing an interest in me, but he would love me to play for Surrey. 'But you'd also be playing for me – and I'm your Dad.' He explained to me what nepotism meant, that some might suggest I'd been favoured because of his involvement. To counteract that, we had to agree to certain behavioural rules. In a work environment, I'd call him 'manager' or 'ger', the shortened version, and he'd call me 'Alec' or 'Stewie'. Because I'd still be living at home, we'd obviously travel together a fair amount. It was fine to talk cricket during those periods – and the more, the better – but I was not to expect any favours from him. If I had done well, I would get the same support and encouragement privately that I'd always had when growing up – but the risk of a perception of favouritism meant that he may have to appear harder on me at work than on any of the others.

From that day onwards, I only called him 'Dad' when we were either away from work or in a family environment. I even used to say to Mum, 'Does the manager know?' if a cricketing matter cropped up at home. Twenty years later, when he was President of Surrey CCC, I'd call him 'President' at the Oval – not to pull his leg, but out of respect for the office he held. No one can ever say I got preferential treatment in my career because of my father, and I'm very glad about that.

It was only after I'd convinced Dad that I could handle

our relationship at work that he felt he could offer me the playing contract he believed I deserved. I'm sure he concealed some of his concerns, trusting to good luck and common sense that we'd be able to handle it, but nothing came my way that was gift-wrapped. Mum would never allow me to have the Surrey feathers on any of my gear until I had signed a professional contract. You had to earn the right to wear them. She was right. I know I'll sound like an old fogey, but I do think that a lot of young cricketers coming on to current staffs have too many things laid out on a plate for them – sponsored cars, free mobile phones, bat contracts, attention from agents… I believe you have to earn status by performances, rather than just because you're now on the staff. I'm glad it was harder for me when I started at Surrey, because I appreciate the perks more.

One thing I was very lucky to have was Dad's advice about planning my career. Although I was only seventeen when he offered me a contract, I was clear about my aims. I wanted to play for England, after succeeding with Surrey. I wasn't so stupid as to assume that any of that would be a doddle, but I was already dedicated, in love with the game and totally committed to giving it everything. Dad set me achievable aims during those early years at Surrey. He said that in the first two years on the staff I should concentrate on my batting, and set out to be a front-line batsman. I should also look to develop my wicketkeeping, which would still be a useful extra string to my bow. Above all, I had to enjoy keeping wicket if the chance came along, or else not bother. One of my heroes was the great Alan Knott; I would try to imitate him by sticking my collar up and having my hankie peep out of my pocket, and all that made keeping wicket fun. It would never be a chore to me, but it was sensible to concentrate initially on my batting.

To be honest, I believe too much has been made of my

relationship with my father as it impacted on both our careers. The fact is that once we had sorted out the parameters on the day I signed my first Surrey contract, we just got on with it. When he left Surrey to be the England coach in 1986, it was to be three years before I came into contention as an international player. After that we had another three years working with England and our only concern during that time was to avoid being photographed together in a staged picture. It was too easy a line for some of the media – the England coach and one of his players, who just happens to be his son – so we wouldn't make it easy for them to run ill-considered articles alongside photographs of us. We just acted professionally when we were at work. I was lucky to have inherited some of his sporting genes and to be part of a sports-mad family, but the rest of my progress was down to me.

When Dad felt I should be singled out for criticism at work, I got it, and in front of my team-mates. In the 1984 season he left me out of the NatWest quarter-final against Warwickshire, when I felt I was batting particularly well. I told him I should be playing but I got the archetypal put-down – 'That's your opinion, but I'm the manager and you're not playing. I make the decisions.' I wouldn't let it go, saying it was the wrong decision, but that was no more than any other frustrated player would say to the manager.

It was Dad who put the call through to me at Bournemouth, where I was playing a second-eleven game against Hampshire, to tell me I was about to make my county debut for Surrey. It was August 1981, and I'd been doing reasonably well in the seconds for my first year as a full-time pro. But our first-choice keeper, Jack Richards, was injured, so I was off to Cheltenham. I was very nervous, although our captain Roger Knight was most supportive and understanding. The first day of the championship match (Saturday) was washed out, so I had to wait for my first-class career to start. The following day was a Sunday League match and I hit the winning runs – only 8 not out, admittedly, but it was terrific. A mate of mine managed to record the finish off the television, and I later watched my first ball, sent down by the Australian Mike Whitney, just shave my leg stump. We scraped home by three wickets against an experienced Gloucestershire attack, and I really enjoyed the tension of those closing overs.

I batted at nine in the championship match and was dismissed twice by David Graveney. Years later, Grav would be the chairman of selectors when I was appointed England captain, and then he'd be the one to make the phone call, telling me that I was to be replaced in the job. Despite a few ups and downs, however, we've had a good relationship – except when he reminds me about my first two innings in first-class cricket!

That was to be my only championship match in 1981 and for the next couple of seasons I marked time. Jack Richards possibly saw me as a bit of a threat as wicket-keeper-batsman, although I don't know why. At the time he was one of the best in the county game, and in 1986 was good enough to score a Test hundred in Australia. But Jack was a hard, difficult individual. He once said to me, 'If you want me to help you with your keeping, then clean my pads for me.' I assumed that was his sense of humour at work.

In 1987 Jack was in contention for the keeper's role for the forthcoming World Cup, with Paul Downton and Bruce French the other candidates. A provisional squad of thirty was announced for the tournament when we were playing at Lord's against Middlesex. My name was in the thirty – as a batsman who could keep wicket if needed. With my father due to be the coach, Jack took it badly, clearly getting hold of the wrong end of the stick. He obviously felt that I was a threat to him as the wicketkeeper-batsman and that I had my father to thank for being in the squad, because he gave me some terrible abuse in the field that day. I couldn't do anything right for him, as he made every one of my throws to his gloves look poor while making disparaging remarks about my fielding. In the end I shouted at him, 'Grow up. I don't pick the squads!'

Ironically, a few months earlier there had been a push to select me for the England squad for a one-day tournament in Sharjah. This was soon after England's triumphant tour of Australia, when Richards had kept in all five Tests and done very well. Mike Gatting, the captain, had told Dad, who was his coach, that he and the vice-captain John Emburey wanted me on the trip. Dad was happy about that but insisted that those in power should realize that the initiative had come from Gatting and Emburey, not the father of Alec Stewart. In the end, my selection was vetoed by Peter May, the chairman of selectors. He rang up Dad, his old Surrey team-mate, and said, 'Let's stick with the chaps who've done so well in Australia – anyway, it might be difficult for you taking your son.' I didn't know about that for years afterwards, but it shows that Dad's involvement with England didn't exactly smooth my progress!

Judging by his sulky performances that day at Lord's, Jack Richards would have hit the roof if I'd been chosen for Sharjah a few months earlier. The fact that I was being considered as a batsman would have made no difference at all to him. I'd scored nearly 1700 first-class runs the previous season, by the way. Jack Richards liked to have something to moan about, even if it was irrelevant. He was not a man for the team ethic and he was out of cricket by the time he was thirty. He's now living somewhere in Holland and doesn't keep in touch with anybody at the Oval. It's a pity, because he was too talented to leave English cricket as early as he did. However, his harshness did me a favour without his realizing it. It helped the toughening-up process that's necessary to survive in professional sport.

Mind you, I did not notice much collective toughness when I played for the Surrey seconds during those formative years. In fact I soon realized how soft and social second-team cricket could be, which made me all the more desperate to get into, then stay in, the first team. The general attitude among the Surrey boys was poor. To them it was an extension of club cricket – play the game, have a bit of a laugh, then go out and have a drink. Some of my Surrey team-mates had great talent, but lacked ambition. They weren't prepared to try everything they could, at the risk of failing.

I've never been one for alcohol, apart from the occasional glass of wine. This is not a case of getting on a moral high horse: alcohol just never suited me. I've just preferred to give myself every chance to succeed as a sportsman and that didn't embrace drinking. When I was in my teens, Mum promised me £100 if I didn't touch alcohol before I was eighteen. I cleaned up easily, and bought her a new fridge-freezer! I'll do the same with my two children, giving them an incentive to make judgements about alcohol when they are older and less likely to be tempted by their friends who do it just for a dare or because they think it makes them appear adult.

So the social culture of second-eleven cricket didn't appeal to me. At close of play, the tray for the Surrey players would consist of eight or nine pints of lager, a gin and tonic, a pint of milk and a soft drink for me. Then it was off to a pub or night club, and when I asked for an orange juice, I'd be told, 'If you're not having a proper drink, then I'm not buying you one.' It all became too much of a macho exercise. I couldn't get my head around the idea of getting drunk, then expecting to perform at your best on the field next day after bragging about how much you'd slung down your neck a few hours earlier. I just didn't believe that would bring you professional success, and thought all that would reduce my chances of being successful in my job.

Not many of my colleagues agreed with me, though, and for a time I got restless at Surrey. There was a lack of professionalism among the players in the seconds, and even when I had a spell in the first team I noticed a lot of moaning and back-biting. There was plenty of competition for places among the batsmen, and the older players seemed to get preference as a matter of course. There was a bit of a 'them and us' attitude, and I felt that we weren't playing positively enough. I was frustrated at not getting a decent run in the first team. I contemplated a possible move to Sussex, who were still interested in me, as I thought I might get regular first-team cricket more quickly there – but I was undecided.

In the end Dad and I sat down to talk about it, and I told him about the interest from Sussex. We sifted through the pros and cons, and finally came to the conclusion that I was a Surrey man through and through. It was the only county that I really wanted to play for, and I would just have to try even harder for a first-team place. I've never regretted that decision.

It was lucky for me that I learned my trade as a batsman at the Oval, when I did. The groundsman Harry Brind had dug up the square in the late 1970s, and brought in hard, true, bouncy wickets which suited my style of batting. I could stand up and play my shots, hitting through the line of the ball. My back-foot play thrived on the even bounce and my timing was ideally suited to the pitches at the Oval. With the ball not moving all that much off the seam, I didn't have to go a long way forward provided that I transferred my weight properly and played straight. I'd go back and across, but not a long way. On other grounds, such as Derby or Worcester, I've been an lbw candidate, where the ball seams around on low, slow pitches. I need to go forward more to nullify the movement and that does negate my effectiveness. But the Oval has been brilliant for my development.

I've always relished the short ball for the cut, pull and hook shots, and when I first started in county cricket, there was no limitation on the number of short balls you faced. There were stacks of world-class fast bowlers in English cricket at that time, and they usually let you have it around your ears. Wayne Daniel, the West Indian, used to take a particular delight in bombing me, hitting my bat as hard as anyone during that period. I faced some fantastic fast bowlers in the early eighties – for example, Richard Hadlee, Clive Rice, Michael Holding, Malcolm Marshall, Imran Khan, Joel Garner, Garth le Roux, Winston Davis, Ezra Moseley – all of whom were at their peak, and not emasculated by the subsequent restriction on short balls per over.

It was an education to bat against any of this lot. Just ask Martin Bicknell – a seventeen-year-old number ten. In one of his first matches for Surrey, Martin faced Hadlee on a typical Trent Bridge wicket – green in the middle, with the ends shaved to help the spin of Eddie Hemmings. His innings lasted three balls and it consisted of a bouncer, a yorker, then another bouncer that was gloved up to the bowler who caught it easily. Hadlee grinned at him and said, 'Now, we can't have you schoolboys hanging around too long, can we?' Welcome to the big time. It was an education for a young cricketer to come up against someone of Hadlee's class, experience and control. Like the others, he would test out your ability and mental strength. Could you cope?

The only time I have ever doubted myself was after Michael Holding broke my jaw and then I had to face him again. In the last game of the 1983 season, we were playing Derbyshire at the Oval and Holding dropped one short that didn't bounce as much as I expected. It came back at me like an off-cutter and at the last moment I turned away. I wasn't wearing a grille with my helmet and it hit me flush on the jaw. I didn't want to come off, but the physio insisted otherwise. Off to hospital for an X-ray, to be told that the jaw was broken. I would be wired up for about six weeks. My winter trip to Perth had to be delayed.

It was a nightmare. I tried to talk, but couldn't. I sipped protein drinks and leek and potato soup through a straw, day after day, and basically existed on a liquid diet. Three weeks after being hit, I said I wanted to go for a net. It was vital to get back into the saddle as soon as possible. I went down to the East Molesey Indoor Centre with Dad, Neil and Geoff Arnold, now second-team coach at the Oval. The first delivery from Geoff was a yorker. I dug it out, the ball bounced straight up off the concrete surface, hit my visor and knocked off my helmet! Nearly back to square one. Then they tested me out on short deliveries. I found it fine and I was relieved to have got through it. But something was still bothering me: facing Michael Holding again.

Typical of a great guy, Holding had already rung Dad to wish me a safe and speedy recovery. But he wouldn't feel that way when he bowled at me next time, and I wondered when that would be. Not for another eighteen months, because in 1984 he toured England with the West Indies and they had no match against Surrey. So it was May 1985 before I came up against him for the first time since the accident. I put on an arm guard for the first time in my career, and as I sat waiting for my turn at number three, I thought, 'Wouldn't it be nice if Mikey isn't bowling when I get in?' It was the first and only time I have ever had reservations about facing a fast bowler, rather than about how I was going to play my innings. When I went in, Mikey was bowling and the first ball he gave me was a quick bouncer. I ducked under it and felt fine after that. There's no happy ending to this story for me, because I got the best nought I have ever made. Holding gave me nothing at all, Paul Newman and Ole Mortenson also bowled brilliantly, and although I lined everything up well, letting the dangerous ones go through to the keeper, I couldn't get off the mark. Eventually I nicked one to slip, and walked off feeling I'd scored fifty rather than a duck! But I'd come through an important psychological test against a great fast bowler.

Over-confidence was often my downfall in those early years with Surrey. Once I got a run in the first team, in the second half of the 1983 season, I started to play very well. I was capped in the 1985 season, scoring 1000 first-class runs for the first time, and there were times that summer when I felt nobody could bowl at me. It sounds ridiculous, I know, but I was only 22. The following summer, I got myself out twice when a hundred was there for the taking.

At Headingley, I played exceptionally until I holed out to mid-on off Phil Carrick for 90. I was really annoyed at missing a deserved hundred, and at the end of play one Geoffrey Boycott came up to me and said, 'You played brilliantly today, but you're an idiot for getting yourself out that way. You'd never see me doing that – hitting against the spin when you're near a hundred!' Later in that game, Boycott showed me how to fashion an innings, when he scored an unbeaten hundred. It was a fascinating exercise and it showed how much he knew about the art of batting.

Later that summer in 1986, at Taunton, I was set for a hundred before lunch. I was timing the ball beautifully on a superb batting wicket and all was right in my world. Ian Botham and Joel Garner opened the bowling for Somerset, but that didn't intimidate me. I got to 78 off 66 balls, then carelessly holed out at mid-off. I walked off in disgust, telling myself, 'I should have got a hundred here, but now it's one o'clock and I've got myself out. I'm going to have to sit in the pavilion for the rest of the day, kicking myself.' And I did. Viv Richards cheered me up, though. He'd watched my innings from slip and later on told me how well I had played. He also told Dad not to curb my attacking instincts. It's safe to say that I haven't compromised all that much in my approach to batting down the years, but turning fifties into hundreds has been a problem. I really admire and envy the conversion rate of batsmen like Martin Crowe and Graeme Hick.

The adrenalin rush as I hit a bunch of boundaries has often been my undoing. I go past my areas of scoring and over-reach myself. Certainly I ought to have scored around seventy hundreds in my first-class career, but instead have made too many attractive seventies and eighties. Geoff Arnold was quite right to advise me against hitting every ball for four, but I'd never forgotten Dad's advice about letting the bowlers know that you're in charge.

So, by the mid-1980s, I had at last established myself in a tough school, the Surrey first team. I was beginning to be thought of as Alec Stewart, rather than the son of my cricket manager. Standing on my own two feet, and being judged on my own merits, were vital for my self-confidence. Now it was up to me to develop mentally as a professional cricketer. That ambition saw me travelling to the other side of the world every winter, but it was something that had to be done if I was going to fulfil my dreams of playing for England.

CHAPTER THREE

my grounding
down under

When Robert Key became an England player in the summer of 2002, he was good enough to mention to the media a conversation I'd had with him a couple of years earlier. We'd bumped into each other at an awards dinner and I talked to him in no uncertain terms about his physical fitness and general attitude to first-class cricket. I rated the Kent batsman and told him so, but also stressed that he wouldn't do himself justice in the game unless he toughened up mentally and physically. My advice was to do what I did years before, which was to go to Perth, Western Australia, and play grade cricket. It proved to be the making of Robert, as it had been for me. As a proud Englishman I don't like to say this – especially after recent hammerings by Aussie cricketers – but I must admit that without the finishing school provided to me out there, I would not have made the leap to becoming a regular England cricketer. There is simply nowhere better in the world to spend an English winter if you have serious ambitions about a career in cricket.

My association with the Midland-Guildford Cricket Club in Perth, which started in October 1981, lasted for eight years as a player and I view the club and the city as my second home. Some people have said that there's a bit of Oz in me, and it's certainly true that my brashness and the competitive spirit that I wear on my sleeve are not exactly in the style of the understated Englishman. The Australian experience really helped to develop my hard-nosed, never-say-die attitude to playing cricket, something that all the best players possess. I make no apologies for playing it as hard as I possibly can, within the rules, because that comes with the mother's milk in Australia. They simply can't accept coming second and in terms of preparation and mental strength they will do everything they can to give themselves the best chance of winning. To a teenager like myself on his first visit to Australia, that was a valuable lesson and it gave me an advantage over others back home who were happy just to take time out and lounge around, waiting for April and the start of a new season.

I first encountered Midland-Guildford in the winter of 1980–1, when I toured Australia with the Surrey Under-18s. The chance came just after I'd signed my contract with Surrey for the following season and Dad, who was to manage the tour, thought it would be a great experience. I had to find £400 to fund the trip, which I managed to do with an assortment of odd jobs that included parcelling up tools in a factory and clearing out furniture in house removals. That helped me appreciate even more the privilege of going out there at the age of seventeen.

We played all over Australia and for the last ten days we were in Perth. I stayed with the Slater family. Keith, an off-spinner, had played for Australia in the 1960s and was also an excellent Aussie-rules footballer. He was terrific to talk cricket with, and I became good friends with his son, Scott, whom I played against when he represented the Western Australia Under-19s. Scott asked me what I was doing the following year after my first season with Surrey, and Keith told me that it would be a good idea to come out there again and develop my cricket. I loved Perth, its climate and its friendly people right away and I was very keen. Dad was equally enthusiastic, and said to me, 'If you play twelve months a year, that'll fast-track your career.' All agreed, then.

Originally I was going to play for the University side in Perth – about the nearest I'd ever get to a university! I'd been hoping to be able to keep wicket as well as being a batsman, but that wasn't available to me at the University club. Keith suggested I went to the Midland-Guildford club, where he had played throughout his career, because the facilities there were excellent and good people were in charge. How right he was.

The most influential person there for me was Kevin Gartrell, a fantastic man of cricket. He'd played for the club for years, then Western Australia, and he had a massive influence on my approach to cricket. Kevin couldn't do enough for me – I called him my Australian Dad – and it was a proud moment for me when I returned to Western Australia as the England captain in 1998, when we played at Lilac Hill, the home of Midland-Guildford. Typically, Kevin was there at Perth Airport at two o'clock in the morning to meet me. I could never understand why he'd do so much for a young English cricketer when I played for his club, but he would say, 'You're not a bloody Pom out here, you're one of us.'

I know he liked my positive attitude and he worked on that, encouraging me to play my shots and not be overawed by anything. He had a great respect for the game. Once Midland-Guildford won the grade final by refusing to play after heavy rain had made the wicket too wet. Kevin felt it was wrong that we had won without the opponents' having had a chance. He refused to celebrate the win, even though he was the club chairman, saying, 'That's not how we should play the game.' Kevin's attitude was that you gave it all you could on the field and, if you lost, you took it like men and licked your wounds. But nobody should have an unfair advantage.

Tony Mann was another tremendous person at

Midland-Guildford. He had played for Australia as a leg-spinner and was a good enough batsman to get a Test hundred as a nightwatchman. He captained the club and his knowledge of the game was excellent. An intelligent man, he was the best captain I have ever played under. He was enthusiastic, a brilliant fielder, a top-class spinner – I got fifteen stumpings off his own bowling one season – and he had that Brearley-esque quality of inspiring his players with clear, decisive thinking and excellent man-management skills. He was in his late thirties when he returned to the club as captain/coach and I was lucky enough to have learnt from him. Tony Mann played it very hard, and it was fascinating, when he was bowling, to see him enjoy the mind games he was playing against the batsmen.

When I pitched up at Midland-Guildford for the 1981–2 season, I was expecting a few hard-nosed characters dedicated to getting stuck into this particular Pom. But there was none of that. They couldn't have been more friendly. That stopped, though, when it came to getting into the first team. It was clear to me that I would have to earn that promotion, after I was picked for the seconds for my first game. I got fifty in that first match, in which I also had to get used to an unfamiliar format: of 96 overs per side over two consecutive Saturdays, and if you batted second you could bat on for bonus points on the second Saturday, even if you had already passed the opposition score. So that went well for me and the following day I played for the Under-21s, keeping wicket well and scoring 60-odd. After that I was in the 'A' team, and I stayed there for the next eight seasons until I was picked for my first England tour.

I loved that first season. The fact that I was a professional cricketer back in England meant absolutely nothing to my new team-mates, and I relished having to prove myself in their eyes and gain their respect. The practice facilities were superb and they were run very professionally. You were expected to be there for practice every Tuesday and Thursday night or you dropped down a grade at the weekend. I would get the train from ten miles away into Perth, then get another one out of the city to Lilac Hill, making sure I got there early, so that I could bat in good light against the best bowlers.

We had a net captain, who was very strict at allocating time. Arrive late and you'd be batting in the dark. You always had to wear whites in the nets and before starting you'd do one lap of the ground as a unit, developing the group ethic. After batting, there'd be full-on fielding practice, on a par with anything I've had at Surrey. And don't forget that these guys were amateurs, trying to get a decent game on the Saturday. There was nothing in it for them apart from pride in performance and a fantastic work ethic. I was in my element.

The standard of grade cricket was tremendously high, way ahead of club cricket in England and of a similar level to county second-eleven cricket. At Midland-Guildford, current Test player Bruce Yardley was a regular when he wasn't away on State or Test duty. Early on I played against Wayne Clarke – Yorkshire coach of the future and former Test bowler – and Bruce Laird and Graham Wood, Australia's Test batsman, and Terry Alderman and Bruce Reid, Australia's opening bowlers. So I'd be up against Test cricketers at the age of eighteen. I couldn't fail to improve. Tom Moody, a tall, gangly all-rounder, was just coming into the 'A' side when I started at the club. Tom was still at school, but they believed in starting you early if you were good enough. Tom and I both had the same willingness to work hard and we practised for hours together at Kevin

Gartrell's indoor school. Kevin would supervise the bowling machine, cranking up the speed when necessary, and you'd bat for at least two hours at a time, getting into the right groove. Kevin wasn't like your typical MCC coach, banging on about the high left elbow. He used to say, 'If you're going to get out, then get out doing something rather than just fiddling about.' He'd set you targets when you batted in the nets – like nominating a specific area of around ten metres in width and making you play the ball in that area, ball after ball after ball. Along with Dad and Geoff Arnold, Kevin Gartrell has had the biggest coaching influence on my career.

Eventually Kevin found me work at the sports shop he ran in Perth with Keith Slater, but for the first two years I had to pay my own way. I'm glad I did. It underlined that it was no holiday for me. My return flight was around £500 – about one third of my county salary – and the whole trip cost me about £1,500. To make ends meet, I took all sorts of unglamorous jobs. One involved throwing sand on to a railway track to collect the oil that had been spilled, then sweeping up the sand and oil. That one only lasted a day, as I got fed up. Then I worked in an animal feeds warehouse, along with my Surrey team-mate Nick Faulkener. One day we were told to sweep out a warehouse that was thick with dust that had accumulated over ten years. We wore masks, but coughed all day as we tried to get rid of the dust. Then I stacked shelves in a supermarket from ten at night till two in the morning. I'm glad I got into the school of hard knocks, because I saw the whole experience as an investment into getting me to play for England. I wanted to see a return on my investment. That's why I told Robert Key, 'Don't see it as a holiday out there – do it off your own bat and it'll mean more to you.' I've never been one to spend my money indiscriminately, but I didn't begrudge the Australian expense for a second.

The hardness you need for top-class cricket was always there. In my first match in Perth, one of the batsmen nicked it to me behind the stumps and I caught it at shin height. No question – he was out. Except the umpire didn't agree. The batsman stood his ground, which he was entitled to do, and he got away with it. So I got the message very quickly. Kevin Gartrell also drummed into me the message of not walking. He was once playing for Western Australia against the MCC tourists and when he nicked one to the keeper he walked straight away without waiting for the umpire to make a decision. He had almost got to the pavilion gate when he heard the umpire running up behind him to shout, 'I've given you not out. You must come back and continue your innings.' Kevin said that he felt in retrospect he had belittled the umpire by making the decision himself. His advice was to leave all that to the umpire and let him get on with his job. That was fine by me and I joined the non-walking brigade. The Australians wouldn't have it any other way. As Mike Atherton remarked to Ian Healy in a Test in Sydney, after nicking a delivery through to the keeper and then standing: 'When in Rome.'

When I played for the first time at the famous Western Australian Cricket Association (WACA) ground at Perth for Midland-Guildford, I creamed one to extra cover and the bloke caught it at ankle height. I stood my ground, hoping I'd get away with a bump-ball adjudication – and I did. Once, in a big cup game, I nicked one to the keeper and, just as the umpire was about to send me on my way, I shook my head. It was a bluff and I got away with it. I got a hundred to win the match, and the opposition exchanged a few pleasantries with me. But I knew that every one of them would have stood there too, leaving it to the umpire.

I tried it on and got lucky. That's accepted as the norm in Australia and I'd have been a fool to try to buck the trend.

That was quite a contrast to the view of my first captain at Surrey, Roger Knight. Now Roger was a lovely bloke and very good to me when I first came into the side, but his background of public school and Cambridge University meant he had an approach to walking that was in direct contrast to that of my Australian team-mates. In a match at Northampton during my second season with Surrey, I edged Sarfraz Nawaz to wicketkeeper George Sharp and I stood my ground, but was rightly given out. As I was taking off my pads in the dressing-room, my captain came over for a quiet word of advice. He said, 'If you want to get on in this game, you need to walk when you've nicked it – otherwise you'll get a reputation and the umpires will start doing you.' I told Roger that in the previous winter I'd got a rollicking from my Midland-Guildford team-mates for walking without leaving it up to the umpire, but he said, 'This is how it works in England, word gets around very quickly.' Well, it may do, but in my time I haven't seen too many who walk when they're on nought, rather than 155. Before I went to Australia, I walked for 90 per cent of the time, but not after 1982. The overwhelming majority of professional cricketers nowadays don't share Roger Knight's view, so why should I make it harder for myself? This may not be very admirable, but surely it's realistic and understandable?

Another reason why you wouldn't walk was that you didn't get many opportunities to bat and if you wanted to stay in the side you needed to make each one count. Over a six-month season at Midland-Guildford, we'd play fourteen matches spread over two Saturdays and eight one-day games lasting fifty overs a side. So you might get three or four innings a month. Compare that to the days when we played three-day championship cricket in England, where you might clock up five innings a week! No wonder the Australians approached every match as a special occasion, even at grade level. They make the most of every opportunity that arises.

My wicketkeeping improved during my time out there. When I first went to Perth, I hoped to get the chance to take my keeping forward, and I managed to retain the all-rounder's role throughout my eight years at the club. Tim Zoehrer, who was a team-mate at the club, kept wicket for Australia during some of my time there, but whenever he returned from Test duty, I kept the gloves, which was very reassuring. They wouldn't have continued to believe in me if they had thought I wasn't as good as Zoehrer, and that got me thinking about my wicketkeeping standards. Bearing in mind Dad's advice when I joined Surrey ('Have two strings to your bow'), I really relished the challenge of keeping wicket out in Perth.

In my last two years at Midland-Guildford we won the grade league, and I'm certain that, in that period, our side was as good as over half of today's first-class counties in England. We had current Test players such as Tom Moody, Brendon Julien, Tim Zoehrer and Joe Angell available, as well as a marvellous captain in Tony Mann. From my time with M-G, it's clear that the Aussies believe that their grade cricket is equivalent to our first-class cricket, and having spent so long out there, I can't give them much of an argument, such is their intensity and competitive strength. As a generalization, I would say that an average grade cricketer is as good as a second-eleven cricketer in England, but with a better attitude. No wonder they are so good at cricket in Australia. Every other state in Australia has the same set-up that impressed me so much in Perth.

This professional approach to their cricket also

extended to drinking alcohol. Now I know the cliché about Aussies downing can after can of beer after a match, but I never encountered a drinking culture at Midland-Guildford, compared with what I experienced in second-team cricket with Surrey. No one ever had a go at me in Perth about having a fruit juice, rather than a stack of beers. Kevin Gartrell, who runs the club, doesn't drink, but there was no peer pressure there. They take their cricket so seriously that nothing ever got in the way of preparing for a match, not even beer. In my experience, those amateurs were more conscientious than a lot of county professionals.

Every year, I returned to England a better player. For the last five seasons I won the awards for champion player and best batsman at the club, and I cherished those honours. One year I even broke the record for most runs, surpassing the great Barry Richards who had played there for two seasons. The interesting aspect of those awards is how the club perceived me, an English county cricketer. On the honours boards it says: 'Alec Stewart, Midland-Guildford and England'. Not a word about Surrey. They don't rate county cricket out there. They believe they helped turn me into an England cricketer and see no reason why Surrey should get any more of the credit. From the minute I walked into that club in 1981, I received no anti-Pom treatment, probably because they decided I was one of them, loaned out to Surrey for half the year, rather than the other way round.

I was so lucky to learn my batting trade on two such excellent surfaces as the Oval and Lilac Hill. The bounce was fast and true – I could play my shots on both squares and trust my attacking instincts. Kevin Gartrell was very good at teaching me to combat the extra bounce I would encounter in Perth after arriving from England. He'd get me in his indoor school, fire up the bowling machine and work on getting on top of the bounce. He had me playing it through extra cover off the full face of the bat, and only using cross-bat shots for the hook, the pull or the cut. So my back-foot play developed out there and helped prepare me for Test cricket, where the ability to play off the back foot is essential. Fast bowlers in Test cricket will try to keep you waiting all day for the chance to drive off the front foot.

The Australian experience meant I crammed in a lot of cricket while still young. During those eight seasons out there, I'd get to Perth by the start of October, just a fortnight after I'd finished at Surrey. I'd be out there till about the last week of March, then I'd be back at the Oval inside two days. I never felt jaded coming back to Surrey because I love the game so much and because you could remain fresh in Perth with just weekend games. Nevertheless I surprised myself when I worked out recently how many seasons I'd played on the trot. After the 1981 English season I played the first of eight seasons at Midland-Guildford, and then I toured with England every winter for twelve years. I took time out only for the 2001–2 winter, so after those twenty summers and winters playing cricket, the 2001 summer made it 41 consecutive seasons. Curiously, I didn't get tired as long as I was playing continually, and it's only when I have come up against a four-week window of rest at the end of a season or long tour that I start to feel tired for a week. I suspect the body is expecting to bat or keep wicket and doesn't know what to do when I'm not in the nets!

The famous Aussie verbal abuse was all water off a duck's back to me. The Surrey school I was growing up in wasn't exactly a place for shy young men, and as a naturally competitive, self-confident character, I was ready for it from the Aussies. I got a lot of stick from opposition players about being a Pom, that we were useless and so on, but it was all fairly harmless stuff. I gave it back with interest and it could get enjoyably heated at times. All part of toughening you up as a cricketer. I think too much has been made of sledging during my time in the game. If you play and miss and the bowler abuses you, so what? As long as it's not personal. In fact, I assimilated myself so quickly into the Australian way of playing that in one of my early games I was told off by the umpire for appealing too much. I replied that I only did that if I thought the batsman was out, which amused my team-mates. I've always believed in encouraging my fielders whenever I keep wicket, and that's a big thing in Australian cricket. Seeing me gee up the guys all the time confirmed their view that I was really an honorary Aussie!

I have nothing but fond memories of my time in Perth. I was only ever homesick on Christmas Day – somehow the thoughts of snow and roast turkey don't fit when you're on the beach in the hot sun. The time I spent there broadened my cricket experience massively, gave me the confidence to succeed and matured me as a person. When young English pros ask my advice now about what to do in the winter, I tell them I'll try to fix them up with a club in Perth – as long as they don't think they're going out on a jolly, to have a few beers, pop down to the beach and just play at weekends. You're there to improve your cricket, not your suntan. Some of them tell me they want their airfare paid, a car and free accommodation, and then I mark their card. You've got to put your hand in your pocket, pay your own way and prove yourself to sceptical people who don't rate county cricket. You must never be a whingeing Pom, but must work hard at the preparation and then stand up for yourself on the field.

From the age of ten onwards, the best young cricketers in Australia are up against each other in their particular age groups. There's no concept of recreational, Sunday afternoon cricket, as you get in England. No one turns up just to make up the numbers; they are all desperate to get a game. You could be playing against Test players in 'A' grade when you're sixteen. That happened to Tom Moody and Brendon Julien, for example. I don't particularly want to build up the Aussies, but they do have their structure right. When I first went out there, England held the Ashes and the Aussies had a bad few years under Kim Hughes, with several of their best players going off to South Africa. Then they won the 1987 World Cup under Allan Border, set up the Cricket Academy and stole a march on the rest of us. So a production line of top cricketers keeps rolling along, backed up by a fierce pride in performance and commitment, with the whole country firmly behind their national team.

Of course, their climate helps, but so too does their attitude, which is very positive. When you ask a typical English cricketer how he got on today, he'll say, 'Oh, I did OK.' Press him and he'll say, 'I got a few.' How many? 'I think it was 130.' An Aussie will say, 'I did brilliantly today – 130 not out, eighteen fours and three sixes.' He's not being an arrogant show-off, just open and enthusiastic about doing so well, knowing that there are plenty of bad days ahead. We should show more confidence in ourselves, more pride in what we have achieved in our profession. The Australians always look at the positives, and that comes out in their sport. The outdoor culture, the obsession with sport, the open spaces available – all that helps them to be fitter and healthier. Even though I'm exceptionally proud of my country, I do respect what Australia stands for, particularly in sport, and I feel very lucky to have experienced it at first hand for eight years. Perth was a great finishing school in every way.

At least I can remember when we gave the Aussies a good contest in Test matches. It felt great to be an England cricketer out there in 1986–7, when England retained the Ashes and won the Perth Challenge Cup. England was the best side in Australia that season during various competitions, and I never let my Midland-Guildford team-mates forget it! Training sessions were particularly enjoyable as I stored up a few more remarks to wind them all up. It was also pleasing from a personal point of view, because this was Dad's first England tour as a coach. So the Stewart family was treated with some grudging respect for a few months! I saw a lot of the England guys when they played in Perth, and two years later I got even nearer to them. In 1988, when England were in Sydney for the Bi-Centennial Test, I flew over to see Dad. I was having a great season in grade cricket, finishing up with over a thousand runs in just fourteen innings, and when Dad said, 'Bring your kit along and have a practice – we'll see how you're playing,' I was very excited. To be training with the England boys, getting a taste at close quarters of what it's like to be playing in a Test match, was wonderful, and I was convinced that my time in Australia had brought me closer to achieving that ambition. Now I needed to get over that next hurdle – and, two years later, I did.

CHAPTER FOUR

an england education

The message every English cricketer longs to get came to me on a September morning in 1989 at the Oval. I was practising in the nets with my team-mates before a county game when someone from the office came over to tell me I was going to India and then the West Indies with the senior England team. We would be playing in the Nehru Cup, a one-day series in India featuring all the major countries, and, two months later, four Tests and a one-day series in the Caribbean. So Midland-Guildford would just have to struggle on without me for the next six months. They got by! It was a good day for young Surrey cricketers. Keith Medlycott was going to be with me in the West Indies, while three more – Graham Thorpe and Martin and Darren Bicknell – would be off to Zimbabwe with the 'A' team.

I don't believe for one moment that Dad's position as coach had anything to do with my selection. He certainly hadn't tipped me off, even though he was in on selection as the coach. He thought I should hear about it in the same way as every other player. Quite right, too. I know he'd been encouraged by my progress, but I didn't discover all that much from him until years later. Apparently he'd been pleased to get a phone call one night in the 1987 season from David Lloyd about my development. David, who eventually became England coach himself, was on the umpires' list in 1987 and he stood in our match at the Oval against Somerset. I scored 105 and 93, and kept wicket well to Sylvester Clarke, the fastest, most intimidating bowler

I've played with or against. David phoned Dad to say, 'Micky, I've just seen England's next wicketkeeper-batsman. Your lad!' Very nice of him, but Dad kept that information to himself until long after I'd established myself in the England side and he'd retired as coach.

I had no problems at all with that, because I wanted to be treated throughout as just another player. Dad was always pushing me to improve myself, and his own competitive instinct came through in 1989, when I scored my first double hundred. It was against Essex, and after breaking my bat in the nets just before the start, I took the wrapper off a new one, didn't have time to break it in – and creamed my first ball, off John Lever, through the covers for four. Batsmen remember moments like that! I made 206 not out and Dad's message was, 'Well done, but you're still twenty-odd short of me!' His career best had been 227 not out. I liked competitive goals like that and when I got to 271 not out against Yorkshire in 1997, Dad at last acknowledged that I'd got one up on him!

His advice was proving to be very sound. He'd told me to keep working at my wicketkeeping as a second string to my bow as soon as I joined the staff, and here it paid off for me, eight years later. That summer I batted at number three and kept wicket. I played well, averaging 45 in the championship, but so did John Morris and Ashley Metcalfe for their counties. They were in contention, but I got in ahead of them, thanks to the extra wicketkeeping option I provided. Bruce French had decided to go to South Africa on Mike Gatting's rebel tour, so a deputy for Jack Russell was needed. Dad did tell me I was going as a batsman and number two keeper if necessary. As it turned out, I kept wicket in only one game in the West Indies, because Jack was so outstanding and he liked to play in every game. But I did offer versatility.

That short tour to India for the Nehru Cup was the ideal way to ease me into the international scene. I didn't really know many of the senior England players and the captain, Graham Gooch, was on a pedestal as far as I was concerned: a wonderful player and a tremendously dedicated one, who set a fantastic example. I was the only Surrey guy in the party, but there were young lads like Robin Smith, Angus Fraser, Jack Russell and Nasser Hussain to knock around with. Nasser and I roomed together – one the scruffy student, dropping his clothes on the floor, the other putting his clothes away neatly in the drawers. No prizes for guessing! We both contrived to leave our treasured England blazers in our hotel room as we flew off somewhere else on that tour, and that remained very like Nasser, but not me!

I was determined to make a good early impression on my first tour. It's the same for any cricketer: you want to settle down and impress team-mates who don't know all that much about you. A new player needs time to gel into the unit. I was pleased to get an unbeaten fifty and keep wicket well for half the allotted overs and even happier when I made my international debut, at Delhi against Sri Lanka. On a boiling hot, humid day I managed a run-out off the first over of the game with my first touch of the ball, coming in from extra cover with an underarm throw. That gave me a big lift, but I was nervous waiting to bat at number five. This was playing for my country, something I hadn't done at any level. I only made four, but we won by five wickets, and I hoped we weren't going to change a winning side.

I stayed in the team for the next game against Australia and, given my connections out there, I was delighted to see Tom Moody in their squad and even happier to crow at him after our brilliant seven-wicket victory. I was 4 not out at the end, totally overshadowed by a magnificent hundred by Wayne Larkins. On his day, 'Ned' was one of the most destructive English batsmen I've seen, and he smashed Geoff Lawson and the others to all parts of the ground.

We also won the next match, against Pakistan, by four wickets and I played well to get 31. Then came the semifinal, against Pakistan again, and defeat by six wickets. This match really brought home to me the massive gulf between county and international cricket. Salim Malik won the game with 66, a really clever innings. His placement was fantastic; with his wristy timing he was literally putting the ball exactly where he wanted. I'd seen Gordon Greenidge get a hundred against us for Hampshire a few years earlier and he was devastatingly powerful. I'd never seen a ball hit so hard; it was going past me at extra cover like a shell. But Salim's innings was different in terms of cricket brains. Allan Border had been just as awesome against us in an earlier game. I'd always thought of him as a tough, nuggety left-hander who didn't give his wicket away and played only a certain amount of shots. But he really hammered Gus Fraser at the end of their innings, hitting the ball like a baseball player. In four balls, he hit Gus for a six and three fours, and few players took such liberties against Gus in those days. It was an education for me to watch top players at close quarters and see how they could go through the gears when the pressure was on them.

That tour brought home to me just how much I still had to do. Dad's de-briefing when we got back home was down-to-earth. He mentioned my innings of 31 against Pakistan, telling me that I got myself out after doing all the hard work. I'd used my feet well against that great legspinner, Abdul Qadir, hitting him back over his head for a one-bounce four – but then I gave it away, going down the pitch and hitting it down the throat of long-off. I was also out with just ten runs needed for victory, which put the new batsman under unnecessary pressure. Dad's point was that in international cricket you need to learn very quickly when to make it all count. I had to grasp that before we turned up in the West Indies in two months' time. There would be no easy runs out there.

I certainly didn't take any unnecessary risks with the food in India after one dodgy experience early on. It was a schoolboy error. The English-style buffet in our hotel looked tempting and the cold meats seemed just the job, but they weren't as fresh as they could have been and I really struggled over the next two days. Now I'd learned my lesson. I've always been a plain, unadventurous eater – I don't think I've had ten curries in my life – and now I was taking no chances. My policy was: peel the fruit, have hard-boiled eggs, no salad and trust in grilled chicken. I did have some problems of communication, though. Once on that tour I asked for a four-egg omelette. After a patient wait, I was presented with four omelettes piled up on top of each other! But I was never ill again on a tour of the sub-continent. I might have gone slightly over the top, however, during the 1996 World Cup, in India and Pakistan. Over 44 days, I had the same meal of grilled chicken, mashed potato and broccoli every evening. Jack Russell had the same diet. Perhaps we did play it a little safe…

When I got back from India, I had two months to prepare myself physically and mentally for the challenge from the best team in the world. Facing Malcolm Marshall, Curtly Ambrose and the other fast bowlers on Caribbean wickets was going to be a massive test for us, and for newcomers like me in particular. Luckily, our preparation was spot-on. Goochy had taken over the captaincy from David Gower and he was convinced we had to be fitter and thoroughly prepared technically for what was going to be a very hard tour. That certainly tapped into Dad's thinking as coach, and they worked excellently together. For me, who had always worked hard in my preparations, this was just common sense. The old days had gone when you turned up in your blazer to sign a few bats the day before departure from Heathrow without any serious training. Goochy's motto was 'If you fail to prepare, then prepare to fail', and that certainly rang all my bells. The way the captain drove himself through the fitness tests at Lilleshall set the finest example to all of us. At the age of 36 he got the best results and when you add that to his magnificence as a batsman, he was the outstanding figure in the squad. Graham Gooch remains the cricketer I admire more than anyone else, for his achievements, his consistency and the professional example he set his players. It was a privilege to play with him.

Another great England opening batsman was very influential to me during the build-up to that tour of the West Indies. Geoffrey Boycott came to the specially arranged Headingley indoor nets eight times over a four-week period and I learned so much from him. Dad had always been an admirer of Boycs, Goochy got on well with him too, and they both believed that the younger batsmen in particular would benefit from his input. I lapped him up – he was fantastic. I'd always been a fan, admiring his classical style of batting, his technical mastery and the fact that you really had to work hard to get him out – but I hadn't realized how good he was in one-to-ones, getting his point over in a simple yet forceful manner. He talked such sense – it was brilliant. He even gave Goochy some good-natured stick in the nets, but when you watched at close quarters the authority and composure of the captain, you realized how much you still needed to learn.

Boycott really put us through it in those sessions. Proper, full-on stuff, with the fast bowlers operating off just 18 yards, each one armed with a new ball and trying to hit you on the head on a bouncy surface. Boycott told the bowlers, 'Hit 'em if you can; they've got a bat in their hands,' and his blunt message to us was, 'This is what it'll be like out there. Four balls an over that you can't score off, the fifth aimed at your rib cage that you might just fend off down to square leg for a quick single, and the last one in the over might be dropped to mid-on or mid-off, so you can steal a run. Nowt to drive, though – forget all those lovely cover-drives! Forget hooking or pulling – they'll all be too quick for you!' You'd bat for twenty minutes against that barrage, and it would feel like two hours. You'd be mentally worn out and thinking, 'Bloody hell, if it's going to be like this out there, where the hell will I get a run?'

I got hit on the visor once in those nets, ducking into the short ball. It was a misjudgement. I shook my head and was ready to face again after about ten seconds. Boycott stopped the net, walked down to me and said, 'When you get hit, check that you're OK and then give yourself as long as possible to re-focus. Ten seconds just isn't enough to be ready for the next ball.'

He was always constructive with me and he made me laugh as well. His ego was large, but it didn't get in the way of his teaching. I remember playing a poor shot and showing disappointment. Boycs came down to me and said, 'Look, you're doing well. You're just starting out in the big time, but I'm impressed. Everyone's entitled to play a bad shot once in a while, even the great ones – like Bradman, Chappell, people like Boycott.' I thought that was so typical of the great former player – his timing was excellent. He'd not try to belittle you, but lighten the mood, saying things like 'You big girl, my grandmother would've played a better shot than that,' but he had a smile on his face. When your net was finished, he'd spend five minutes or so with you face to face, making encouraging remarks but also suggesting how to cope better against the short, rising delivery or how to play with softer hands.

Early on, he told me, 'Look, I'll not try to turn you into a Geoffrey Boycott, I'll turn you into a better Alec Stewart than you are now. I've seen you play, I know you're a fine timer of the ball and that you like to hit the ball hard. But the higher the level you're playing at, the fewer bad balls you'll get to hit, so you need to tighten up in certain areas. I'll never talk you out of hitting the bad ball for four – some of the shots you play I couldn't. I won't change your style.' Despite his reputation as a dour batsman, Boycott valued flair, and when he coached us, you could see that he genuinely wanted us to improve, while still playing in our own personal styles. I never saw any of the selfishness that many of his contemporaries said they experienced.

I did wonder, however, where I'd score my runs when I got to the Caribbean. Geoffrey would reassure me, stressing the need to concentrate and work hard. When we got out there, it wasn't quite so difficult for batting as it had been in those nets at Headingley. Boycs was out there too, working as a summarizer for television. We had dinner together one night and he said to me, 'Headingley was harder, wasn't it? I only did all that to prepare you. If you work harder at the things you're not used to, then it helps your batting and it does become easier.' I thought that was spot-on. This was one of the few times that I worked with Boycs in an organized, structured way for England, because his TV commitments took him abroad a lot. Certainly he was always welcome when Dad was coach, and I continued to ask his advice when we bumped into each other.

Boycs never waffled but got straight to the point and talked common sense. I know he rubbed many people up the wrong way with his abrasive manner, but that was just his Yorkshire character. I understood and enjoyed his humour. He knew he had a powerful ego, but laughed at himself as well. When I was an established England batsman, having a good trot, and passing a few milestones, he wandered over to me and said with that familiar lop-sided grin, 'Hey – you may soon go past my Test runs, but it'll take you nearly twenty more matches!' No harm in that – we had mutual respect. He once paid me a fantastic compliment as we stood out on the square one Test match morning. Boycs had done his pitch report for the telly, I'd had my throw-downs, and we were talking cricket, as usual. He turned to me and said, 'If you'd been able to open for England all the time, rather than getting distracted by your wicketkeeping, you'd have gone down as one of England's greatest openers.' That, from a great England opening batsman, was a remark I still treasure. No one ever doubted that Geoffrey Boycott knew what he was talking about. Down the years he was always helpful to me. I know that if ever I rang him for some advice, he'd be there for me. I was delighted when he turned up to honour me on the *This Is Your Life* TV programme in May 2003 after he'd spent six months battling against throat cancer. He looked well after going through some bad times and I was very touched that he made a rare public appearance to say some kind words. I'll never have a bad word for Geoffrey Boycott.

Would he have been a successful coach for England? Not everyone would have been able to accept his man-management style and he would probably have driven a very hard bargain financially, but it would have been good to have him more available than he was in the 1990s. I wouldn't know how good a team coach he was, but on an individual basis I found him outstanding. I know that Nasser Hussain and Mike Atherton also had sessions with him at times and they found him excellent as well.

Boycott's input in the build-up to the West Indies tour was matched by the tactical and physical work that we put in, especially at Lilleshall. Colin Tomlin and John Brewer really worked hard on our fitness. We were, in effect, the guinea pigs for future England players, because this was the first time that England had got into scientific preparation, thinking about attaining proper fitness and how to maintain it. Looking back on all that, I can't understand how anyone could criticize Gooch and Dad for pushing us harder than any other England squad. Such professionalism is the norm nowadays and the two of them were ahead of their time. If a great player wanted to improve continuously and give himself the best possible chance by preparing properly, who could seriously disagree?

Over a four-day period at Lilleshall, we didn't just run around and do the bleep tests in the gym, checking on our recovery rates. We talked tactics. The coach and captain talked about the 'corridor of uncertainty' – that phrase that everybody seemed to adopt around the cricket world. Basically it meant that our bowlers had to bore their batters out by concentrating on a line just outside off-stump and tempting them for the drive. We were told that West Indian crowds love attacking batting and that they'll start getting on to their own players' backs if they try to block it. Seal off their scoring areas by avoiding middle and leg stumps and the supporters will unsettle them by giving them some stick. So the responsibility on our seam bowlers, Angus Fraser, Gladstone Small and David Capel, was to nag away at their batsmen, while the greater pace of Devon Malcolm was to be used to ruffle them up – give them a taste of their own medicine, something we hadn't done all that much in previous series. As for our batsmen, the advice was bleak. Expect to take a few blows from the short ball. The wickets won't be particularly reliable, the bounce will be variable, and when you get the rare bad delivery you must put it away. There would be no easy runs to be had off these guys.

Before I left for the Caribbean, there was one more important date in my diary. I got engaged to Lynn. We went to Bath for the weekend to make it official – there must have been a good deal with the hotel, or perhaps the sales were on at the jewellers'! Seriously, Lynn has been a fantastic wife. When we got married in 1991, she knew what she was letting herself in for. I'd met her up in Durham, when Surrey were playing a NatWest game and she was doing some promotional work for the sponsors. She knew from very early on what cricket meant to me and how deep were my ambitions. She often jokes that she's a cricket widow, but secretly I think she came to terms with my regular England tours, because it gave her a chance to spend my money! Lynn has never pressurized me when I've been thinking about my future in the game, and how long I should keep making myself available for England. She knows that you're a long time retired. Luckily, she's not interested in cricket, so that when I come home to her and my two lovely children I can switch off from my job. I've been incredibly lucky with my family. They may not always think they come first, but they do.

So when I arrived in the West Indies for my first Test series, I was fulfilled personally. Now I needed to see whether I could cut it as player. I made a good start, getting runs in the warm-up games, and the day before the first Test in Jamaica, Graham Gooch came to see me in my room. I was going to play tomorrow. To get that special news from such a special cricketer was fantastic. When Goochy had left, I sat on my bed and let it all rush over me, thinking back to those times when I wondered if I'd ever make the grade at Surrey, never mind for my country. All those years in Western Australia had been worth it. Then Dad knocked on the door. He said, 'Well done,' and then: 'From your Dad – well done, son.' That was a very private, personal moment between the two of us. He'd been tremendously professional in his dealings with me over the past decade, so much so that no one would ever have known that my coach was my father – unless you had prior knowledge. I could tell he was proud. We both were.

I then made three phone calls – to Lynn, to Kevin Gartrell in Perth, then to Mum. She reacted as if she knew nothing about my news, but I suspect the old man had tipped her the wink before coming to see me. It was a special day for me. Mum certainly had no doubts that I'd do well, and that the team was going to surprise almost everybody. She gave an interview to Cliff Morgan for BBC Radio 4's *Sport on Four* programme in which she said she was certain England would beat the West Indies and that my Test career would start on a high. She was spot-on with that prediction. Mum always was a shrewd judge of sport!

I slept well that night. That was strange, because normally I don't sleep as well the night before a Test as I do once we've started. I'll be restless if I'm due to bat next morning, or if I'm out overnight, I'll be playing my innings that day over in my mind, but apart from that I'm a good sleeper. I never really switch off, though – Lynn tells me that although I talk in my sleep, it's always about cricket, so she can nod off in boredom!

On that first day we caused a sensation by dismissing cheaply the best side in the world. Our plan to bore their batsmen out worked and they queued up to get themselves out. We knew that this tour would be the chance to make a name for ourselves and it was a fantastic way to start the series. I was glad to field first to have a chance to get used to the atmosphere of Test cricket, rather than sit with my pads on right from the off, ready to go in first wicket down. By the end of that first day, however, I was out. As I waited to go in to bat, I was more nervous than I've ever been, before or since. I was asking myself all sorts of questions. Am I up to this? Where will I get my runs? Just how quick are those bowlers?

The answer to that last question was 'very quick'. When I went in, Patrick Patterson was bowling very rapidly indeed in front of his home crowd. Off a very long run, with the crowd chanting 'Patto! Patto!', he absolutely steamed in. At the time he was one of the world's fastest bowlers, and after Wayne Larkins had wished me 'good luck' as I passed him, my heart couldn't stop pounding. Normally I could block out the noise from the crowd, but not this time. That was due to my nerves.

I got off the mark first ball, steering Patterson through gully and point to the boundary. At least I wouldn't get nought. Boycott's advice about how to combat these seriously fast bowlers kept coming back, but this was all so new to me. I'd got to 13 when Ian Bishop did me with one that rose up sharply, caught me on the glove and was taken at slip. A wicket falling to 'chin music', as Graham Gooch called that line of West Indian attack. I hadn't been overawed, but it was a nervous innings. All those sessions with Boycs could only get me so far. It prepares you, but not entirely for the mental challenge of actually having to go out there, in an intimidating atmosphere, and do it against four hostile fast bowlers, with the crowd on your back. At least I had realized my schoolboy dream, but I was none the wiser after this innings as to whether I was up to it.

Allan Lamb was certainly up to the challenge. He scored a fantastic hundred, backed up by Robin Smith. Lamby scored his fifth Test hundred against the West Indies in this innings, a wonderful achievement, and it was inspiring to see the way he counter-attacked. He seemed to have no fear, even to relish the challenge. That innings of his was something to aspire to, one of the best I have seen in Test cricket. It brought home to me what was needed at that level, first to survive, then to make an impression.

So we had a lead of 200, thanks to Lamb and Smith, and then we again bowled them out cheaply. It was an astonishing performance and we were actually going to win, in my first Test. The rain that washed out the fourth day frustrated us, but we only needed a few, and there was certain to be time left on the final day. We won by nine wickets and I was there at the end – nought not out. It could so easily have been a duck for me on my Test debut, because I was convinced that Courtney Walsh had me plumb lbw, but I escaped. At the end I managed to grab a stump and it remains a proud part of my cricket memorabilia at home, along with my first England cap. That first match in my Test career is still one of the special highlights of my time in the game.

That Test victory was a huge one for us. No one had fancied us against such tough opposition, yet we had stuck to our game plan intelligently. The scenes in the dressing-room were as chaotic as usual, with champagne and beer being sprayed everywhere to please the press photographers. That win meant even more to the likes of Gooch and Lamb, who had endured many a hammering from the West Indies down the years, and we were all delighted for them. The opposition were impressive in defeat. Jeff Dujon, Viv Richards, Desmond Haynes in particular were gracious. They had been hammered, and Viv as captain was now going to be under a lot of pressure from the volatile home supporters, but they didn't slink away from us. They were sincere in their congratulations, sat down and talked about cricket with novices like myself, showing proper respect for the game's traditions. I never forgot the way those guys fronted up, and it's something that I've tried to do with the opposition, win or lose.

Enjoying the company of opposition cricketers that you respect and like doesn't mean that at any stage you are compromised on the field of play. I think some of our younger England players in recent years have missed out by keeping away from the good guys in the other dressing-room when it's all over. You learn so much about cricket by swapping stories when there's time to spare, and you also develop lasting friendships with players from other countries. I know that in years to come, I can call up the likes of Curtly Ambrose, Courtney Walsh, Brian Lara, Stephen Fleming, Nathan Astle, Chris Cairns, Shane Warne, Steve Waugh, Adam Gilchrist, Justin Langer, Damian Martyn and Wasim Akram and go out to dinner with them, either in their country or mine. That doesn't mean I ever failed to give my very best against those blokes when representing my country. It's just that there's usually a time in a series when you can switch off and enjoy the company of your opponents, and I wouldn't have missed those opportunities for anything.

That friendly chat in Jamaica with Desmond Haynes was soon forgotten, though, when we had a frank exchange of words in the Trinidad Test. The press photographs of me, in only my second Test, going head-to-head with the veteran Haynes did me no favours. I honestly believe I was unlucky to get dragged into it all, and that one second that led to that damaging photograph led many to form a false impression.

Dessie was under pressure on the final day of that Test.

He was standing in as captain for Viv Richards, who was out owing to health problems. Dessie, from Barbados, was not very popular in Trinidad. That is the way of it in the Caribbean – they do love their local heroes. We again bowled and fielded marvellously, and we had the whole of the final day to get just 151 to win, to put us 2-0 up in the series. That would have been a sensation and Dessie, as captain, would be held responsible for any defeat.

That was the background as we started off confidently in pursuit of the target. We lost Wayne Larkins early, and then – damagingly – Graham Gooch was hit on the hand by Ezra Moseley. I was at the other end, and Goochy was in agony. That was him out of action, and, as it turned out, his Test series was over. But Allan Lamb and I kept attacking and our victory seemed assured. Dessie Haynes was getting very agitated by now. As I settled at the crease, he was fielding at silly point, waiting for Ezra Moseley to bowl. He shouted, 'Let's get the youngster out, he's only playing because he's Daddy's boy. This ball's going to kill you.' I pulled away to compose myself. Before the next ball, he was at it again. I said to him, 'Say what you like between deliveries, but when he starts his run-up, shut up!'

Soon afterwards it began to rain, and we had to troop off. Dessie carried on at me again. Allan Lamb, an old mate, told him to pipe down as the two of us walked off, shoulder to shoulder. Then the photograph was taken, with me looking straight ahead and Dessie in my ear. It gave the distorted impression that we were both rucking at each other, with the new boy giving as good as he got. In fact I said nothing at all, and Lamby was the only England player talking during that incident, telling Dessie to behave himself. All I had done was fail to back down at the verbal intimidation on the field of play. I suppose it's bred into me, but I wasn't going to let a senior player try it on with me, when he was seeking an unfair advantage, trying to distract me when the bowler was on his way. But I had only spoken one sentence during all the kerfuffle.

To be fair to Dessie, he called me over when we went into the West Indies dressing-room at the close. He apologized, saying, 'I was out of order. I was under pressure out there. I'm from Barbados and we looked like going under again, with me in charge. You did well to stand up for yourself.'

There were no hard feelings, even though the West Indies' blatant timewasting robbed us of a deserved win. When we came back out after the rain, we needed just 78 off the remaining thirty overs and had eight wickets in hand. In the first over Moseley ran up then stopped three times, complaining about the damp footholds. They were clearly intent on slowing the game up, and I'm sure we would have done the same. I was out for 31 in the second over after the break, caught at third man having a dart at Walsh. I saw it as basically a one-day game now and was determined to be as uninhibited as possible, but it wasn't to be. We all had a go, but eventually got frustrated by ten overs an hour, accurate bowling and deteriorating light. As the laws stand today, we would have won, because there would have been a minimum amount of overs to be bowled and the umpires would have hurried the game along, as Steve Bucknor did on our behalf in Pakistan in 2000, when Moin Khan was trying to slow things down. Back in 1990 there were no neutral umpires or match referees, and the Windies got away with it. It's a grey area between gamesmanship and cheating, but the bottom line is that when you know you can't win you just want to avoid losing, so England couldn't moan too much. We would have been equally keen on bowling our overs slowly. It's amazing how concerned you can get about the damp surrounds when you're looking at the prospect of defeat!

So it ended in a frustrating draw for us, but there were many consolations. Our fast bowling for a start. It was during this period that Angus Fraser and Devon Malcolm blended superbly as a unit of contrast and stamina. They took fifteen wickets between them in that Trinidad Test, and none of the West Indian batsmen looked comfortable against them. Dev really unsettled them in that series with his pace, and they took the attacking option, getting themselves out. He was our wild card, not bothered about the 'corridor of uncertainty' that was the plan for the other fast bowlers. Dev didn't have a classical action, so when his radar went astray, he'd spear it down the leg side or bowl four-balls, short and outside the off stump. But he was the most naturally strong cricketer I've ever played against. When he got it right, Dev could be devastating, a match-winner. I appreciate that he could be frustrating to captain, because you never knew when he'd be on top of his game, or for how long. One of the loveliest men you could wish to meet, Dev could be stubborn, despite being very intelligent. He would want to stick to his way, even though he could be very expensive. But I think he could have been handled better in the latter stages of his England career. We couldn't afford to be so inflexible with our match-winning bowlers, because we haven't had that many in my time.

To get the best out of Devon Malcolm, you had to pick a bowling attack that would work around him, imposing discipline from the other end, so that the frustrated batsmen would try to take on Dev. That's where Angus Fraser was so good for him. They were a very good pairing because they were so different. I'd seen Gus Fraser in second-eleven cricket for Middlesex when he first started his career, thought he was an outstanding prospect and wasn't at all surprised that he came straight into Test cricket as if it was all perfectly straightforward. Before he injured his hip on the 1990–1 tour of Australia, Gus was a consistent wicket-taker for us, who got the best batsmen out. He was our version of Glenn McGrath, moving the ball around just enough, hitting the pitch hard and landing the ball every time on an area the size of a piece of A4 paper. He gave the captain control and leadership, because he cared so much and would never give in. Gus would moan about bowling thirty overs a day in extreme heat, but you knew he didn't mean it. He'd be looking for one final spell before close of play, then expect to open up the following morning. Before his hip injury, Gus was quick enough to ensure the batsman couldn't adjust if he'd done them with movement off the pitch. On flat wickets, when you're looking for discipline from your bowlers, Gus Fraser was a captain's dream.

I believe Gus could have ended up as one of England's greatest-ever bowlers, just as McGrath has for Australia, if that hip injury hadn't dogged him for so long. It was criminal that it took so long for it to be diagnosed and treated properly. When he finally got back into the England team, he had lost that nip on flat wickets that had made him so formidable. He still had great success on pitches that aided seam bowling, especially in 1998, but elsewhere they could cut and pull him, as they did on his last tour to Australia in 1998–9 – something he had never allowed in his early days. If Gus had stayed fit, he would have taken more than 300 Test wickets, instead of 177 in just 46 Tests. Over nine years he missed as many Tests as he played. Gus was a true professional who expected his team-mates to feel the same way, and if they didn't, he'd climb into them during team meetings. He was as straight and honest as any player I've known, and I wish we had unearthed more like him. In that case, we wouldn't have had the regular inquests into England failing against Australia. With a fit Fraser, and with every player having his standards and heart, we would have matched them.

On that 1990 tour of the Caribbean, the absence of Gus Fraser for the last two Tests was almost as crucial as losing our captain. Gus picked up a rib injury and his control was badly missed. Allan Lamb captained instead of Gooch, and he led the side as he batted – positively, with attacking fields. He didn't get into the bowlers' ears as much as did Goochy, who was stronger on the basic disciplines. Lamby had great talent as a batsman and worked very hard at his own game, but Gooch thought more about the overall picture and we missed his leadership. Eventually the West Indian batters got the measure of our bowlers and we ran out of steam.

I opened in the Barbados Test, replacing Gooch. I'd hardly ever done the job with Surrey, usually slotting in at number three, and I found it a big difference mentally, needing to think about my batting when in the field with nine opposition wickets down, working out how I was going to play on that wicket. I took the attacking option in Barbados, going for the upper cuts down to third man. I made 45 and 37, but I was a little too loose and ambitious. You couldn't take too many liberties as a young player against Ambrose, Marshall, Bishop and Moseley without getting done.

We were unlucky to lose that Barbados Test right at the death, as the shadows closed in on that final evening. Ambrose bowled absolutely magnificently to take eight wickets, but the bounce got lower and lower and more inconsistent. We were also unlucky with some umpiring decisions, especially the one that nailed Rob Bailey towards the close of the fourth day. I was at the non-striker's end, when Ambrose sent one down the leg side. It brushed Rob's thigh pad, to be taken by the wicketkeeper, Jeff

Dujon. Viv Richards then ran from slip, whooping and hollering, eventually ending up at my end. To my amazement, umpire Lloyd Barker gave Rob out. I had a clear view and Rob got nowhere near that delivery. In my opinion the umpire had allowed himself to be intimidated by Viv. Before the next ball, Barker asked me, 'Do you think that was out?' and I told him no. He didn't say anything more; he knew he'd buckled under the pressure exerted by the captain. Now I've never had a problem with people appealing – as anyone who's seen me on the field will agree! – but I do get annoyed when the umpire isn't strong enough and gets influenced by strident appealing. That's what happened at Barbados. Today, the ICC Code of Conduct rules against behaviour like Viv Richards' that day, and it was incidents like that one that probably helped bring about the tightening-up that was needed.

So many things have changed since that first tour of mine. Preparing for a Test match for a start. There were only two days between the end of the Barbados Test and the start of the final one, in Antigua, and what did the dedicated young professional Alec Stewart do to while away the time? Played football and beach cricket by the sea in scorching heat! I was just one of several of the younger ones who were restless hanging around the hotel and wanted to let off steam. Great preparation for a Test the next day – as Allan Lamb told us, in no uncertain terms! These days an England cricketer would go nowhere near the hot sun in similar circumstances. So when I'm praised for my attention to detail and thoroughness in preparation, I think it's only fair to point out that, when I was younger, I did some daft things. So did another future England captain, Nasser Hussain, who was also involved in the beach games!

We were hammered in Antigua by an innings. The

wicket was the quickest and bounciest of the series, and their fast bowlers knew too much for us. We'd run out of momentum and luck with injuries. But if anyone had said we'd go to the West Indies and give a great account of ourselves to stretch the world's best side, we would have settled for that. A fairer result would have been 2-2, because we would have won in Trinidad if it hadn't rained.

My two cheap dismissals in the final Test – caught in the slips, playing away from my body, then slapping one to cover – summed up my first series. I had played positively, but kept getting myself out. I averaged 24, which was not good enough. Dad told me at the end of the tour that I never looked out of my depth but I had to toughen up my approach, make it harder for the bowlers to get me out, while keeping faith in my aggressive instincts. I'd sampled Test cricket against the best team in the world and knew deep down that I could play at that level, but I also knew that there was a long way to go before I could be a regular. I felt comfortable at the crease as the series progressed, felt I was handling myself well in the tough environment, but needed to stop wasting all the hard work with rash judgements. Now I had to kick on, and make the selectors keep picking me.

For me, that tour began a love affair with cricket in the Caribbean. I loved the aggressive cricket that was played out there, and the way that the crowds appreciated you if you entertained them. It didn't matter if you played for the opposition – they'd be rooting for you if they liked your style. And they were all so knowledgeable. Everybody seemed to have an informed opinion about the cricket. At one stage on that tour, I was just padding up for a net when a rotund gentleman in his sixties came over. 'I like the way you play, man,' he said, 'but you've got to tighten up.' He then proceeded to dissect my batting, praising my footwork and back-foot play, but warning me about being too loose around off-stump. He'd only seen me in a game once, but he was spot-on. I had no problems with him expressing his views, because he was so polite and obviously loved his cricket. He was typical of the knowledgeable fans I've met on three England tours to the West Indies. It's a great place to play Test cricket.

Within a week of returning from that tour, I was playing for Surrey. I had just turned 27 and was desperate to taste Test cricket again after my first series. I knew that the captain and coach were keen on continuity of selection and that the younger guys had impressed them in the West Indies, but now it was up to me to cement my place that summer with consistent batting early on. I only featured in the first part of the international summer, playing in two one-dayers against New Zealand and three Tests before losing my place against India. First I had an ankle injury, then my path was blocked because of the return of David Gower and the need to give John Morris an extended run in the side. Fair enough. Apart from scoring my first Test fifty at Lord's, I did little to justify my place for the whole summer. Dad told me to go back to county cricket once I was fit, score enough runs to be noticed again and force my way back in. I didn't think that was the end of my international career. Although I thought I could play at the highest level, I needed to keep learning, and quickly. How was I getting out? Was there any pattern? When does an attacking shot that works for Surrey become a loose one when you're playing for England?

My wicketkeeping was to prove a bonus for me when the selectors sat down to pick the squad for Australia at the end of that 1990 summer. That option allowed them to pick me as a batsman while I could also be the reserve keeper, allowing them to pick an extra batsman or bowler.

I was seen as an all-rounder, not for the last time, and Dad's advice to keep working at my wicketkeeping had got me on my first Ashes tour.

It was fantastic to return to Perth an England player early on that tour. We played at Lilac Hill, Midland-Guildford's home ground, and I got 70 not out to help us knock off the runs to win. They even christened one of their new stands 'The Alec Stewart Stand' and I was very proud of the support the locals gave me. They saw me as a Midland-Guildford cricketer returning to play for England. After all, I had spent eight successful seasons with them, and they were determined to claim me as one of their own. They still do, in fact! When I appeared on *This Is Your Life* on BBC TV, they flew Kevin Gartrell and his wife over to appear in the programme, and Kevin presented me with life membership of Midland-Guildford. He made it quite clear to me that this honour was a rare one for a Pommie cricketer!

I played well in patches in my first Ashes series. I got 79 at Melbourne, then missed my first Test hundred in Sydney, when Peter McConnell adjudged me out lbw. I wasn't too pleased. I'd made a positive start, using my feet well against the off-spin of Greg Matthews. My first scoring shot was a hard sweep off Matthews in front of square leg that went for four, and I was going well at 91 not out when we came off for the tea interval. Off the second ball after the break, Terry Alderman got me lbw to one that was going down the leg side. I still haven't forgotten that decision all these years on. I know these things even themselves out, and I've been lucky with umpires many times, but I was bursting to succeed and it would be another seven years before I scored a hundred in a Test against Australia.

My scores then tailed away in the last two Tests, and I

made only 29 in four innings. That may have had something to do with my keeping wicket for England for the first time in Test cricket, but I'm not sure. Probably I still wasn't tight enough or able to concentrate hard enough for long periods. But Jack Russell was sacrificed for those last two Tests because we were 2-0 down and needed to get back into the series. So, to accommodate an extra bowler and give us a better chance of taking twenty wickets in hot weather, a great specialist was left out. I never saw it as Jack being dropped, more a case of the selection policy dictating the final eleven. Jack was the best in the world at that stage and he was understandably gutted to miss out.

So that began the situation of a quality performer like Jack Russell being seen as surplus to requirements because of the deficiencies elsewhere in the team. If the specialist bowlers and batters had done their job as well as Jack, there would have been no need to hand me the gloves. His stumping of Dean Jones in the Sydney Test was amazing. Deano was batting outside his crease to combat the low bounce, and Jack decided to challenge that by breathing down his neck, standing up to the stumps even when the quicker bowlers were on. Gladstone Small sent one down the leg side and Jack stumped him brilliantly in a flash. I was fielding at square leg and Jack jumped into my arms in delight and triumph. It was the work of a genius, and yet he missed the next two Tests.

I felt so sorry for Jack. It didn't affect our relationship, because we both knew it was out of our hands. He gave me excellent support in my training at Perth and Adelaide, but I did have doubts about taking over from such a wonderful performer. I'd batted very well in the two previous Tests, so would this new role affect my batting? Was I in fact good enough to keep wicket in a Test match? How would it affect my concentration levels? This was the biggest test of my wicketkeeping abilities so far in my career and although the tour selectors appeared very confident in me, I wasn't so sure. I didn't voice my doubts to anyone because I had been asked to perform a role for the team to try to get us back into the Ashes series, but I was worried.

In the end I kept wicket well. I was very pleased to catch Greg Matthews, standing up to the stumps off Graham Gooch, and I didn't miss anything in either Test. But it would be another five years before I started preparing as thoroughly for wicketkeeping as I did for batting before and during a Test. Only then would the doubts be banished. Meanwhile, Jack Russell, our best man at the job, would continue to be sacrificed for me when we were behind in a series and desperate measures were needed. That was unfair on Jack and, at times, on me as well.

Our morale and team spirit on that Australian tour weren't as high as in the West Indies a few months earlier. A ridiculous run of injuries didn't help, and the long itinerary of four months sapped our stamina. We needed to be fresh and ready for the challenges, but the captain and coach felt we had to work harder in practice because we weren't playing well. You need to draw a fine line between rest and work on such a long tour, and I know that Dad and Goochy would now admit that we trained too much. At the time it was second nature to me, because the work ethic had been part of my make-up for years, but having had the experience of many tours, and seen from Duncan Fletcher's advice what rest periods can do, I also agree that we spent too many hours at practice. Touring Australia is hard enough with all the travelling involved, but we would fly in to another city and then find ourselves in the nets within a couple of hours of getting off the plane. Some of the senior players like David Gower and Allan Lamb grumbled about the lack of days off, and in retrospect they were right. Goochy and Dad knew that you live and die by results, and with those going against us, they felt that their way was best. But we needed a better balance between time off and hard work.

David Gower and Graham Gooch never came to a harmonious working relationship on that tour, which was very sad to someone like me who admired them both so much. David took the mickey out of the management with his infamous trip to the skies in a Tiger Moth plane while we were playing a match on the pitch below. He and John Morris left the ground without permission while we were batting, which was wrong – and returning to pose for photographs in the plane wasn't a good idea, because it looked as if they were giving two fingers to the management. From a blinkered cricket point of view, it was right that they were fined £1000 each.

I loved batting with Gower on that tour. He was such a sweet timer of the ball, so effortless. I'd watched him bat for England when I was still at school and it was a thrill to have two good partnerships with David in the Melbourne and Sydney Tests. He was very relaxing to bat with, and happy to give helpful advice and support. He was very complimentary to me when I played some good shots, and I'm really glad that I spent some time out in the middle with David Gower towards the end of a great England career. No one made it look so easy in my time with England.

The results went against us on that Ashes tour, ending in defeat by 3-0. Little did I realize that this was to become a familiar pattern for the rest of my England career. The seeds of Australian greatness were being scattered under Allan Border's tough captaincy, with Mark Taylor and then Steve Waugh benefiting in later Ashes series. Ian Healy was blossoming as a top-class wicketkeeper-batsman, and

Mark Waugh made his debut in the Adelaide Test, scoring a lovely hundred. Those two would be serious thorns in our sides for the rest of that decade.

Yet I didn't feel out of my depth in that series, despite scoring only two half-centuries. Bruce Reid took 27 wickets for them and was devastating at times, but I'd scored heavily against him in grade cricket when he played for Bayswater-Morley, so he didn't bother me all that much when we played in a Test. It helps when you've played against a Test opponent at a lower level. It was the same with Merv Hughes. He came over in the early 1980s on an Esso scholarship to play for Essex. He was very sharp and never short of a word or two. I always enjoyed batting against Merv because I'd give him verbals in return for his banter, and then he'd eventually shut up. He bowled six bouncers in a row at me during the Melbourne Test and it was very funny to see him get so worked up. I had a lot of time for Merv – a very fine bowler, a huge team man and a great bloke for a chat with at close of play – but knowing him for years meant I wasn't fazed by him.

I felt I was getting there. Greg Matthews was very complimentary to me when we chatted in the dressing-room at the end of the series. He thought I'd used my feet well to him and that I looked confident. I was throughout – until I got out. I hadn't forgotten the supportive words from David Gower when we'd batted together. But I still had a long way to go before I had Gower's knack of taking on the bowlers and yet staying at the crease. Too often, I'd flatter to deceive. A total of three half-centuries in twelve Tests didn't suggest consistency. I couldn't keep my place in the England side with the occasional cameo performance.

CHAPTER FIVE

england fixture
at last

I came back from Australia hoping to stay in the England side, but not expecting anything. I hadn't yet established myself as an England player and my batting had tailed off in the last two Tests of the Ashes series. Graeme Hick was about to make his long-awaited England debut, young Mark Ramprakash was knocking at the door, and there were many other fine batsmen worthy of selection ahead of me. In the end I had to wait until August before I was picked by England in that 1991 summer. It was worth it because that started a fantastic run for me over the next twelve months.

Hick and Ramprakash did in fact begin that series against the West Indies and I was omitted. By the time the final Test came round, however, we were 2-1 down and the selectors were looking for ways to square the series. They went for inspiration in returning to Ian Botham, then backed a hunch in picking me as wicketkeeper-batsman. Hicky and Jack Russell were dropped. I was pleased to be in, of course, and playing in the same side as a legend like Botham was wonderful. He may have been way past his best – it was his first Test in two years – but he was a legend to me, who had watched him win so many Tests while I was still a schoolboy.

Jack's omission was significant. I had thought that playing me for those last two Tests in Australia would be a one-off, given his brilliance, but he only averaged ten in the first four Tests of the West Indies series and he was vulnerable. The selectors decided to bat me at six, and Botham at seven, which would allow them to pick four front-line bowlers as well as getting a few overs out of Beefy. I could see what they were getting at, but the pressure was now on me in both areas, with the gloves and the bat. I was confident that I could acquit myself in the dual role in one-dayers, but not so sure over a five-day Test, especially if the ball was going to turn for the spinners. Jack was an absolute star in such situations, yet he had been sacrificed for me – again. This was to be the pattern in several series over the next few years – send for Stewart to keep wicket when we have to square the series, and leave Russell out. Even when he'd done nothing to deserve being discarded. Basically the selectors wanted to get twelve players into eleven, but when Jack wasn't scoring runs, he was always in the firing line, despite his great skills as a specialist wicketkeeper.

I kept my concerns to myself when we gathered for the Oval Test. I know that if I had confided in Dad he would just have told me to get on with it and justify the faith of the selectors. His only tip to me in the build-up was: 'Go out and play like Alec Stewart.' Luckily all the media coverage in the days leading up this Test was about Beefy Botham: could he roll back the years and inspire England to victory yet again? Well, we did win, and although Beefy made the winning hit in true storybook fashion, he'd be the first to admit that he played a minor part in a great win.

It was my first Test on my home ground and the atmosphere was superb on that first day. The Oval may not be the most scenic of cricket grounds but when it's full and the crowd are on England's side, it's a great place to play. Also, in 1991 its wicket was the best in the country and, with its even bounce and pace, ideal for someone like me who likes to play shots. Or someone like Robin Smith. He scored a great hundred in that first innings and I really enjoyed my partnership with him. Robin loved to keep the score flowing and he would always support his partner. No batsman at that time cut the ball harder, and he had a fine record against the West Indian fast bowlers because he was fearless and his back-foot play was first-rate.

Robin was a great team man. A few years later he was discarded, far too early in his England career, at the age of just 33. He was in his prime, averaging more than 43 when Raymond Illingworth, the supremo of English cricket at the time, decided he was on the scrapheap after the 1996 World Cup. Good judges said he was dodgy against top-class spinners, but everybody gets dominated by them at some stage in their careers, and Robin was a great fighter and would get through the various crises. And you don't average 43 just by being able to play the quicks. I've had my reservations about England picking players who were born outside our island, wondering about the depth of their commitment, but I never had any worries on that score with Robin Smith. He gave everything to England when we played together and was one of the most popular guys I've known.

It was very rewarding batting with him in that first innings. I admired his tight discipline, his patience and his refusal to be dictated to by the fast bowlers. His was the sort of approach I wanted to adopt at the highest level. My dismissal was sadly typical, however. Having played very positively, and weathered the second new ball to be not out overnight, I then slapped one to cover off Patterson. That was becoming too regular a dismissal for me in Test matches. I wasn't going to get too many more chances unless I started to bat with controlled aggression, showing the necessary judgement.

I did manage to meet my biggest challenge when the West Indies batted. Even though Phil Tufnell turned the ball sharply, I concentrated hard and kept wicket very well. I was particularly pleased to catch Viv Richards as he went down the pitch to Tufnell – so far that it was also a stumping chance. I kept my eye on the ball and didn't snatch at the chance, even though Viv's body obscured the ball for an instant. In the second innings, when they followed on, I was again tidy and efficient behind the stumps with good concentration levels. But would I get another chance with the bat?

They came back hard at us in their second innings and on the final day, we needed 146 to win. That would be tough against Ambrose, Patterson, Marshall and Walsh. Only Patterson could be expensive at times, but he was also a potential match-winner with his extreme pace. It was never going to be easy and, with England at 80 for 4, the game was in the balance as I came to the wicket to play the most significant innings so far in my Test career. It was only 38 not out, including a partnership of 62 with Ramprakash, but it saw us through to victory.

I was very pleased with the way I fashioned that innings, when I was under the sort of pressure you associate with Test cricket. The crowd was noisy and appreciative, the wicket was still good for batting and I relished the challenge. I felt at ease at the crease, their style of bowling on that fast pitch suited me, and at last I batted with controlled aggression. There was one shot that I played which Ramps still talks about. Ambrose bowled a bouncer that I saw early and I hooked it in front of square leg to the boundary. Ambrose followed through and actually applauded the shot! He may have been a man of few words on the cricket field, but he did respect certain batsmen and we always had a good relationship. He would say 'well played' if you'd got fifty or a hundred by playing well. I slapped that ball really hard and had a massive surge of adrenalin when it careered over the boundary rope. I felt I'd at last arrived, and I was loving the heat of the contest.

That shot off Ambrose remains one of the best three that I've played in my Test career. The others were a pull off Merv Hughes in the 1993 Oval Test that simply raced away and a straight drive off Aquib Javed in the Edgbaston Test in 1992 against Pakistan. Somehow I timed that one beautifully, just leaning on it, and it zipped past the bowler. That was a classic stroke, whereas the other two were meaty, macho shots off the middle of the bat, with a satisfying crack. Ramps was also batting with me in that Oval Test against Australia and he'll happily go on about both shots to anyone who'll listen!

So we beat the West Indies by five wickets, squaring the series, and I was there at the end with Ian Botham, on my home ground. Fairytale stuff! I do believe that we would have lost if Ramps or I had gone cheaply and it was enormously satisfying for me to prove at last that I could dig in and make significant runs when the battle was at its fiercest. Many times those great West Indies fast bowlers have won a Test against the odds, and they had already had more than a sniff of victory, with the likes of Gooch, Smith and Atherton out cheaply as we stuttered in search of the 146 needed.

It was Viv Richards' last Test and I was flattered when he took time out to speak to me while we were all having a drink afterwards in our dressing-room. He said he liked the way I'd played in the second innings and that this should now be the start of my proper Test match career. Coming from someone like Viv, that was very special. He'd been very good to me when I was just starting out at Surrey, and also told Dad that he rated me. Viv's words gave me extra confidence. I knew I'd done well in this Oval Test, dealing with the pressure of combining the dual roles, but he didn't hand out praise to many English players. He seemed to understand how important that Oval Test was to me. I needed to make an important contribution to the result. At last, after thirteen Tests, I had done that.

And my fourteenth Test a couple of weeks later was equally memorable. I scored my first Test hundred against Sri Lanka, at Lord's – my favourite ground in the world. Jack was reinstated to keep wicket and I batted at number three, my Surrey position. That was encouraging. Clearly the selectors felt I'd done enough at the Oval at number six to be considered a front-line batsman. We were in a spot of trouble at 183 for 6, in overcast conditions, but Jack supported me in his eccentric way in a stand of 63, and then David Lawrence – dear old 'Syd' – talked me through the nervous nineties. I was on 99 for a fair amount of time, as the field was brought up and they waited for me to take a chance. Syd said, 'I'm backing up a long way, mate,' and finally we took a chance on the single as I nudged one on the off side. The throw just missed Syd's stumps and he scrambled in. It was a huge relief and I shall never forget the contribution of Syd, a fantastic team man. When he joined me there was only Phil Tufnell to come and my score was still in the eighties. But Syd was no mug with the bat and his broad smile as I raised my bat was typical of the man. To get my first Test hundred at such a fantastic, historic ground was even better. Lord's has usually been a good place for me, but I'd still rate it the best even if I'd got more noughts than hundreds there (which I haven't!).

When I walked out to bat for the second innings, I at last felt like a proper Test cricketer, and it showed as I made 44 and added over a hundred with Goochy. This was the most confident I'd felt in fourteen Tests. I knew there'd been a lot of stick coming my way about the way I would score flashy twenties and thirties, only to play a loose shot and get caught at cover or the slip region. The easy line was trotted out that I was only in because the coach was my father. It had been vital to me to start kicking all those remarks into touch by making runs and looking the part. I'd played seven Tests, then was dropped, then another five, then got dropped again – all in the space of eighteen months. After Lord's I no longer felt as if I was on trial. In fact England didn't drop me again until 1996, and that was for just one Test.

Taken together, those two Test Matches were hugely significant in my career. I had passed the test of temperament at the Oval, then kept my place as a batter at Lord's, doing what you expect from a Test batsman: scoring a hundred – and winning the Man of the Match award. With a tour to New Zealand coming up, and then the World Cup, I had wanted to cement my place for both the short and the long game. Perhaps I really had turned the corner and become a genuine Test match performer in the space of a fortnight.

It got better. Before we went to New Zealand, I was asked if I could be vice-captain to Graham Gooch. We'd been training at Lilleshall and Goochy just stopped me in my tracks with the direct question. I was shocked. Only a few weeks ago, I couldn't even get in the side! It had just been announced that I was to captain Surrey for the 1992 season and I had done it now and then in 1991, but I wasn't prepared for this. Goochy said he liked my approach to my cricket and attitude to playing as a team and asked for my reaction. I was honoured and accepted straight away, but was flabbergasted. Dad later told me that he had no input at all in the decision, which was entirely down to the captain. To have the confidence of Gooch, a player I admired so much, was a great boost. Allan Lamb, the vice-captain in the West Indies and in Australia, was also going on the tour, but perhaps Goochy thought that, with several youngish players in the squad, it made sense to have a deputy who was only 28. I don't know his thinking on that to this day, but I have always shared his attitude to cricket. I would remain vice-captain of England, home and away, for the next five years.

I had another piece of information to digest before we left England that winter. I would be Goochy's opening partner. Mike Atherton was missing the tour because of a back operation and I was surprised to get the role, having just got a hundred in the Lord's Test batting at three, a position that had been my regular one for Surrey. I had opened in only two Tests, on the 1990 tour to West Indies, and that was just filling in for the injured Gooch, so I asked the old man for the reasoning. Dad's answer was straight and to the point. 'First, you take it as a compliment that Goochy and I think you're up to it technically, and second – you do as you're told.' That soon sorted me out!

That trip to New Zealand convinced me that I preferred opening the batting to any other position. I'm sure having a good Test series had a lot to do with it. Very quickly I changed my mind about batting at three, agreeing with Goochy that going in at the top of the order is the best place, even though the new ball will occasionally clean you up. You can set the tempo of the innings at the start, and capitalize on attacking fields that the new ball warrants. After 1992, if the selectors had asked where I always wanted to bat, it would be opening. It's a matter of regret that I didn't get to do that often enough, but the needs of the side dictated otherwise. However, I'll always remember the pleasure I got from opening for England, first with Graham Gooch, then with Mike Atherton.

The first Test was perfect for me. We won by an innings and I scored a hundred. The only jarring note for me in my 148 was that I got out just before the close on the first day, caught at slip off a good ball from Danny Morrison.

Having played so well, cutting out the loose shots, I was conscious of Graham Gooch's advice – 'When you bat, you've never got enough' – and a double hundred was there for the taking. Not long ago I would happily have settled for a big hundred opening for England.

New Zealand handed that Test to us by some strange batting from their two top players, John Wright and Martin Crowe. Wright was 99 not out at tea on the last day, when they only had two wickets down and the match was destined for a draw. But then Phil Tufnell bowled a magic spell after tea and they cracked under pressure. Wright was stumped for 99, going down the pitch to Tuffers, but as long as Crowe was there we surely couldn't win. Crowe will always be in my world eleven from my time in the game because of his simple, pure technique and mastery of playing the short ball, with so much time to spare.

I was fielding at short leg and it dawned on me that, with just a couple of minutes left, all Crowe had to do was play out the next over from Tuffers and the game was drawn, with New Zealand nine wickets down. They also needed just four more runs to make us bat again, so I shouted out from under the helmet, 'They only need a four and the game's saved!' I made sure that Crowe heard me. He then went down the wicket, looking for that boundary and holed out to Derek Pringle at wide mid-off. I couldn't believe he had got out so tamely, but it was first-hand experience of how even the top players can react strangely to pressure.

In the third Test, at Wellington, I got another hundred on a slow wicket. I was very happy with that innings, as I adapted well to the conditions, reining in my shots. When I reached my century, Ian Smith, their veteran wicketkeeper, clapped his gloves and said, 'Well played.' I could tell he meant it, as he had been a very tough competitor down the years and didn't say things like that just for the sake of it.

I was now so confident that I was disappointed to make only 63 in the second innings. Two hundreds in the same Test now looked feasible to me, which was a sharp contrast to how I had felt a year earlier, when I was still searching for a proper game plan as a Test batsman. I had now made three hundreds in my last five Test innings and, for my own peace of mind, I'd answered a few questions over my right to be in the side. Getting the respect and support of my team-mates and the congratulations from opponents like Ian Smith made it even more gratifying. It seemed I'd gone from 'promising' to 'established' overnight.

Sadly, that Wellington Test will linger in my memory for reasons other than my hundred. I witnessed the worst injury I've ever seen on a cricket field, as poor Syd Lawrence suffered a fractured knee-cap. The game was dead in the last session of the match as they batted out time but, typically, Syd knew no other way than to try his heart out. He'd complained about a sore knee earlier in the game, but still steamed in to bowl 27 overs in the first innings. I was at cover when he collapsed as he was about to bowl and the noise he made was like that of a wounded animal. He screamed in agony, and even now, after all these years, I can't forget that terrible, terrible noise.

He was carried off the field on a stretcher, still screaming. Coming from such a strong man, that sound was awful. Then Dad got involved in an incident with a TV cameraman who wanted to get too close to the stretcher. Dad shoved him out of the way, feeling that the bloke was being too intrusive. The papers handed out some stick the following day along the lines of 'England Coach Punches TV Cameraman', but he could have been a little more sensitive.

After that Syd was never the same again, even though he tried a comeback a few years later. His bowling action was all muscle and hustle and his knee just couldn't sustain the physical stress placed on it when he bowled flat out. It was shocking and a huge reality check for me. At a time when my England career was at last taking off, after a lot of chances and frustrations, there was a lion-hearted colleague lying in a hospital bed, finished with the big time. Syd, a top bloke and fantastic team-man, was the original 100-per-center and brilliant to be around. He combined a great sense of humour with total dedication to his team-mates. Cricket throws up many cruel moments, and Wellington 1992 is sharp in my memory.

Next stop Australia, for the World Cup. After winning the Test series 2-0 against New Zealand we were justified in thinking we'd go all the way. And we nearly did it. We lost to Pakistan in the Final after being the best team in the tournament until the day it really mattered. Pakistan deserved to win that match, but I'll always wonder if we peaked too early in the competition and went off the boil just at the wrong time. That England side was the best I'd played with in one-day cricket throughout my career. We had top batsmen in Graham Gooch, Allan Lamb, Robin Smith, Graeme Hick and Neil Fairbrother, all-rounders in Derek Pringle, Chris Lewis and Dermot Reeve, a wicketkeeper-batsman in myself and a canny spinner in Richard Illingworth. And a player called Ian Botham.

Now there was no doubt that Beefy was past his very best in the 1992 World Cup, but he still exerted an astonishing influence over the opposition. He turned up, a little overweight and unfit, after preparing by appearing in a pantomime season in Bournemouth! Only Beefy could manage that. I don't blame him for looking after his own interests by seeing it through in panto after signing the contract with the theatre. He hadn't had any indication from the England selectors months earlier that he was in their thoughts for the World Cup, so he signed the deal. But after the Oval Test against the West Indies he was back in favour. He had promised to keep fit by training with Harry Redknapp's players at Bournemouth FC, but judging by his shape when he arrived in Australia, he'd talked Harry out of training a few times! The deal was that if you weren't playing in the next match, it was your job to keep him amused in the evenings so the rest of us could prepare properly. Thank God I was involved in every game, as I couldn't have kept up with Beefy! One night we all piled into a restaurant and found Neil Fairbrother doing the honours, drinking wine with Beefy. Neil groaned, 'I'm dreading tomorrow, but I'm doing it for the team!'

Of course, Beefy could have prepared more professionally for the World Cup, but he was too old a dog to learn new tricks and the management knew the score and what they'd get from him in return. None of the players minded, because he still gave us a match-winning dimension. Ian Botham was definitely a man to have alongside you in the trenches, and he was great value in the dressing-room, with his patriotism and positive thinking. Also he still had a hold over the opposition, even though his bowling was medium pace. He won the Man of the Match award in the first match in Perth, getting rid of Sachin Tendulkar, and then in Sydney he overwhelmed Australia with the force of his personality. He took four wickets and scored 53 as we hammered them by eight wickets. It was amazing to see how frightened the Aussies were of him. He could have walked out to bat with a stump and would still have scored runs against them that night. His bowling was not too frightening, but they played the reputation and they were ridiculously tentative against him, as if he was still the miracle worker of 1981. For the first time I was seeing at first hand the effect that Beefy could produce, and

I could appreciate what a force he must have been in his prime.

With Beefy still weaving his spells, we were a very confident, professional unit. We had been well prepared and feared nobody. I captained England for the first time in an important match when Graham Gooch tweaked a hamstring. I opened against South Africa, scoring 77 and picking up the Man of the Match award. Then, if it hadn't rained in Adelaide, Pakistan would have been blown away by us. They were all out for 74 and we weren't far off the target, having lost just one wicket when the rains came. Pakistan were very fortunate to share the points. They would have been eliminated if the rain hadn't intervened, but from that day on they never looked back, as if they were inspired by the reprieve. In contrast, we started to go slightly off the boil after that match.

We lost by seven wickets to New Zealand, then were embarrassed to lose to Zimbabwe when we couldn't get 135 to win. We had already qualified for the semi-finals by then, because of our excellent form earlier on, but it wasn't ideal for team morale, even if the batting order was juggled around. In the semi-final, the South Africans were frustrated by the rain, as they needed another 21 off twelve balls to beat us, with four wickets in hand. When they came back on, it was 22 off just one delivery! The rain regulations for that World Cup were baffling, and there was a great deal of sympathy for the South Africans. Not from me. I still felt we would have won it because they would have had to bat out of their skins to get the runs against our experienced, big-match bowlers. We were there to win the game, and the rules were known in advance. They would have had no sympathy at all for us if the boot had been on the other foot. And what about Pakistan's great escape against us in Adelaide? How did they get precious points after being bowled out for 74? They were almost on the plane home, yet they survived to meet us in the Final.

I suppose that World Cup Final was in a way the pinnacle of my one-day career, but it was also the lowest point. To play in front of 87,000 spectators under the lights at the Melbourne Cricket Ground, in a game being watched by millions all around the world, was awesome. We had fantastic English support at the MCG, which made our lap of honour afterwards all the more poignant. We had let them down. We should have won the World Cup for the first time.

We had them 24 for 2 at one stage, and with Imran Khan and Javed Miandad batting very slowly, we were looking favourites at the halfway mark of their innings. To this day, I still don't know why umpire Steve Bucknor failed to give Javed out lbw off Pringle off only his second ball. He stood in front of his stumps and it would have knocked the lot out. It was an astonishing decision and Javed admitted afterwards to Pringle that he was out. Slowly he and Imran turned it round and towards the end Wasim Akram and Inzamam-ul-Haq thrashed the bowling. They ended up with 250, which was more than they should have got. In those days, before batting in one-dayers became more daring, that was a daunting target. We started badly, with Ian Botham going in the first over, caught behind by Moin Khan. It was now a full-on, passionate atmosphere.

I came in at number three and should have been out straight away, edging one off Aquib Javed to Moin. Luckily Brian Aldridge took a leaf out of Steve Bucknor's book and I got away with it. This was no time to walk when you knew you'd nicked it. Nobody else on either side would have given it up in those circumstances, but the Pakistanis were furious at me. A few pleasantries were exchanged between us and I told them that the umpire was there to make the decisions and no one else. A few overs later, however, my luck ran out. I nicked one with an ever bigger deviation and not even I could stand there and try to bluff that one out. I walked. We were now in trouble.

Soon Wasim Akram was making the ball talk with a wonderful display of reverse swing. From around the wicket, he bowled quickly and swung it late. He was devastating. He got Lamb and Lewis with consecutive magnificent deliveries, and they were the killer blows. Wasim was the obvious choice as Man of the Match, and he deserved it for the all-round flair he had shown on the biggest night of his career. Great cricketers make it happen at the really crucial moments.

At the awards ceremony, Imran hogged the podium, talking about the cancer hospital he was trying to build, and although many thought he went on too long about it, without mentioning his players, I wasn't bothered. I wasn't listening. I just blocked the words out of my mind, trying to keep my emotions in check. It was so disappointing to lose after being the outstanding unit for the majority of the tournament. We had tailed off just when we needed fresh impetus. Perhaps fatigue did play a part. We had been on the road for almost four months. But we had got so close. Next day I was still brooding about that defeat. I've never been so disappointed at losing any other match in my career. It was no consolation at all that I could look forward to a few more cracks at the World Cup before I retired. I had geared myself up mentally to winning it this time and we'd failed. I wasn't to know it, but I would never get as close again in three more attempts at the trophy.

I felt sorry for Dad as well as the rest of us. He was due to retire as England coach in a few months' time and would have loved to go one better than in the previous World Cup, when England had also lost in the Final. So his record as coach was played two, lost two Finals. Yet he and Graham Gooch couldn't have done anything more to prepare us; their planning had been spot-on. I did spare a thought for Goochy as well – he'd now played in three World Cup Finals and lost them all. And still England haven't won it after eight tournaments, stretching back to 1975. That is so frustrating.

We saw a lot of the Pakistanis in 1992. They came to us for a five-Test series that involved lots of brilliant cricket, passionate exchanges on both sides that at times spilled over, and an ongoing controversy about ball-tampering by the Pakistani players. Whatever the rights and wrongs of that – and I got sucked into it at the end of the season with Surrey – there's no doubt that Waqar Younis and Wasim Akram bowled wonderfully against us that summer. Add the world-class leg-spin of Mushtaq Ahmed and they had three match-winning bowlers. That made my consistent performances against them even more satisfying.

I'd started off in just the right manner with 190 at Edgbaston in the first Test, my fourth hundred in five Tests. On a flat wicket I carried on my good form of the early part of the summer and cashed in. I was timing the ball well throughout that innings, and my confidence was now so high that I remember being disappointed not to get a double hundred. I pulled a ball to mid-on for 190, when I should have batted out the final afternoon, finishing on something like 240 not out. In fact that 190 remains my highest Test score.

It was Graham Gooch who drummed into me that you must value your innings. He said you can always get cleaned up cheaply with the new ball, so you should never flirt with your form. 'You can never score enough' was his motto. It was fantastic opening the batting with Gooch that summer. He was 39, but still a brilliant batsman. He looked massive at the crease, compared with when you saw him off the field. He just had this dominating presence when he had a bat in his hand. His concentration levels were fantastic; he'd talk away to himself, telling himself to watch the ball as the bowler came in. Dominance in a secure way was his style. He appeared to have a very broad bat, and you felt that bowlers were intimidated by him because of his achievements over a long period.

Goochy was great to bat with. He didn't just think about his own game; he was always encouraging and supportive at the end of the over, and it gave me huge confidence to do well in partnership with one of the world's best players. As captain he set a great example to the other players, both in fitness terms and then making it all count on the field. I had always shared his professional attitude and love of the game, and he was an inspiration to me in my early years in the England side.

He copped a fair amount of criticism as England captain, and finally resigned during the home Ashes series in 1993, saying he could do no more. Critics forget that you can only captain the side that you've been given. If you don't have match-winning bowlers, it's hard to be a flamboyant, exciting captain. In my time with England, we have lacked bowlers who can turn a game in a short space of time. I can think of Gus Fraser, Darren Gough and Andy Caddick who have all won games on their own, but other countries have had geniuses for far longer. So then they beat us, and our detractors, instead of wondering why, settle for blaming the captain.

Goochy would get down if he felt players in his team weren't giving everything to the cause. He couldn't understand why those who get picked for England didn't give themselves the best chance of success – whether by extra physical training, more work in the nets or taking a few extra catches. I've never had a problem with someone who's given his all yet missed out on runs and wickets, and Goochy felt the same way. He was ahead of the rest in England when it came to preparation. All that is taken for granted now, but he and Dad were kindred spirits and after they started working together in 1989 we were certainly better prepared. It used to annoy me when the press satirized Goochy, saying that the way to prepare for a Test match was a thousand press-ups on the morning, then a couple of miles lapping the outfield, without ever picking up a bat or ball. That was absolute rubbish. People in all sports have got better because they prepare more thoroughly. If you are fitter, do you perform worse? Of course not. Whatever job you are in, the fitter you are, the more alert you are, and the more likely to do well in that job. If you're playing a Test in Australia or Sri Lanka and the temperature is over forty degrees and you're not fit enough, then you get found out. You must be a better player if you can keep your concentration in the final session. In turn that attitude can also help to prolong your career. That was certainly the case for Gooch and me.

The supporters of David Gower – who disagreed with Gooch's philosophy of hard work – will always say that he and Ian Botham were examples of another attitude being equally successful. No one was a bigger fan of those two than me, and no one can say for certain that they would have been better if they'd been closer to Gooch's example. But they wouldn't have been inferior players. For me, professional cricket is about doing everything in a professional manner, to give yourself every chance.

This 1992 Test series was to prove the last for both Gower and Botham and the second Test at Lord's saw

Beefy bow out sadly, with a groin strain that prevented him bowling when we could really have done with his ability to conjure wickets out of nothing. We lost a dramatic, tense match by just two wickets, with Wasim Akram and Waqar Younis tormenting us as they added over 40. We were down to three fit bowlers as Botham and Phillip DeFreitas were both troubled with injuries. Having played at Surrey with Waqar, I was surprised to see him bat so capably. But we should have won.

This Lord's Test was the first time that Waqar and Wasim had operated together against us, and they were awesome. They had mastered the art of reverse swing – whereby you keep one side of the ball dry and it swings the way you are not expecting. The later the ball swings, and the faster the pace, the more dangerous you are. That summer there was a lot of chat about the Pakistanis roughing up the ball illegally to aid the reverse swing, but one thing we couldn't argue about was that Waqar and Wasim were wonderful fast bowlers. It takes huge talent to master reverse swing and they were whizzbang bowlers. They could bowl you out for 250, when you'd been coasting along at 215 for 2 by making the old ball go round corners at speed. The best place to bat against them in 1992 was at the top of the order, when the ball was still shiny and they couldn't control the swing. They always attacked, with fielders close to the bat, so the gaps were there. We folded like a pack of cards against them regularly, but that was due to wonderful bowling, not bad batting.

I'd seen Waqar first hand at Surrey in the two previous seasons, when he picked up an astonishing percentage of dismissals by lbw or clean bowled. He was the most devastating bowler I have seen over a period of time. When you batted against him and Wasim in 1992, you'd be straining to spot the shiny side of the ball to tell you if it was going to be an inswinger or outswinger, but then they'd bluff you by hiding the ball with both hands. They'd place the ball at your toes or the foot of the stumps with brilliant yorkers, then vary it with the short ball. They bowled spells against us in the 1992 series that were as fast as anything I've faced. They were a pair of contrasts – Waqar with his long, powerful run-up and a slingy action, Wasim bustling in off just a few yards, pinging it at you with a very fast arm action. They were a great sight and the ultimate test for any batsman around that period.

The challenge of those two great bowlers was one of the main reasons I was so pleased to get runs in that series. I was now doing well against top Test bowlers. In the Lord's Test, I scored 143 for once out and my second innings of 69 not out ranks as one of my best, because of the quality of the bowling I faced and the need to chisel out some sort of target for them to chase in the fourth innings. It took me almost 53 overs to get that 69, with the next highest score just 15. I became the first English batsman to carry his bat in a Test innings at Lord's, which amazed me. The satisfying element was to keep out Wasim and Waqar during their various hostile spells, then deal with Mushtaq's leg-spin. I knew a little about his style of bowling and how he liked to set you up with the odd flighted delivery, so it was a case of watching the ball very closely. Against the two fast bowlers, I made sure I got my feet out of the way, to avoid being lbw, and kept the bat on line, so I wouldn't get bowled. Above all, watch the ball. With wickets falling regularly at the other end, it was difficult but challenging. I loved it.

Wasim and Waqar were just as hostile in the next Test at Old Trafford, and this time they nailed me – but not before a memorable spell of cricket that I relished. On the

Saturday night they had about an hour and a half in which to bowl at us, with a rest day coming up on the Sunday and a big total already posted by their batsmen. They really came hard at us on a fast, bouncy wicket. They bowled at the speed of light, with short-pitched bowling that really tested your reflexes and physical mettle. This was proper Test cricket, light years away from what you get in county cricket. Nothing you encounter on the circuit with your county could prepare you for this. It was torrid, yet exhilarating, and I was disappointed to get out after an hour, caught at slip. But that was one of the most demanding spells I have been involved in down the years in Test cricket. It's why you want to keep playing at the highest level – to keep matching yourself against the very best.

By the middle of that series, the atmosphere between the two sides was degenerating. Some of our guys were particularly annoyed at what they saw as deliberate ball-tampering by the Pakistanis while the opposition weren't happy with our umpires. At Old Trafford, Aquib Javed behaved disgracefully when he ran through the crease to bowl a beamer at Devon Malcolm, who had no pretensions to being a batsman. After being warned by umpire Roy Palmer, he abused Roy, backed up by his captain Javed Miandad, and then snatched his sweater out of the umpire's hand. Roy had been put in an impossible situation and it was inexcusable the way that Aquib and Javed behaved towards him. The bowler was fined half his match fee, and their manager, Intikhab Alam, was reprimanded for adverse comments to the media. Then we got dragged into it. The match referee, Conrad Hunte, reminded both captains of their responsibilities to play the game in the right spirit, which led to a stern reaction from Graham Gooch. In my view he was right to take exception, protesting that we had done nothing wrong in that match and that we were being tarred with the same brush. We agreed, believing that this was a weak effort from Conrad Hunte.

It certainly did nothing to calm things down. The aggressive bowling of the Pakistanis, together with their intimidatory style on the field under a captain who believed in provoking the opposition, was bound to lead to a few flashpoints. They would continue chattering among themselves when the bowler was running in, which didn't show enough respect for the game. We weren't exactly angels either, and there was no love lost between the teams at various stages in that series. They were unlucky with some umpiring decisions at Leeds in the next Test, when Ken Palmer failed to give Goochy run out when he was yards out of his crease. Then, when we were struggling to get 91 to win, with wickets falling cheaply, they were convinced that David Gower had been caught at silly point. They went spare. Rashid Latif was fined for throwing down his cap, the wicketkeeper Moin Khan got a warning for his verbal abuse, and they left Headingley, having lost, with a strong sense of grievance. I had a fraction of sympathy for them in this Test, but more importantly we were back in the series, the score 1-1 with just the Oval Test to come.

Because we were behind in the series going into the Leeds Test, I was the wicketkeeper there, with Jack Russell again missing out. It was becoming a familiar scenario, following Adelaide and the Oval the year before. Most of our batters weren't bowlers, which meant that with Jack in the side we were restricted to four front-line bowlers. In the absence of a Botham in his pomp, we lacked a high-quality all-rounder who could bat at six, so they went for me as the next best option, a batsman who would keep wicket. It didn't seem to matter that Jack could keep wicket better than me. His omission meant we could play the extra bowler or batsman. I felt it was short-sighted and unfair to both of us, but better for the team. I'd done very well in the previous twelve months, either at number three or as an opener. Now I was to be shuffled around the order, depending on how many overs I had kept wicket for. I batted at four in the first innings at Leeds, at five in the second, then opened in both innings at the Oval. A batsman needs to know where he's going to bat in a Test match; he's entitled to peace of mind about that. From a selfish point of view I wanted to carry on opening the innings, but the team's interests came first and I just got on with it. Meanwhile, Jack Russell, an outstanding wicketkeeper, again suffered through the failure of others in the side.

We were hammered at the Oval by ten wickets, so the experiment of playing me as wicketkeeper-batsman didn't bring us any joy this time. Waqar and Wasim again bowled brilliantly. It was not often that David Gower got bowled off-stump, playing no stroke, but Waqar's reverse swing foxed him. Our collapse from 182 for 3 to 207 all out demonstrated just how dominant those two bowlers were. By now, however, the whispers about ball-tampering were getting louder. We'd been talking about it in our dressing-room all season and Richie Benaud made a significant comment on television that summer. The ball had crossed the boundary rope and the cameras caught one of our opposing players running his fingernails over the ball. Richie, in his laidback manner, said, 'I'm not sure that's allowed.' For him to say that was an eye-opener.

We all knew that ball-tampering was going on, and some of the counties weren't innocent. Mine, for a start. Ian Greig had been our recent captain and he had seen it at first hand when he played for Sussex alongside Imran Khan. The practice was to get the fingernails into the ball and rough it up on one side so that the ball would swing late when the other side was soaked in sweat. There was talk of bottle tops being used, secreted into the pockets of players out on the field. When Waqar came to Surrey in 1990, he was the ideal man for reverse swing and we made sure that we had the ball in the ideal condition.

Fingernails were also used to scratch the ball. I was keeping wicket for Surrey at that time and knew all about it. You didn't have to throw the ball to the umpire at the fall of a wicket as you do nowadays, which meant there was plenty of time to alter the ball's condition. Before a drinks break or a scheduled interval like lunch or tea, one of the Surrey players would wet the ball with saliva to try to disguise any scratch marks from the umpires. The idea was for the ball to be in an acceptable condition, then we'd work at it later. I've seen a ball that was fifty overs old look as if it had been used for 250 overs. One side would look like suede and the other like a normal cricket ball.

Surrey weren't the only ones at it. I wonder whether the Lancashire boys used to rough up the ball in the same way, while the abrasive, dry surface at Old Trafford was also ideal for scuffing up the ball. A few years after the ball-tampering saga, Mike Atherton went on record with the opinion that bowlers should be allowed to use a ball that had been worked on. Certainly Wasim Akram bowled many a magnificent spell for Lancashire, swinging the ball alarmingly, with his team-mates possibly performing a valuable back-up service!

During that 1992 series, as the ball-tampering allegations swirled around, we would watch the Pakistanis with our binoculars from our dressing-room balcony. But players from Surrey and Lancashire were less critical than some of our colleagues! After all, English counties down the years who have been blessed with swing bowlers have been known to use lip-salve or sun cream, and more recently the sugar from mints and wine gums on the ball to help it move around late in the air. Is that cheating? Is that altering the condition of the ball?

Ian Botham and Allan Lamb felt particularly strongly about ball-tampering. That may have been partly because the Pakistanis were far from being their favourite opposition, and partly because they were getting away with it. During that summer we played a one-day international against Pakistan at Lord's, when the ball was changed at lunchtime. At the time the ball was being used by their bowlers, and umpires John Hampshire and Ken Palmer decided that enough was enough. It had been a rain-affected match, spread over two days, and with a lush outfield the ball should not have been roughed up. I was stand-in captain, because Gooch was injured, but no one informed me what was going on officially. Dad went to see the umpires about it, and the match referee, but he didn't get very far. If that had happened later in my career, I would have been less inclined to toe the line by leaving it to the umpires and match referee. We'd been watching them work on the ball and it was obvious what was going on. They'd run up to bowl with their hand over the ball, scratching it with a thumb nail. Very clever, but we were familiar with all that. While I was batting at Edgbaston, in the first Test, I kept picking up the ball and examining it closely on both sides before throwing it to a fielder. The Pakistani fielders kept saying, 'Leave it alone, we'll get that,' but I wanted them to know I was on to them. Playing with Waqar at Surrey had been an advantage and they knew it. Throughout that summer, I picked up the ball regularly when batting, much to the Pakistanis' annoyance.

There's no doubt there was a cover-up in that Lord's one-dayer. The Pakistanis maintained the ball simply went out of shape, but the match referee, Derryck Murray, refused to make any public comment at all. Lamby and Beefy were particularly incensed about this and they tipped off the *Daily Mirror*. Over the next few days, all sorts of allegations appeared in the press, and the ICC had to make a statement that the matter was closed. Pakistan was neither exonerated nor condemned in the ICC statement, so you can draw your own conclusions. I suspect the ICC was delighted that the tour was almost over, so that the fuss would die down.

There was a danger that England could be seen as whingers over all this. Certainly the Pakistanis saw it that way. We always talk about the Pakistanis learning how to scratch the ball at an early age because the brown, dusty wickets out there do nothing for seam bowlers. Tales abound in the county dressing-rooms about Sarfraz Nawaz teaching all the tricks to Imran who then hands the tips down to Wasim and Waqar. When Aquib Javed played his first game for Hampshire against one of the university sides, Robin Smith found four huge scratch marks on one side of the ball after just three overs. Robin told him, 'It's a bit obvious if you're doing it so early on in the innings – and anyway, don't waste your time doing it against schoolboys!' So we weren't naïve about ball-tampering, but perhaps frustrated because we had nobody as good as Wasim and Waqar. It's part and parcel of the game that if the opposition has an advantage over you, you moan about it. In that 1992 series we just didn't have the firepower ourselves, even if we had doctored the ball. Ball-tampering had become a hot topic because of the sheer quality of Wasim and Waqar. Whatever you do with the ball, you still have to make best use of it, and they certainly did.

Amid all the controversy, I'm sure the Pakistanis were delighted to hear about one county side being done for ball-tampering, and not for just an isolated occurrence.

That team was Surrey and I was the captain summoned to Lord's to explain. We had been caught and had to take our medicine. Just after that final Test at the Oval, I captained Surrey against Leicestershire at the Oval. I was called into the umpires' room during the game and told by John Holder and Barry Duddleston that we had been altering the ball's condition. They showed it to me and I had to agree. One of the ball's quarters had been opened up to help reverse swing and it was badly scratched. I had been keeping wicket and didn't know how much work had been done on the ball by our fielders, but I had to hold up my hand. We were reported to Lord's. I called a team meeting and told the guys they had been stupid to get caught. There was no point in scuffing up the ball because we had nobody in our team who could reverse swing it as effectively as Waqar, so why do it? Perhaps it was just an ingrained habit from our days with Waqar in the side.

So we went to Lord's to face the music. Other offences were laid at our door. Don Oslear, an experienced umpire with a particular bee in his bonnet about ball-tampering, had reported us on two other occasions – the year before, in successive matches at Guildford. Waqar had taken a lot of wickets in each game. I was acting captain in one of them. There had also been a third occasion when Lord's had been alerted about us – against Gloucestershire at Cheltenham in 1990, when Waqar again played, Ian Greig was captain, but I wasn't playing. As the 1992 Surrey captain, however, I was in charge of conduct on the field when playing, so I had to take it on the chin. To be fair, I had also known what was happening on the previous occasions.

There was no doubt that we were guilty, and it was irrelevant that other counties were at it as well. We'd been the ones who were caught out. John Holder and Barry Duddleston were both at the Lord's hearing, and I took the opportunity to say, 'I hear what you say about what we did in the Leicestershire match and we'll take our punishment. But can you tell me why you two umpires, who have both stood in matches involving the Pakistanis this summer, haven't done a thing about them? It's been obvious what they've been up to. Yet a county gets done for the same thing.' I didn't get a satisfactory answer. Surrey were fined £1000, suspended for two years and we agreed to return the ball to the umpires at the end of each over, hoping that other counties would do the same. We were also told that nothing said in that hearing would go past those four walls. Next day, it was all over the papers, although nothing came from those representing Surrey. We kept our side of the bargain.

But it was open season on ball-tampering in September 1992, and everything got rather hysterical. English cricket didn't come out of it all that well, especially as we were not exactly saints ourselves when it came to getting an advantage. Ball-tampering hasn't been stamped out in world cricket since 1992, but the greater number of TV cameras and increased vigilance from match referees have reduced it. Umpires are now entitled to ask to see the ball at any stage and they get it at the end of every over. I don't believe that England have been guilty of actually scratching the ball since 1992, partly out of fear of getting caught, partly because we haven't had that many reverse swing bowlers. Darren Gough has been the best in that line, while Chris Lewis and Craig White have been good at it for a time, but there's been no one like Wasim and Waqar. It would have been good to have expert reverse swing bowlers firing out opposing teams regularly, but it wasn't to be.

I couldn't be too het up about ball-tampering at the end of the 1992 summer for two reasons. It would have been hypocritical, given my Surrey involvement, and I had also batted very well against the best fast-bowling combination in the world. I'd topped the averages against them, coping with reverse swing bowled by two outstanding performers in a technique that was devastating on a consistent basis.

atherton or stewart?

In 1993 everybody got very excited about a change in the England captaincy. Obviously Graham Gooch, who was nearly 40 years of age, couldn't go on much longer and there would soon be a vacancy. By the summer it had come down to two main candidates – Mike Atherton and me. By then I had been on the tour to India and Sri Lanka as Goochy's vice-captain again, which may have put me in pole position in many people's eyes, but I had more than enough on my plate to be bothering with speculation. I didn't play very well, for a start. In common with the rest of the batsmen, I didn't play the spinners all that confidently. I wasn't sure about how much pad to bring into my defensive technique and never really knew what was permissible in the judgement of the umpires. I was more tentative than I'd previously been against the spinners, pushing forward rather too firmly at times, and giving catches to close fielders on either side of the wicket.

We lost all four Tests by wide margins, got hammered in two one-dayers in Sri Lanka and drew the one-day series in India. There were all sorts of distractions on that tour, with a load of rubbish being churned out by the press about our image. We were deemed to have been dishevelled and surly on several occasions while in the public eye, but anyone who was on that long, tough tour with us for any length of time would agree that we were unlucky in the way that certain things were portrayed. It didn't help either that our chairman of selectors, Ted

Dexter, kept putting his foot in it, to the delight of the media. On a slow news day, Ted could be relied upon by the journalists.

It was a very difficult tour for Graham Gooch. Right at the start, he confirmed that his marriage had broken up. That was a shock to all of us. We had assumed that Graham's long marriage that had brought him three lovely daughters would withstand the pressures of being away from home so often, and we were all very sad for him. I'm sure Graham would now admit that, because of his personal problems, he was more insular than usual on that tour. He spent a fair amount of time in his room, with his great friend John Emburey for company, and I'm sure he found the demands of captaincy harder than usual.

The captain was under fire from many quarters even before a ball was bowled in India because of the squad he had helped pick. There was no place for Jack Russell or David Gower, and that caused a big fuss. Jack was still the best keeper around, and would have relished the job on turning wickets, but Richard Blakey of Yorkshire got the trip because he was a good batsman too, as number-two keeper to me. Dick and I had both started our careers as batsmen before taking up wicketkeeping. Were we good enough to warrant dispensing with someone of Jack's class? Or Gower's. It seemed a strange decision not to choose David, given his experience of batting on the subcontinent and his huge natural ability. It was presented in the press as a contest between the Roundhead and the Cavalier, while Goochy's supporters felt we ought to build for the future. David was 35, and had been struggling with a shoulder injury, but he was surely still too good to ignore. I had no say on selection, even though I was vice-captain, but when I saw the squad I was concerned about the omission of Jack and David.

Goochy also had a new coach to work with. Dad had retired and a familiar face to the captain, Keith Fletcher, who had captained him for many years at Essex with enormous success, had been appointed. Goochy obviously knew him very well from Essex, but it was bound to mean a change of emphasis after working alongside Dad. Fletch was certainly quieter, an old-fashioned cricket man who was big on working at cricketing skills rather than physical training. He felt that you played cricket to get fit. I liked Fletch very much and he was particularly good in one-to-ones with the players. You could see how much Goochy respected him, but I think it all got on top of Fletch eventually in his two years as coach. He wasn't dominant enough in team meetings and couldn't get across his coaching philosophy as easily as he would have wished. He got frustrated with some of the players he had to work with during those two years. Having had nothing but success in county cricket, it was difficult for him with England.

Phil Tufnell caused the tour management a few problems. At Vishhakhapatna, he had a bust-up with an umpire for being no-balled continually, then he climbed into Dick Blakey on the field for failing to stump Sachin Tendulkar. That was unforgiveable – you just don't say what he said to a team-mate. Tuffers had got wound up because he wasn't bowling sides out on turning wickets, but instead of looking to sort out his own game and adapt, he took it out on a lad on his first senior tour. That really upset the apple cart and he was hauled up in front of Goochy, me, Fletch and the tour manager, Bob Bennett. Tuffers' psychological make-up was very shaky on that tour. He said we'd got it all wrong about the Blakey incident, then he turned round and said he was really sorry. We fined him £500 for ungentlemanly conduct towards the umpire, but that was not the last time that

Tufnell was to cause the tour management severe grief in his England career.

In Australia, on the 1994–5 tour, he was having serious marital problems and while we were in Perth he just flipped. He trashed his hotel room in frustration and Mike Atherton, his captain, went to see him. He found Tuffers sitting naked on his bed, with a towel around his shoulders and a cigarette in his mouth. He was crying his eyes out and in a terrible state. The management met to consider the situation, knowing that it was unfamiliar territory. Phone calls were made to Lord's about what to do. Should we take the huge step of sending him to a psychiatric ward? Should he be sent home to sort out his personal problems? In the end, it was decided that he had to go to hospital. One hour later Tuffers burst through the manager's door, back from hospital. He had a can of beer in his hand and proceeded to give the management massive earache about what had gone on. He insisted that he was fine and persuaded everyone that he did not need to return to hospital.

That was the trouble with Tuffers – he could be very hard work at times. You were never too sure just how he'd behave when he was running up to bowl early on in an England tour. He came across as a Jack the Lad, full of streetwise front, but I don't think he was ever that confident on the international stage. On his day he was a top-class slow bowler, and he did win us a few Tests, but on many other occasions he was just another bowler. He was not a great fielder and was a poor batsman who didn't fancy the quicks at all, so all he had to offer was his bowling. Tuffers was so desperate for success that he saw it as a personal slight if anyone misfielded off his bowling, conveniently forgetting that he did it at times himself. His Test record was patchy and you had to work out whether it was worth putting up with all the baggage that is Phil Tufnell.

I never picked him when I was England captain because I wasn't convinced he was then bowling as well as he did when he first played in the early nineties. I was also big on getting a team on to the park in every sense of the word, rather than eleven individuals. The question I asked myself was: what will give us the best chance of winning?

There was one occasion when I was totally on his side in the field after a spat with an umpire. It was in Australia during a Test on the 1990–1 tour when he got into a ruck with Peter McConnell. Tuffers asked him how many deliveries were left in the over, only to be told, 'Count them yourself, you Pommy bastard.' That was ridiculously rude and unprofessional, and Graham Gooch had a go at the umpire about that.

Having given Tuffers some stick, I must also point out that he was the funniest man I ever played cricket with. He would have me in stitches with his gift of story-telling, his daft mannerisms and his phrases. He could tell a tale superbly, straight out of the London Streetwise Manual, and whenever I meet up with him, he still makes me laugh. However, in top-class sport you've got to pick those players who'll fight for you when it's really tough. And Phil Tufnell didn't come through for you often enough.

Tufnell was left out of the first Test, in Calcutta, and so was John Emburey, as we decided to go in with four seamers. Not a good move. We thought that the cracks on the wicket would widen, that it would go up and down for the quicker bowlers. It didn't. The ball turned sharply for the Indian spinners on a dry, firm pitch, and we lost by eight wickets.

The next Test, in Madras, was an even bigger hammering, by an innings. Not the ideal way for me to mark my first Test as captain. Graham Gooch had to drop out just before the toss, feeling dizzy and ill – all because of a plate of prawns. I'd been at the same table the night before in the team hotel, when a few of us ordered about eight separate Chinese dishes. We kept spinning the plates around, trying them all, but only Mike Gatting and Goochy were ill the following day. Gatt made the final eleven, but he didn't feel well and had to leave the field at one stage. So did Robin Smith, who'd eaten in his room. Perhaps it wasn't the prawns that were dodgy after all; maybe Goochy drank his water out of a dirty glass. The press certainly climbed into us, saying that we'd been unprofessional in not following the recommended diet for that part of the world. But it was a high-class hotel, Chinese food was not banned, and these things happen in India. If we'd won the Test, it would all have been forgotten.

So my promotion to skipper happened in a rush. I was still doing all the pre-match training work when I was suddenly told to dash off and toss the coin, because Goochy wasn't going to make it. For once, I was caught out in the presentation department. I'd always prided myself on being smart when on official duty, but I had no time to put on a cricket shirt and had to make do with a white T-shirt under my England blazer. So the circumstances were far from ideal. We also had a dilemma about our final eleven. Who would come in for Gooch? Atherton was an option as opener, or Blakey could come in and keep wicket instead of me. I had opened and kept wicket in Calcutta, but I didn't believe I'd be able to give of my best in Madras if I added the captaincy responsibilities. So Blakey came in at number six; I opened but didn't keep wicket, and Robin Smith moved up to partner me.

When I walked out ahead of the team, it finally sank in that I was captaining England in a Test match. I was proud, of course, but that was all there was to it. I'd captained Surrey sides at various age levels, and had done the job at county level for one summer, as well as deputizing twice for Goochy in the World Cup. But this was rather different. In any case I had already made the cardinal error. I had lost the toss on a wicket that was set to turn. It did, their spinners took seventeen of our twenty wickets, and although we managed to prolong the game until the fifth morning, we just weren't in the game at any stage.

The third Test at Bombay was another innings defeat for us, but for many in the media that was all too predictable now. The run-out fiasco involving me and Athers was the story. Yet it was just one of those things that happen every day on a cricket pitch somewhere. Athers had come in to bat at number three for this Test and he was obviously desperate to make up for lost time, having drifted through the tour without playing much cricket. He seemed a lonely figure at times, wandering around with a big book under his arm, and I'm sure he was very disappointed to have missed out on the previous Test when we had to revamp the final eleven in a hurry.

We came together when Gooch was out cheaply on the first day. I played a ball to cover and called for a quick single, but Athers didn't want it and turned back. I carried on running to his end and actually beat him into the crease. Someone was run out, but who would go? Technically it ought to have been Athers, but he wasn't going to give it away, understandably, after his frustrations on the tour. We didn't exchange a word while umpire Venkataraghavan adjudicated, but that was quite normal. A batsman in these circumstances thinks to himself, 'I don't want to be the one to go.' In the end I had to go, and I admit I wasn't best pleased about it. It's one of the worst ways to get out, especially when you believe you've been sold short. I'm sure it made a great photograph, but he and I talked it over that night. We agreed to disagree about the merits of my call for that run, but there was never a falling-out.

With Gooch nearing the end of his captaincy reign, it was suggested that this stand-off between me and Athers symbolized the struggle for the succession, and that we didn't get on. That was rubbish. We didn't know each other that well, because we'd only toured once together owing to Athers' back problems, but there had been no difficulties at all between us and there never were subsequently. Some might say that I was being selfish in standing my ground and waiting for the decision, while others could feel that Athers was also looking after number one. It was simply a piece of decision-making that went wrong. We've laughed about it many times since, and Athers wrote an amusing article about it for my 1994 benefit brochure. Yet, a few months later, when our respective claims for the England captaincy were being considered, that run-out at Bombay was dragged up. In fact it had no significance at all.

Losing that Test series 3-0 was a huge disappointment to us, because we knew we hadn't played to our capabilities. From then on it was open season on us. Ted Dexter became Mr Rent-a-Quote at times and the media lapped it up. After we'd lost in Calcutta, he said that air pollution experts should commission a study on the effects of smog on England cricketers in India. Certainly the smog wasn't pleasant, but we didn't go on about it as much as Ted did. He then held forth on designer stubble, indicating that he thought we should have looked smarter on that tour. I thought that was trivial and unfair. Because of a prolonged strike by pilots with Indian Airways, we were flying vast distances all round the country to get to destinations that would normally have been relatively easy to reach. Sometimes we'd go on train journeys that lasted about eight hours in filthy carriages. We'd turn up at some unearthly hour on a railway platform somewhere and then have to do the stage-managed photo on behalf of our sponsors, Tetley's Bitter. Next thing we know is that the papers back home are crucifying us for looking scruffy, the general line being that we not only can we not play cricket, but we don't even look the part.

Then poor Bob Bennett, our manager, had a serious back problem. He couldn't move and he was in agony. As tour manager he still had to deal with the media on one specific occasion, so they all piled into his hotel room. Bob struggled on to the sofa to give his statement, wearing a polo shirt and a pair of shorts, and the photographs were damaging. Now the angle was: it's hardly surprising that the team's playing so badly when the manager looks like he's on holiday. It all goes hand-in-hand with losing. If you're winning, you can turn up in jeans, T-shirt and five o'clock shadow and no one in the media will bat an eyelid.

We were all in a bit of a siege mentality as the Indian leg of the tour drew to a close. I took exception to some remarks about me on the radio by Jonathan Agnew, the BBC's cricket correspondent. I was told by friends and family back home that he had laid into me during the radio commentaries, saying I was guilty of dissent when given out. Well, none of us was walking, that's for sure. We felt we were getting a raw deal from the Indian umpires as we pushed forward, playing bat and pad. I said to Agnew, 'There's a difference between dissent and disappointment.' He hadn't played much international cricket and I wondered just how much he had cared about his career. I certainly did about mine. I said to him, 'I'm entitled to show disappointment. If you want me to walk off with a smile on my face, that won't happen. Just because I stand at the crease and look up to the sky when given out doesn't mean I'm guilty of dissent.' He kept going on about it the following summer and I was annoyed. He was a recently retired cricketer, who felt he was now an authority on the game and that he could pontificate about how I was feeling. Yet he barely knew me as a cricketer, let alone as a person.

When I get out, I always look over my shoulder at the giant electronic screen, but Agnew seemed to think that was dissent. I told him, 'Check my reaction whenever I'm out: I always look at the screen, even if I've been bowled. I'm not in the dressing-room quickly enough to see my dismissal on the TV replay, and I want to see it there and then.' I had no qualms about fronting up to Agnew. I do it whenever I think someone in the cricket media has got something factually wrong about me. Opinion is a different matter – I'll listen to anyone's views on cricket, as long as they care about the game.

By the time we arrived in Sri Lanka to play a one-off Test and two one-day internationals, we were a tired, dispirited squad. Goochy had gone home, as had been prearranged before the start of the tour and the announcement of his marriage break-up, and I took over as captain for the Sri Lankan leg. It was hard and we lost those three games easily. No excuses – we played badly. But the humidity was remarkable. From my experience of playing cricket around the world, I would say that in terms of humidity Colombo is the hardest place to play. Keith Fletcher said it was almost too humid for Europeans to play there and although that was taken as just an excuse, I could see his point. You had to change batting gloves every five or six overs. Robin Smith batted over seven hours for a hundred in the Test and I reckon he changed his shirt every half-hour – it was just sticking to him. We certainly didn't have enough time to acclimatize. The Sri Lankans have the same problem when they come to the cold of England in April and May. They rarely do themselves justice.

Standing in for Goochy as skipper was a difficult task for me. I knew I was only the fill-in, and I struggled to impose my own style over such a short period of time with a beaten, tired group of players. The wickets turned and we weren't up to it – it was as simple as that. I kept wicket and batted at number five, scoring 63 in the Test, but it wasn't a spell with England that I look back on with great fondness. It was good to get home.

We returned to the inevitable inquests at Lord's about our failure on the sub-continent and there was a lot of adverse comment about our image. There was speculation that Ted Dexter would resign as chairman of selectors and that Graham Gooch would stand down as captain. The rumour industry worked overtime and the media had a great time for weeks. The spotlight inevitably fell on Mike Atherton and me as the possible saviours of the England team, with many saying that Goochy was past his sell-by date. Athers and I both felt embarrassed at all this, because of our great respect for the captain, and we just tried to get on with our jobs. With the Australians visiting us that summer, we had enough to think about.

We were thrashed again by the Aussies. We managed to get one back in the final Test at the Oval, but the 4-1 margin didn't flatter us. In two of the Tests we were still in the field on the third morning of the Test and my abiding memories of that series are watching them rack up massive scores, and Shane Warne's fantastic spin bowling. He announced himself at Old Trafford with his first ball in an Ashes Test that turned square outside Mike Gatting's leg stump, and then bowled him off-stump. He has been a wonderful entertainer, the smartest bowler I've ever faced and great for the game worldwide. And in that 1993 series he showed his dual value by taking stacks of wickets – 34 of them – and bowling long, accurate spells, sometimes for two hours. If you had Shane Warne in your side at his peak, you had a head start on the opposition. He has to be one of the greatest bowlers of all time, and that's not just my opinion. Older players whose judgement I respect share that view.

We just never got into that series. England used 24 players, compared to Australia's thirteen. Only three of us – Athers, Goochy and myself – lasted the entire series. They beat us at Lord's by an innings with just ten men. Craig McDermott, their top fast bowler, was taken to hospital with a twisted bowel on the second morning as they piled on the runs, and he took no part in the rest of the match or the series. Mark Waugh, of all people, had to open the bowling. And still they hammered us. At Leeds we had four pace bowlers with a combined experience of five Test Matches. The Australians scored over 600 and lost just four wickets: another innings defeat.

It was all too much for Goochy and he resigned before leaving Headingley. We felt we had let him down, but he wouldn't be talked out of it. It was time for a change, he felt, and with two Tests left in the series, the successor would have something to work on. Quite a challenge for the new man!

For the next ten days, everyone had their say about who should be captain. I was deemed to be the favourite, because I'd already done the job as a stand-in on several occasions over the previous eighteen months, and I had some county experience – unlike Athers. The general feeling was that we were both automatic choices in the side, so that the eleven wouldn't be weakened. There was a lot of talk about the need for fresh blood and more dynamism in the field because some believed that Goochy's body language was too passive and careworn. I never took any notice of that; you captain what you have available. No one would have given a monkey's about body language if we'd been winning.

Some of the stuff in the newspapers was ridiculous. Some tried to drag in the class system to contrast me and Athers. Simon Heffer wrote a silly piece in the *Daily Mail*, contrasting the southern oik with the sophisticated Cambridge graduate from the north. The implication was that I was tough and uncompromising, coming from the School of Hard Knocks, whereas Athers was the calm intellectual who could rise above it all. Now, among Athers' most admirable traits are his mental toughness and hard competitive instinct, and Heffer's generalizations were ridiculous. Mum, uncharacteristically, got very upset at the article and wrote to Heffer to point out that I had gone to a grammar school and didn't lack for anything in my upbringing. She felt there was an implication that I hadn't been brought up all that well by my parents, and she told Heffer he needed to check his facts. It certainly was a lazy piece, but it was unlike Mum to get involved.

We were all relieved when the decision was finally made at the start of August. I was playing at Taunton in a championship match and Ted Dexter rang me in the evening to say that Athers would be the new captain and that it would be announced in the morning. It was a short, polite conversation. I didn't feel the need to ask Ted the reasons for the decision, because I wasn't exercised by it one way or the other. Of course, I would have accepted if offered it, but there was a slight doubt in my mind whether I'd have been up to the job at that stage of my career. At thirty, I was five years older than Athers, but I was still inexperienced in captaincy and wasn't sure I was ready for it. Staying in the England team and playing well have always been the primary targets for me. I've set myself achievable goals, things that I can influence – whereas the

England captaincy depends on the opinions of the selectors and others behind the scenes.

I've since found out that Dad pushed for me. He was on the England committee, because his new role was looking at young players and reporting about them to Keith Fletcher. He thought that as Athers had been out of the England set-up for a time due to his back problems, I'd be the better bet because I represented continuity. He believed that I should step up from the vice-captaincy and that my extra experience gave me the edge. I would never have discovered this if Ted Dexter hadn't blurted out at the press conference that 'Micky fought hard for his son, as you'd expect from any father.' Dad heard that on the car radio and wasn't too impressed that a confidence had been publicized. To be fair to Ted, he realized his error straight away and rang up Dad to apologize. Apparently, he was very shame-faced and Dad soon got over it and they remained friends.

Athers and I had a good laugh about that when we met up. I'd left him a message of congratulations on his answer-phone at home, pledging my full support. I was privately relieved not to get the job and wished Athers well, because we were short of the necessary top-drawer, experienced players to turn it round in a short space of time. It would be a long haul. But there was never any competition between us for the post. I was totally behind him throughout, just as he was behind me when I took over from him in 1998.

Looking back on it now, it's amusing that many media people thought that Athers' appointment would herald an exciting period for English cricket, with a young, dynamic leader thrusting us forward. Many were convinced he would be fresh and exciting in the job, contrasting his boyish appearance with the withdrawn, ageing Gooch. Now Athers may have remained youthful in looks, but within a year he was getting all sorts of adverse comment about slouching around with his hands in pockets, looking detached from his players on the field, even lacking inspiration. All that is so superficial. He always had a shrewd, mature head on his shoulders and would do the job in his own way. Athers would never pretend to be anything other than his natural self and he was right to captain England in his own particular fashion. He was understandably dismissive of all the superficiality associated with the change of captaincy.

I thought he got it spot-on with his first tour party to the West Indies in 1994. He wanted young players with spirit who could grow into the responsibilities under a skipper of the same age. He therefore went for Matt Maynard, Nasser Hussain and Graham Thorpe, rather than the more mature batsmen like Mike Gatting and Graham Gooch, and I think he was right. That was the squad that Athers wanted and he seemed comfortable with them in the Caribbean. It was a little similar to the party that went out there in 1990, with a lot of youthful promise to back up the experienced guys. It was always going to be tough against bowlers like Ambrose and Walsh, but it made sense to trust in young players.

With Jack Russell back in favour, I was going to open the innings, which suited me. I'd kept wicket throughout the Ashes series while batting at numbers four, five and six, but the position I really fancied was opener. I hadn't done that for eighteen months with England, but I was looking forward to opening with Athers for the first time. It would prove to be a rewarding partnership.

Right from the first Test, I had first-hand evidence of his immense guts. At Sabina Park, Courtney Walsh gave him a serious working over, peppering him with short deliveries aimed at the ribs and heart. Targeting the captain has always been a favoured West Indian tactic – the

Aussies followed suit when they became the world's best – and Athers was in the firing line. Walsh went around the wicket and just aimed at Athers' body. He'd end up on his back, but jump up, flashing that toothy grin at the bowler, and they couldn't rattle him. I knew Athers was a quality batsman, but I could now see at close quarters just how mentally strong he was. Bowlers of the calibre of Walsh and Ambrose would try to get you out in normal ways, then revert to short-pitched bowling to see if you had enough guts to stay in line and watch the ball closely. They'd stop you getting on the front foot and test your ability to find areas to score runs. After Athers and I had put on over a hundred for the first wicket at Sabina Park, Walsh and Ambrose never tried those intimidatory tactics against Athers again for the rest of the series, and he ended up scoring more than 500 runs. He was magnificent, leading from the front and setting a fantastic example.

I loved opening the batting with Mike Atherton and I just wish we had done it more often. Our styles complemented each other. I'd play my shots if all was right in my game, whereas he'd just bat and bat, playing some fine strokes himself. He would take on the short ball and hook and pull as much as me. Both of us could defend and play off the back foot, which is essential in Test cricket. Athers' concentration levels were the best I've ever known among English batsmen. Nothing was ever allowed to get into his bubble to distract him. Between overs, on the other hand, we would relax and have a joke, just to lighten the tension. Once, in the Trinidad Test of 1998, I got whacked on my elbow by Winston Benjamin. A photograph shows Athers wincing, clearly thinking 'that must have hurt', and then, when he realized I was OK, another photo shows him bursting out laughing. We always enjoyed banter out in the middle, at the right time.

We knew each other's game well and used just to run on the nod for the sharp single. That run-out at Bombay in 1993 was soon a distant memory. The only time he and I were involved in a run-out as openers came in the Jamaica Test of 1994 when I took on Kenny Benjamin's throw from long-off on the third run – and lost a direct hit. I was so annoyed at myself that I showed anger for once in the dressing-room, punching a hole in the locker-room door. It was only made of plywood, so I didn't break any knuckles, but I was raging in frustration. That dismissal was totally my fault.

It was good to be able to have someone keeping an eye on my technique on tour, both in the nets and out in the middle. On practice days we'd stand at the side of the net and look closely at each other's work, to make sure we were doing the basics right. Footwork was always something we examined carefully. Athers was very good square on the off side, and he had a lovely cover drive. I really admired the way he could switch on and off with his concentration levels. He had fantastic willpower, enormous bravery and all the other attributes of a top-class opening batsman. That duel with Allan Donald in the 1998 Trent Bridge Test remains the best piece of Test cricket I've ever seen – a great fast bowler furiously trying to prise out a batsman who just refused to buckle. Athers mastered the perfect response to sledging or psychological intimidation from the bowler. He would just stand there looking the bowler in the eye, or smiling, well aware that eventually the bowler would lose eye contact because he would have to turn around and walk back to his mark. So Athers would always win the staring contest.

The Australians could never master Athers in psychological warfare. Merv Hughes would huff and puff, blustering in his face, and Athers would completely fox him by quoting Shakespeare at him. Merv had no comeback to that. On his first England tour to Australia, Athers nicked one and didn't walk. Ian Healy, the wicketkeeper, went absolutely spare. Athers turned round, smiled his cheesy grin and said, 'When in Rome, Ian.' He was only 22 at the time, and Healy was silenced. There's nothing better than winding up a keeper by telling him you've nicked it after getting away with it. And the Aussies are past masters at that.

If Athers was very secure in his batting in 1994, before his back started to trouble him, he had a severe wake-up call as England captain. He had to learn the hard way right from the off, at the age of 25, in his first two series against the best two sides, Australia and West Indies. We went 2-0 down in the Caribbean, because our batting was not tight enough against the quicks, our catching was fallible at crucial moments and we were unlucky with the toss of the coin. But then we were blown away at Trindad, getting bowled out for 46, to go 3-0 down.

That nightmare at Trinidad will never be forgotten by any of those English players. It was absolutely devastating. We were in a winning position, as the West Indies were just 60-odd runs ahead, with half their side out. On the fourth morning, we were a very confident team as we prepared to go to the ground. The Sky Sports TV cameras recorded us getting into our team coach at the hotel, and when someone shouted out, 'Good luck!', I said, 'We'll be all right today – we'll win.' Idiot! That night, when we returned to the hotel, we needed only another 154 to win – but we knew we almost certainly weren't going to make it. We were 40 for 8.

They got about 70 runs too many on the fourth day because two dropped catches at slip by Graeme Hick reprieved Shivnarine Chanderpaul and he hung around to make valuable runs. Even so, a target of 194 was well within our range. But it rained between the two innings and two hours' play was lost. They had fifteen overs at us before the close, so Ambrose and Walsh could come out guns blazing and really slip themselves. When the bowlers only have about seven overs each before the close, they can bend their backs, and for a batsman, with close fielders breathing down his neck, all that adds to the pressure. But none of that explains the unbelievable bowling of Ambrose.

He got Athers out to the first ball of the innings, and he was at his very best – knees pumping, running in smoothly, profiting from a wicket of uneven bounce. He gave us absolutely nothing loose in a remarkable demonstration of brilliant fast bowling. I top-scored with 18, playing a shot or two, until Curtly bowled me on the back foot with one that nipped back.

The dressing-room was deathly quiet at the close. We couldn't believe it. The game had gone away from us in just over an hour. If we'd been just four down overnight, there might have been a chance for us, but not at 40 for 8. In the space of eight hours, my foolhardy comment to the cameras had come back to haunt me. Room service was the order of the day that night.

We lasted for a quarter of an hour next morning but we were finally all out for 46. We were embarrassed and the pictures of us standing around at the awards ceremony, looking very sheepish, appeared in a lot of newspapers back home. There was no excuse and no hiding place for us. We felt very sorry for the hundreds of English supporters who had flown out to Trinidad and were desperate to see us win. All we could hope for was to give them something to cheer in the next Test at Barbados.

Before that, however, we lost again – and very badly. We went to Grenada to lose by eight wickets to a President's eleven on another poor pitch. I captained the side and kept wicket. This game was the low point of the tour. It came too soon after the humiliation of being bowled out for 46 and was no sort of preparation at all for Barbados. That only makes our victory there even more remarkable.

Barbados was an amazing turnaround by us. We were playing for our pride, to heal some of the wounds of Trinidad, while the support we had at the Kensington Oval was fantastic. Around six thousand English fans were there every day, and the noise and colour were marvellous. We became the first visiting side to win a Barbados Test for 59 years and, just to make it even more memorable for me, I scored a hundred in each innings. It was one of the great occasions of my career.

I love Barbados anyway. They're crazy about cricket and the locals banter with you in an affectionate way. They show you respect, they are very knowledgeable and they like to laugh. Lynn and my son Andrew had flown out to join me, and their presence just added to the superb five days I had.

We batted first on a very good pitch, and the reception Athers and I got when we went out to bat was brilliant. I felt so proud to be English that day. When we got to 47, the crowd erupted and we didn't realize why straight away. We had managed to go one better than Trinidad, and Athers and I had a good laugh about that. We just batted on and on and were chuffed to go into lunch, still together. Another wonderful ovation from the crowd. We put on 171 before Athers went, and I carried on playing very well. I got to my hundred by pulling Ambrose through mid-wicket, and the reception I got from both sets of supporters was unforgettable. All this on my 31st birthday – and Chelsea got to Wembley that day by beating Luton in the FA Cup semi-final! With my wife and son out there as well, it was one of the red-letter days of my England career.

Dad was coaching the England Under-19s at Lilleshall and he rang me before we batted again with some typical old pro's advice. 'Now then, it's start-again time' were his words. I hoped so. It was an excellent pitch, ideal for my shots, with short, square boundaries. I'd played as well as I'd ever done for England in that first innings and I felt in tremendous nick. We'd see how it went in the second innings.

For the first time in my career, I got two hundreds in the match. The fact that it was against high-class bowlers in a Test match that we eventually won just made it a perfect game for me. My 143 in the second innings wasn't as fluent as my first hundred, but I battled hard for almost eight hours. When I reached three figures, a group of English supporters invaded the pitch and bowed down in front of me in the fashion of those characters in the film *Wayne's World* – 'We are not worthy.' Not sure about that. At the moment of exhilaration, I looked towards the TV commentary box where Geoffrey Boycott was working and waved my bat in his direction as a mark of gratitude for all his support through the years. We'd had dinner earlier on the tour, in Jamaica, and his advice had been as sound as usual – 'Just play naturally; you're good enough to do well against this lot.' Back home, Mum was rushing around, trying to get someone to watch my innings with her, to share the moment, because Dad was still up at Lilleshall. I think he was pleased that I had indeed started all over again!

I felt a huge release of emotion as that back-foot force went through the covers for four. I'm usually quite calm when I reach a century but this time I punched the air and shouted out in my exhilaration. What a time to do something for the first time in my career! The acknowledgement from the crowd was fantastic and I felt very proud. The West Indies players were great to me as well, very sporting. It's moments like this that make you play the game. I've always loved playing in front of large, excitable, noisy crowds, and the desire to do well in a big game is what makes the top players different from the others. You must want to thrive on the big occasion – really want it.

I was on a high that night, absolutely elated, and the reaction from one West Indian supporter summed up why I've always loved playing out there. I walked into the hotel foyer that evening, grinning from ear to ear, and this giant Barbadian shouted out, 'Where's big bat Stewart? Respect, man!', followed by the obligatory high fives. And respect to Barbados people from me, too, for the way they appreciate the game of cricket. It's one of the best places in the world to play.

Even better, we went on to win the Test, with everyone contributing at some stage in the game, especially Gus Fraser with 8 for 75 in the first innings. Of course, it was a surprise to win, but we had pressurized them throughout. Pressure acts as your twelfth man, no matter how good the opposition is. When the side batting last has to chase a large total in the fourth innings, the fielding side can get into their ribs by grabbing some early wickets. That's what we did, our confidence soared, and we were unrecognizable from our poor effort in Trinidad. I also ended up with a stump as a memento when Curtly Ambrose was bowled to win us the game. He was so angry at losing that he smashed his stumps down and one of them came in my direction in the gully. Amby ended up with a £1000 fine from the match referee for showing how much he hated losing, and I got something to commemorate one of my happiest games!

I was particularly pleased for Athers that we won in Barbados after all the flak he had taken when we went 3-0 down in the series and for the hurt he would have felt after that abject collapse in Trinidad. The captain always feels defeat more than the rest of the team, and he could be proud at the guts and self-respect his players had shown in bouncing back. We celebrated in glamorous style – sitting on the floor that night at Barbados Airport. We had to hang around for hours, waiting for a connecting flight to Antigua, because the final Test was due to start in a couple of days' time.

That Antigua Test will always be remembered as Brian Lara's match. He scored 375, the highest-ever Test score, in an amazing display of batting. The wicket was one of the flattest of all time, but that shouldn't detract from Lara's awesome batting. He made it look so easy and didn't play a false shot until Gus Fraser beat him outside the off stump when he was at about 340, prompting a classic remark from Gus: 'I can't really call you a lucky sod when you're on 340, can I?' Lara's bat appeared to be about four feet wide, and his bat speed and placement of the ball were amazing. To bat for a whole day in a Test match is hard enough, but to do it into the third day, with all the pressure building up on you, is magnificent. I'd been aware that he was a special talent – we'd played against him on the previous tour to the Caribbean in 1990 – but this was something else.

The nearer he got to breaking Garry Sobers' score of 365, the more I wanted Brian to do it. You want every game you play to be a win, and every opposing batsman to get nought, but I look back on Brian's feat with pleasure and with appreciation of the fact that I was on the field to see him do it. The presence of the great Sobers at the ground only added to the sense of occasion. When the crowd spilled on to the pitch to celebrate the record, we were glad of the delay, because it meant that for a few minutes Brian wouldn't be thrashing us around the park! But it was great to have first-hand experience of a wonderful performance.

After the match, Brian very generously gave me a signed shirt that I could auction for my benefit that year. Everybody was after him to sign things, and he was exhausted, but he couldn't have been more helpful. The shirt was one that he had fielded in during that historic Test. There was some unfavourable publicity about that shirt when it was auctioned off and I want to set the record straight about it. The man who bought it knew that it wasn't the actual shirt that Brian wore when he scored his 375 and he confirmed that when I managed to track him down a few days later after the story appeared. He had no problem with that.

On his day, Brian Lara is the best player I've ever seen, and I say that as a huge fan of Sachin Tendulkar. While Tendulkar is classically correct, and superb to watch, Lara just destroys you. People have criticized his rashness but a strokemaker is always likely to get out, going through his full repertoire of shots, compared with someone who nicks it off a forward defensive stroke. I believe that Brian has done himself justice, despite his dips in form. He does average more than 50 in Tests, which sets him apart. After that 375 and then his 501 a few weeks later – the highest score in first-class cricket – it was inevitable that he would go off the boil at times. I'm also not sure if he was advised all that well in trying to cash in on his new fame. It's understandable that he should try to make money off the back of his amazing achievements, but you can easily lose your focus. You make a lot of money because you're good at cricket, and perhaps Brian lost his way a little. His management should have asked if he wanted to be known as the greatest batsman ever and told him to concentrate on what he does best while they looked after the financial matters.

He was given a fantastic house by the Trinidad Government and I went there for a party. He was a very good host and excellent company. I'll only judge people on what I see of them, and I like Brian Lara very much. He's a very good, caring person. I suppose it was unrealistic to expect him to maintain those amazing standards he set in 1994, because mental fatigue was bound to become a factor. I like to think that he'll look back on his career with satisfaction. He has a great record against Australia, who are the best in the world. Brian has such a special natural talent. For a small bloke, he gets the ball racing off the bat. He's so wristy and he times it so well off his hips that he can demoralize bowlers. And that trademark swivel pull stroke has demoralized bowlers for many years. It's been a privilege to observe his genius at first hand.

Lara's inspiration and some great fast bowling were the decisive factors in West Indies winning that 1994 series 3-1, but there were genuine signs of promise for England. That terrific win in Barbados demonstrated that we were moving in the right direction under a young captain who looked as if he was growing into the job. A year earlier, Athers had been unsure of his place in the England team, and in India he had looked disheartened at times. But he had shown his character by making it all count as a batsman, and that would help his confidence as a captain. There was something to build on there. We were all completely behind the new skipper and he had our total respect. But things are never as straightforward as they appear. A new chairman of selectors was about to make his impact – a former England captain was about to complicate things for our young skipper.

CHAPTER SEVEN

life with raymond

It was never dull when Raymond Illingworth took charge of English cricket, and some might even say it was fun. Mike Atherton wouldn't agree, though. Ted Dexter, Raymond's predecessor as chairman, who had appointed Athers captain of England with an eye to the future, had many quirky ideas but was fundamentally someone who'd go with the captain's will, because he was the one who had to carry out the philosophy where it really mattered – on the pitch. When Raymond took over from Ted in the summer of 1994, it was clear that his would be a hands-on influence. The next couple of years were to be turbulent for the regular England players, with indifferent results and a lot of strain on Mike Atherton.

When we returned from the Caribbean, it was clear that Raymond's new broom wasn't going to be idle for very long. I had no problems with the new chairman bringing in fresh ideas, and anyone who had listened to Illy's work as a summarizer on radio and television knew that he had a great knowledge of the game. He'd also been a highly successful captain of England. A tough character who believed in speaking his mind, Illy was a godsend to the media. That didn't do Athers any favours. Raymond believed in open discussions about England players, whereas Athers understandably preferred to keep things private. Raymond brought in Fred Titmus and Brian Bolus as selectors, two former players from the 1960s and 70s, who were trusted by the chairman – but the captain wasn't impressed. Athers, who was 26, felt that they were too rooted in the past, and I could sympathize with him. He was particularly against Bolus, who had a tendency to fire from the hip to the media. Bolus was often the 'England insider' quoted in the press, and the captain didn't approve of all those leaks.

So Athers had to face a change of policy right from the off under Raymond. The young players who had been in the Caribbean, coming to terms with what's needed to survive in Test cricket, were elbowed out, including Nasser Hussain, Mark Ramprakash, Matt Maynard and Graham Thorpe. Older players such as Graham Gooch and Mike Gatting came back, and Raymond took a punt on two Yorkshiremen, Steve Rhodes and Craig White. Athers admitted he'd never seen White play, but Illy insisted he could do the all-rounder's job. The role of Keith Fletcher as coach appeared to be threatened and the sound working relationship between Fletch and the captain was tinkered with by outsiders. Athers wanted to take a young squad forward, showing them trust in the Australian way, but Raymond had different ideas, which brought tension into his dealings with Athers. Generally they got on well, but strains did appear regularly during their partnership.

At times Athers gave the impression that he wasn't always happy with the eleven that he had been given, that he wasn't going on to the field with the final selection he wanted. Some of the borderline choices as bowlers suffered – such as Mark Ealham, Paul Taylor and Craig White – as Athers chose to rely on others whom he knew better. It wasn't the fault of either captain or player, more a reflection of the fact that Athers didn't feel he was getting 100 per cent support from all the selectors. The honeymoon for the new young captain was well and truly over.

In fairness to all parties, it's really difficult to keep backing a hunch successfully in international cricket. Raymond got it right with Craig White, because he did eventually prove himself, years after the chairman had lobbied for him. More recently, Duncan Fletcher was spot-on in his assessment of Marcus Trescothick and Michael Vaughan, even though they hadn't scored many runs in county cricket. Duncan identified something special in them and backed his judgement. For every successful punt, however, others just don't make it. Take Mark Lathwell in 1993 against the Aussies. A great natural talent, he was the one England player of my era who I believe just didn't want to be there. He played in two Tests and in that period barely said a word. He changed next to his Somerset teammate, Andy Caddick, and despite all our efforts to involve him in conversations, we couldn't drag anything out of him. If Lathwell had possessed the right mental approach he could have been anything in the game, because he certainly had the talent. Sadly, he just appeared to be overawed by the whole Test match scene. It was no surprise to me when he drifted out of county cricket when still so young.

Although you can use wickets and runs to gauge a player's quality, you can't measure temperament. You have to go on judgement, then see how players react to challenges that they've never faced before. It's a leap into the unknown and whether you can bowl the outswinger or play a good cover drive is taken for granted. You must relish being centre stage. That's one of the reasons why I was still playing for England at the age of 40. I love big crowds, and the challenge posed by top opponents; I'm motivated by a deep desire to make it a good day for me and my team. That's why I have every sympathy for the selectors, as they try to assess who's got the bottle.

To be fair to Raymond Illingworth, I thought he was an excellent judge of a player's qualities and potential. I enjoyed talking cricket with him. He could be dogmatic, but he's a typical Yorkshireman. The senior players loved pulling Raymond's leg when he got on to his own playing career. Now, he was obviously a fine all-rounder, and terrific captain, and Raymond wouldn't give you any arguments on that score. Dad, who was a playing contemporary, told me that Raymond had an excuse for every mistake he made on the field and a photographic memory for each impressive individual performance by him. Every time we had a team dinner before a Test, the likes of me, Athers, Gus Fraser and Robin Smith would find a *Wisden*, check up on one particular season and test Illy on his own record. Someone would say, 'Did you ever play at Dover, Illy?', well aware that he had scored a hundred and taken ten wickets there. Off he'd go, talking us through every cough and spit of that game. Then we'd ask him about playing at Ilford, knowing he'd got nought. He wasn't fazed, though. 'Ay, but I got twelve wickets next time I played there!' He knew what we were up to, but he took it in good spirit. We used to scramble over each other to grab a seat next to Raymond at the team dinners, because he was so unintentionally hilarious. But it was impossible not to be fond of him.

I hatched a plan to take the mickey out of him in the 1994 Trent Bridge Test against New Zealand. Raymond had announced a ban on those new-fangled contraptions, mobile phones, in the dressing-room and he let it be known that he thoroughly disapproved of us wearing shades on the field. Nor did he think much of the use on tour of the Revd Andrew Wingfield-Digby, the director of 'Christians in Sport'. Andrew had been a sort of spiritual advisor to some of the boys recently. He was there if anyone needed to chat about things that were concerning them. Certainly Phil Tufnell talked a lot to him on his troubled tour to India in 1992–3. Illy would have none of that – 'If anyone needs a bloody vicar to play for England, he's in the wrong job.' It was raining one morning at Trent Bridge and I knew the TV cameras would be tracking around, looking for something unusual, so I got some white tape, wrapped it around my neck to make it look like a dog collar, put on the shades, grabbed a mobile phone and sat on the players' balcony, waiting for the cameras. I was bored and fancied a bit of a laugh and Illy took it in the right manner. Once you've been part of a dressing-room, you never forget the sort of humour you encounter in there.

Raymond was dead right in his assessment of one new player to the England dressing-room in 1994. Darren Gough made his one-day debut at Edgbaston and I took a catch off his bowling in his first over. He looked as if he'd been playing for England for years that day. He'd bowled at us in the nets in the World Cup of 1992 in New Zealand and, unusually for a youngster, he bowled bouncers at the senior batsmen. He wasn't worried about doing the right thing he tried to ruffle Gooch and the others. I liked that. He had the necessary temperament and heart right away. I'm a huge fan of Goughie, who is a wholehearted cricketer and a larger-than-life character. Every team needs someone like him, whether it's rallying us in the dressing-room, making us laugh or giving everything with the ball in his hand. Like a true Yorkie, he likes a moan, but five minutes later he's smiling again, having forgotten what upset him.

Goughie is essentially a lovable bloke and can speak before he thinks at times. His 'Goughieisms' have become legendary in the England dressing-room. 'Why's your nickname Rhino, Goughie?' – "Cos I'm as strong as an ox.' 'Don't forget, a leopard never changes its stripes.' 'Don't we get low when we land in an aeroplane?' We've laughed all around the world with Darren Gough. He really hasn't changed a bit. He's been a fantastic cricketer for us and an unlucky one. If he hadn't had so many injuries, we'd have been more successful because Goughie could bowl any side out. He's been the best reverse swing bowler for England, and we missed him when he wasn't with us.

I didn't keep wicket for England during that 1994 summer. Illy wanted Steve Rhodes in because he admired the Yorkshireman's pluck and grit. Jack Russell hadn't had a great tour of the Caribbean, so he missed out. The West Indies is the worst place of all to keep wicket. The ball generally stays low when it passes the stumps, and the area surrounding the wicket is rough, so that throws from the deep can be a nightmare if they pitch just in front of you. Rhodes got his chance, therefore, and stayed in the job until the end of our Ashes tour. As I didn't have to keep wicket, I hoped and expected that my opening partnership with Mike Atherton would continue. We had gelled excellently in the Caribbean and it was surely important to build on that strength, with another trip to Australia just around the corner. In fact I didn't last the summer as an opener and I still don't know why. I got a hundred in the Lord's Test as an opener against New Zealand, but for the last two Tests of the summer, against South Africa, I was down to number five, with Goochy opening with Athers. My admiration for Goochy had been well documented, but I thought my opening partnership with Athers was one for the future. I had done very well a few months earlier against top fast bowlers, but now our partnership was being broken up – why not invest in something that had clearly worked?

No one took me to one side when I got to Leeds to explain why I had to drop down to number five. It was irrelevant that I scored 89, 62 and 36 not out in those last two Tests. I was very disappointed to be moved down the order through no fault of my own. Three hundreds in four Tests as an opener earlier that year had established my credentials, I would have thought. Despite Goochy's stature, I had earned the right to open the innings. This decision was to start a pattern over the next few years in which I never really knew where I'd be batting for England. It seemed to change every series and sometimes after every Test.

Unfortunately Athers had a lot on his mind by the time we got to Headingley. He'd been in deep trouble over what came to be known as the Dirt in the Pocket Affair during the Lord's Test and the feeling was that Raymond had saved his neck. Athers had been caught by the TV cameras dropping dry soil on to the ball. Was he altering the ball's condition? All hell broke loose on that Saturday night at Lord's and Raymond had to pacify the match referee, Peter Burge, after Athers had been a little creative with the truth. Illy ended up fining Athers, but he could have been suspended. To this day, I can't think what Athers was trying to do. I asked him about it and he said, 'I was just trying to keep my hands dry by having some dust in my pocket.' Certainly it was a very humid afternoon and our hands were clammy, so it was difficult to keep the ball dry enough for Gough to reverse-swing it. Two years earlier, we'd been on our high horses about the Pakistanis allegedly tampering with the ball, and now here we had the England captain acting suspiciously in a Test match at Lord's.

Illy always hinted that he'd saved Athers' captaincy by squaring it with Peter Burge, who'd played against him in several Ashes matches in the 1960s. Certainly, he must have been a great help to his young captain over those difficult 24 hours at Lord's. But what it meant was that Athers was now in his chairman's debt – he owed him one. That reduced Athers' independence and authority, and meant that Raymond would get his way even more over selection issues. Perhaps one of those issues was moving me down to number five and pushing Gooch up as opener. Athers had enjoyed opening with me, I know, so I assume that his hand was forced by Illy and he couldn't fight the issue.

Goochy's influence in the dressing-room was still strong, and he was particularly supportive of Athers in the next Test at the Oval. Peter Burge clearly hadn't forgotten Athers' questionable behaviour at Lord's and he was keeping a sharp eye on him. When Athers was given out lbw in the first innings, even though he got a big inside edge, he walked off, looking at his bat. This was not blatant dissent – it was the sort of thing every batsman does at some time – but Burge fined him for dissent. Athers was gutted at that, really disappointed. Goochy spotted how down he was and, on the fourth morning, gathered us together when Athers was out of the dressing-room. He said, 'Look, Athers is really down. We've really got to put in a performance today to drag him up again. We've got to win for the captain.' It was an impressive effort by Goochy. As a former captain, he read the situation well.

And we did raise our game that day, hammering South Africa by eight wickets. Typically, Athers made 99 and 63 in successive Tests after his self-induced embarrassment at Lord's, but the real star was Devon Malcolm. He took 9 for 57 in the fastest spell I've seen from an English bowler. He really unsettled their batsmen, roaring in with great rhythm and fantastic support from a full house. For me there is nothing better than seeing a quick bowler steaming in for England on a home ground, handing out the sort of punishment we've had to face around the world. The South Africans didn't fancy him at all. I remember Craig Matthews getting the slightest feather on to his glove, to be caught by Rhodes down the leg side, and walking straight off without waiting for the umpire to give his decision. You don't see that very often in a Test match. It was the highlight of Devon's career and we were thrilled for such a lovable bloke. It was a pity that a year later when we went to South Africa various things would conspire against him and he couldn't repeat his performance against them.

Athers didn't get the precise squad he wanted for the 1994–5 tour to Australia. I don't think he wanted both Gatting and Gooch, preferring just one of them. He wanted younger players but Illy lobbied for Gatting, presumably because he was such a good player of spinners, with Shane Warne obviously a threat. As it turned out, it was probably a tour too far for both Gatt and Goochy. The Aussie spectators were merciless, taunting us for our unathletic fielding, and it was a tour to forget for all of us. We were torn apart by injuries, with six players coming out as replacements, but clearly the gap between Australia and us was growing.

I started off the injury run by breaking my finger on the third day of the tour. We had a practice game among ourselves in Perth and Craig White smacked me on the right index finger with a ball that just took off. It was broken, my first proper injury since the fractured jaw I'd received in 1983, courtesy of Michael Holding. So I missed my return game at Lilac Hill, where I'd played for Midland-Guildford, but still enjoyed the day. There were banners saying 'Welcome back, Alec' and I gave it the large one all day, meeting and greeting old friends. I got a hundred in my comeback game, in Hobart, and so was fit for the first Test. Little did I realize that I'd only play in the first two that series. The broken-finger jinx was about to kick in with a vengeance.

In the Brisbane Test, I was back to opening, with Goochy down at number five. No, I don't know why either, but I was just happy to be back, partnering Athers at the top of the order. In the second innings, Shane Warne bowled me with one of the best deliveries I've ever faced. I'd cut a long-hop from him for a boundary the ball before, and I thought the next was another four-ball. It appeared to be another short ball, but it was his slider that went on quickly and clean bowled me as I tried to pull him. It was a fantastic piece of bowling and he completely outwitted me. Such a clever bowler, Warney. When Athers and I were both out we went up and sat in the stands behind his arm, but we were none the wiser. He had great variations, concealed them brilliantly and was also so accurate. A phenomenal bowler.

In the next Test, at Melbourne, Craig McDermott hit me straight on my right index finger and that re-opened the fracture I'd picked up at the start of the tour. In the second innings we were up against it, desperately trying to save the Test, and I went in lower down the order. To help numb the pain, I'd had three injections. It certainly wasn't a pleasant experience and brought me out in a bit of a sweat – some of the boys who crowded round to watch me suffer soon disappeared when the needle went in! When I batted, I stood at the other end while Warney took a hat-trick and the game was over in a rush. All that pain for a meaningless not out!

Normally a broken finger takes six to eight weeks to heal, but I was desperate to get back earlier than that. I was pain-free when I returned three weeks after the Melbourne experience, at Bendigo against Victoria, even though the fracture wasn't 100 per cent healed, and I batted at number six to protect me against the new ball. So as soon as I came in, I faced the second new ball and I got hit again on the same spot! Another trip to hospital, more X-rays and the same verdict – a fractured finger. My tour was over. I stayed on, hoping it would heal up so that I could play in the Perth Test, but it wasn't to be. It was going to bother me for a few more months as well.

So that was a very frustrating time. I did all the twelfth-man duties but whenever I tried to bat against some throwdowns on the outfield, the pain would return. I did lots of gym work and running, with the carrot of a quick return being dangled, but it was hopeless. My recurring injury summed up our tour. It was a nightmare. We managed a consolation victory in the Adelaide Test, and could have won the Sydney Test, but ended up losing 3-1.

Athers' decision to declare at Sydney with Graeme Hick stranded on 98 not out cost us dearly. That was the worst thing that could have happened to both the player and the team, because it left us so flat when we went out to field, needing quick wickets on the fourth evening. I was acting as twelfth man and took out the message to Hicky that we'd be declaring in five overs' time, so score the required runs if you want your hundred. He was already in the nineties but he didn't show much aggressive intent over the next three overs, and he was losing the strike as well. Suddenly, Athers stood up and clapped our batsmen in. 'Are you sure?' I thought, and I know the other lads thought the same. Hicky was spewing when he came in and you could have heard a pin drop as we prepared to go out to field. We should have been bubbling, delighted that a team-mate had scored a hundred in an Ashes Test, but we went on to the field very flat. We couldn't believe that Athers had declared.

A hundred at that stage of his career would have been

vital for Graeme Hick. On the previous tour, to the West Indies, he'd made a magnificent 96 in the Sabina Park Test and he was starting to look the part. But Sydney knocked him back and he was soon forced out of the tour with a back injury. We used to talk a lot about batting. Graeme liked the way I could clip the ball to the boundary off my hip when I was on the back foot and asked me how I did it. I told him I didn't know, but it was just a matter of timing. Graeme thought a great deal about his batting. He had awesome talent. I thought he was a fantastic batsman, but perhaps the run of huge success he'd enjoyed before he qualified for England rebounded on him. The pressure of being in the limelight and coming up against the West Indies and Pakistan in his first year was completely unfamiliar to him, and he struggled. He'd been built up as the great hope for English cricket, but you can never be sure of someone until they've been tested consistently at the highest level, against top-class opposition. So this was the first time that Graeme had faced real adversity and perhaps he started to question himself too much. If he'd just trusted in his own huge natural ability and avoided complicating his game, that might have got him through.

Those high-class quick bowlers soon spotted that Graeme was sometimes uncomfortable against the short ball. Then it was a test of nerve and temperament for him. If you've been hit by the short ball, you must demonstrate that you can play the next one, because you can be sure you'll be tested out again straight away. That can add to the doubts that cloud your mind while the opposition relish a target to aim at. As a tall man, Graeme had to decide whether to duck under the bouncers or take them on. He never really resolved that. He didn't get out all that much to the short ball, but didn't play it as confidently as other shots. Aggressive bowlers like Merv Hughes, Wasim Akram and Waqar Younis appeared to unsettle him at times and while he looked for the short delivery, they'd slip in the yorker and get him bowled or lbw. So one of his strengths – his front-foot play – was undermined by clever bowling. It may sound harsh, but six Test hundreds in 65 Tests wasn't a proper return for someone of Hicky's massive ability, and someone whose talents I admire greatly.

I came back from Australia well aware that my finger needed time to heal. The right index finger is in the firing line when you bat right-handed, and at the back of my mind was the necessity to get it 100 per cent. The West Indies were the summer opposition, followed by a tour to South Africa, and I knew that Messrs Ambrose, Walsh, Donald and Pollock would be testing me out for any vulnerability in my fingers. But it was to be another difficult summer for me. I broke the finger twice more and didn't play again after early July.

Before then, I was back as England's wicketkeeper for the first Test at Leeds. Steve Rhodes hadn't fully grasped his chance, Jack Russell was still out of favour, so I was given the gloves again. After opening in my last two Tests I was shunted down the order to number five. Robin Smith opened with Athers, which seemed odd to me. Robin was a very fine player of fast bowling, but in forty-odd Tests he'd only opened once. This was also his first Test for almost a year, which was enough pressure on a seamer-friendly wicket with cloud cover. After we lost at Headingley by an innings, Robin and I swapped places in the order for Lord's. The selectors said they wanted me to open, and I certainly agreed with that, but they were concerned about my workload as keeper. If we batted first, I would open, otherwise we'd see how long I'd been in the field. If I was unsure, with a few hours left in the day and no time to get myself psychologically attuned to opening, then Robin would go in first. It was an unsatisfactory arrangement, and this problem of my place in the batting order would linger on for a few more series.

But we beat the West Indies at Lord's, and I took a key wicket, that of Brian Lara, with one of the best catches of my international career. They were chasing 295 to win and were close to a hundred with one wicket down and Lara looking very dangerous. I dived full length to my left to catch the edge off Lara, inches in front of Athers at first slip. I impressed myself, not just because it was a very good catch but also because it was a match-winning one. Lara could win a match off his own bat and we had to get him as soon as possible.

That game was Dominic Cork's Test, and also his first. He batted positively twice, then took 7 for 43. A star was born, it seemed, and comparisons were soon made with the great all-rounder, Ian Botham. Corky was a terrific competitor, who gave his all whether bowling at Brian Lara or against a number-eleven no-hoper. In his first year with England, he was a match-winning bowler with a big heart who always wanted to bowl. He swung the ball late at a sharp pace, and bowled wicket to wicket, which enabled him to get a lot of lbws and shape the ball away from the right-hander after pitching middle and off. He had all the attributes of a top-class swing bowler, our equivalent to Australia's Terry Alderman. And he could bat with spirit as well, although the attempt to bracket him with Botham in this respect was just silly.

Corky wasn't the most popular of cricketers with the opposition because he was always in your face, but I liked that. When I captained England, he gave me everything and he was good to have around. I restored him to the team for my first Test as skipper, at Edgbaston in 1998. He and Goughy were great mates, always having a go at each other, and there was never a dull moment with those two around. Unfortunately, he stopped being able to swing the ball late and his bowling declined in effectiveness. He lost the purity in his action at times and then, when he'd lost that swing, he tried to compensate by bowling too fast. Even so he never lost his will to win.

Athers was also a big fan when he first captained him, but Corky blotted his copybook when he came out to join us in New Zealand in 1997. He had been permitted leave of absence for the Zimbabwe leg of that winter tour, because his marriage had just broken up. He was put on trust to do all the necessary work back home, but when he came out to New Zealand it was clear that he was struggling. Athers had a go at him and Corky told him where to get off, which wasn't a good idea because he was in the wrong. He was close to being sent home from that tour because of his attitude, even though he was so important to us as a bowler.

Success came very quickly to Corky, and I think he'd admit he didn't handle it all as well as he might. Perhaps he forgot that it was his performances on the field that bought him the trendy sunglasses and the smart, sponsored car. If you keep delivering where it counts – out in the middle – all sorts of perks come your way, but you must maintain the high level of your performances. For me, it was always a case of aiming for a long, successful career and everything else will look after itself.

Within a few weeks of that triumphant Cork debut my season was over. Just before the third Test, at Edgbaston, I'd played against Middlesex at Lord's and Richard Johnson hit me on the same index finger. The X-ray was inconclusive. There was a line on the X-ray but I was told it wasn't a fracture. So I reported fit at Edgbaston. If you played only when you were 100 per cent, you'd rarely get on the park, but I honestly felt I was over my run of bad luck.

That Edgbaston pitch was a shocker. Shaved at each end, it was grassy in the middle. Two years earlier, we had played there against the Aussies on a pitch that turned square for Shane Warne; now we were on a wicket tailor-made for Walsh and Ambrose, with uneven bounce. Off the first ball of the match, Athers got out of the way from an Ambrose delivery that went for four byes over the keeper's head! We grinned at each other, tapped the offending spot just back of a length and had a laugh about what lay in store for us. We were all out for 147, and by the end of the first day I was nursing another broken finger, this time from keeping wicket.

Darren Gough bowled a short one that kept flying, I got my right index finger to it but it still flew for four byes. I had exactly the same feeling as when it was broken previously. But I had to keep wicket next day, because there was no one else who could do the job. Injections numbed the pain, but when I went for an X-ray that evening, the fracture was confirmed. I brought the X-rays with me that had been taken during the Middlesex match and the Birmingham specialist confirmed that it had indeed been broken. So I went into the Edgbaston Test as an opener/keeper with a fractured finger: what you might call a medical cock-up.

I didn't bat in the second innings, when we were dismissed for 89, to lose by an innings just after midday on the Saturday. The Birmingham cricket-lovers were not impressed. Normally we can count on fantastic support at Edgbaston, but not this time. When we were having lunch in the dining-room, looking out on the outfield, some came up to express their displeasure in a rather aggressive manner, shouting, 'We've paid good money to see that rubbish!' I appreciated their anger, but no one had chickened out on what Athers described as the worst Test pitch he had yet seen. Robin Smith's 41 not out was an incredibly brave knock in the circumstances, as he was battered and bruised by Ian Bishop in particular. Athers was very annoyed that he and Illy had to walk over to the indoor school to do the press conference. Even with a police escort they had to run the gauntlet of jeering spectators, and we experienced the same when walking to our cars, carrying our gear. Yet no one gave the groundstaff any abuse for preparing that dreadful wicket.

So, after breaking the same finger five times since the previous October, I was finished for the summer. There was a lot of talk at the time about me having brittle fingers, but it was only the one digit that was vulnerable. It just wasn't healing strongly enough. I saw various finger specialists and inquired about extra protection but the problem was how to cushion the impact of a ball delivered at more than eighty miles an hour crashing into my finger, which then got squashed against the bat handle. One specialist told me that if the finger was smashed once more, it could finish my career because there are only so many times you can fracture a bone before it gives up trying to heal. I honestly thought that was a little over-pessimistic, but I was certainly worried.

At the end of August, I got the breakthrough I needed and it came from an unlikely source. I went to the BBC TV studios to appear on *Grandstand*'s 'Cricket Focus' and got chatting to the broadcaster and writer Ralph Dellor. Ralph said he had just the thing to solve my finger problem. He had invented a shock-absorbent mould that goes over the glove on the first two fingers of the bottom hand. In my case, the right hand. It was designed to ensure that when the finger gets hit, the sides of the splint are pushed out on to the bat handle. That absorbs the impact of the ball, so that the finger doesn't get squashed. Ralph sent me one of the moulds and I tried it. On the South Africa tour, I was hit several times in the usual area and the mould took the blow satisfactorily. When I came home, I took it to a splint maker and he made me five moulds with hard plastic in them. I've used them ever since and haven't had to replace them. Cheap too at the price – £25 a throw. I must have been struck about fifty times on that precise area since and not felt a thing. Ralph sold the patent eventually and I hope he got a good deal. He certainly saved my career.

By the time I was finally fit to leave for the 1995 tour to South Africa in October, I'd had the longest break I'd ever had from the game, and it did feel strange. I'd been in the nets as usual with Dad, but you can't beat match conditions. Early on I got a century and 90-odd in the warm-up games, but I didn't feel right. That feeling never left me on that tour. It's the only tour where my timing, footwork and balance were never in harmony. I kept being stuck on the crease, going nowhere. My initial movement is back and across my stumps so that I can come forward, evenly balanced, but now I was stuck on the back foot, with my weight planted there. So I couldn't really handle the short-pitched delivery as confidently as usual, and when you're an opener, that's a horrible feeling. My strength has always been off the back foot and the South African fast bowlers were never shy of testing me out, but at no time on that tour did I play them the way I can.

I'd ask the lads in the nets to hammer me with the short ball and I'd get so much weight on the back foot that I'd struggle when they pitched it up to me. I felt lost, largely through having been out of the game for almost four months. There was a real battle going on in my mind – I knew I was out of sync but tried not to show that I was worried. I spoke to Athers a lot on that tour, asking him to watch me closely in the nets and out in the middle. In that whole series, I only played with freedom once, at Port Elizabeth when I took on Donald with the hook and pull to smack 81. For the rest of the time, I was a shadow of my usual self.

It was ironic that Athers played so superbly while I struggled. We had gelled as openers so well in the Caribbean and, with Jack Russell restored, I was really looking forward to resuming my opening partnership with Athers. I did at least manage to get a close-up view of part of his remarkable 185 not out that saved the Johannesburg Test. I scratched around for 38 while my partner was totally unmoved at the other end. We had to survive for five sessions to save the Test, and Athers never looked like getting out. It was a fantastic display of concentration and mental tenacity, as he simply refused to buckle against hostile bowling by Donald in particular. Don't forget that this was the fourth innings of the match, and he'd been captaining the side as well, which brings enough mental pressure. But he just stood there and took the lot. Nothing seemed to distract him, and we were more nervous in the dressing-room than Athers. Out of superstition, we didn't move from our seats, and those watching the TV in the dressing-room also had to stay put. During the various intervals, Athers would sit there quietly. As a player he was never a man of many words, but from his demeanour you wouldn't have known that he'd been batting for so long. I was also delighted for Jack Russell that he fought it out for more than four hours to help secure us the draw. He'd been out of the side for too long and he really made everything count. But the captain was unbelievable, and his stature was even higher in our ranks after an innings that took an awful lot out of him.

I'm afraid that, at times, that tour wasn't a great one for Raymond Illingworth. His frustrations boiled over, particularly regarding Devon Malcolm. Joining Raymond in his tour brains trust were two players who knew him from his days as England captain, John Edrich, who would help out the batsmen, and Peter Lever, who was the bowling coach. They were all too set in their ways, and mercifully our physio Wayne Morton and the manager John Barclay were more progressive in the practice sessions. Without those two, the tour could have been a disaster.

The tone was set after our first training session in Johannesburg. After we had done the batting and bowling work, we then moved on to fielding practice. The ground backed on to a golf course and while we worked hard, I looked up to see Illy, Lever and Edrich teeing off next door! The same thing happened in the World Cup in Pakistan a few months later. We met up in the hotel reception in Lahore for our practice session and wondered where Illy was. We looked a few yards to our right and there, sitting by the pool in his swimming gear, was our guru, catching a few rays! Illy's response was, 'I'm here for the cricket. Wayne Morton will take you for the physical stuff.' He was a funny character, Illy. I liked him and respected his cricketing nous, but this South African tour and the World Cup showed how out of touch he was with the modern game. By contrast, Bob Woolmer in the South African camp was never off his laptop, always exploring new ideas. If Illy had just been the chairman of selectors, that would have been all right, but he had now been promoted to tour manager, with special responsibilities in cricket that reflected his stature. Yet he sometimes seemed to be stuck in a seventies timewarp and this was now the mid-nineties.

I don't think he handled Devon Malcolm at all well. Right from the start of the tour, Raymond gave the impression that he felt Devon's head had been turned by all the attention he was getting as the only black man in the tour party. Nelson Mandela had recognized him when we were all introduced to him and the photo was widely printed. I don't think Devon was distracted at all. He had dealt with all the publicity very well when going back to his native Jamaica with England in 1990, and he was too intelligent and sensitive a man to think that he was above the rest of us. Raymond and Peter Lever belittled Devon in their chats with the media, pouring scorn on a bowling action that had brought him more than a hundred Test wickets and terrorized the South Africans a year earlier at the Oval. They also thought that Devon was taking too long to get fit after a minor knee operation before the tour had started. After meeting President Mandela in Soweto, they pulled Devon out of the match and sent him off to Centurion Park to work on his bowling action. That was cheap and unnecessary. It was a little early in the tour to go public on him. If they thought he was letting the squad down, they should have dealt with it privately, rather than humiliating an immensely popular player.

Raymond almost lost it with Dev in our dressing-room at Cape Town, immediately after we'd lost the Test to give South Africa the series 1-0. Dev had bowled loosely with the second new ball earlier in the day, after which Paul Adams and Dave Richardson added precious runs for the last wicket to give them a lead of 90-odd. We then batted badly to lose by ten wickets inside three days. After the game it was announced that we had agreed to play a one-dayer against Western Province on the scheduled fifth day of the Test, to compensate all those who had bought tickets for that day. Athers knew nothing about it and tackled Illy in the dressing-room. Raymond then lashed out at Devon: 'I don't know what you've got to be proud of – your bowling cost us the series!' That was nonsense. Dev was playing his first match for a month, and he was taken off after three overs with the second new ball, while others also bowled poorly and our batting was just as disappointing. I'm surprised that Dev didn't deck Illy, but he just stared at him. It was understandable that Raymond was frustrated at the way we played, but he was wrong to take it out on Dev – we were all at fault. That moment harmed Illy's standing in the England dressing-room and he never regained total respect from the players as we lurched through a shambles of a World Cup in India soon afterwards.

Our preparation for the tournament was very amateurish. We played seven one-day internationals in South Africa and at no stage did we know our settled, first-choice eleven. The batting order constantly changed and there was no continuity. No wonder we lost the series 6-1. We didn't know the World Cup squad until the evening of the last one-dayer in South Africa, just three weeks before the start of the World Cup. Nothing to our advantage was learned from that one-day series, so that we were never sure of our best team when the World Cup started. We got to the quarter-finals, where we were thrashed by Sri Lanka, but we only got that far because of the format of the tournament. Beating just Holland and the United Arab Emirates was hardly cause for celebration.

Our planning simply wasn't good enough, and we were going round in circles. The players weren't sure who was running the show, the captain or the manager. Athers opened sometimes, then batted down the order, while I batted at five, six and as opener. Jack Russell stayed at number six after a good Test series in South Africa, but that was probably a place too high and a little inflexible. Neil Smith operated as a pinch-hitter in some matches, but not in others, while the fast bowler Phil DeFreitas bowled off-breaks in the quarter-final, with predictable results. The Sri Lankans hit us all over the park. They'd taken the one-day game to a new level, with their dynamic batsmen teeing off right from the start of the innings. We had just stood still in contrast. They thoroughly deserved to win the World Cup.

We were short of laughs during that disastrous World Cup, although Dermot Reeve provided one in a team meeting. We were talking about the best way to play the Pakistan leg-spinner, Mushtaq Ahmed. We agreed he bowled a good googly and Raymond asked if anyone could pick it. Only Dermot put his hand up. Next day, off the third ball he faced from Mushy, he went down the pitch trying to hit him over extra cover. He was bowled through the gate by the googly. Later we all had a chuckle over that one. Dermot never lacked confidence in his own ability.

That World Cup showed how much we'd slipped behind in progressive thinking and organization. Raymond had to bear some of the responsibility for the failure because he had insisted on the final say. That eventually affected his relationship with Athers, which was definitely frayed around the edges by the time we'd crashed out of the competition. We needed a new coach with modern methods and ideas, and Raymond must have sensed that because he resigned as the England supremo as soon as we got home. He said he wanted to remain as chairman of selectors, which at least ensured more amusing dinners on the eve of the Tests – but it was time to move on.

CHAPTER EIGHT

family worries

Mike Atherton couldn't believe it. When he rang me to tell me I'd been dropped by England, he expected to get a volley from me. Yet all I said was, 'Fine, no problem'. He found out later why I was so unconcerned that Sunday, early in June 1996. My wife was in agony at home, suffering from what turned out to be a brain haemorrhage. Just to complicate matters further, she was six months pregnant. Ahead lay months of anguish and fear that Lynn wouldn't ever be the same again. Losing my England place at the time seemed irrelevant.

Just to get the cricket in context – Athers had to make that difficult call to me because the chairman of selectors, Raymond Illingworth, wanted new blood after the massive disappointment in the World Cup. Illy had pointed the finger at me, Angus Fraser, Robin Smith and Devon Malcolm as the most experienced players who had probably passed their sell-by date by the summer of 1996. At the age of 33, I was considered to be part of the old guard. I knew that it must have pained Athers to pick up the phone to me to break the news before the squad for Edgbaston was announced, and he's told me since that he couldn't believe I was so calm. Playing for England had always meant so much to me, but now there was a different agenda to follow.

Lynn had woken up early that morning in tears with a splitting headache. That wasn't like her at all and we called out our family doctor. He thought it was a migraine and gave her some painkillers. Mum and Dad came round to

look after three-year-old Andrew but we were all concerned about Lynn's pregnancy as well as the pain she was
in. They all persuaded me to go to the Oval, where I was
due to captain Surrey against Derbyshire in a Sunday
League match. I didn't want to go, but it was felt that a
quiet period and the painkillers would bring some relief to
Lynn. So I played, scored an unbeaten hundred, as if to
show the selectors I was still a good player, and we ended
up winning the match. With ten overs left in their innings,
however, our twelfth man came on to the field to tell me
that Lynn had been rushed to hospital. I immediately left
the field of play and sped over to Lynn.

She had suffered a burst blood vessel in her brain. She
was now seriously ill and in a bad way. After numerous
tests, she was kept in overnight, under observation. A CT
scan next day revealed the haemorrhage. A blood vessel
had not sealed at birth and had now burst. Apparently this
could have happened at any time. The dilemma was that
Lynn was six months pregnant. When would be a safe time
to seal off the artery that had burst? After Lynn was
transferred to the Atkinson Morley Neurological Hospital
in Wimbledon – because this was now considered a
life-threatening case – she had more tests and scans. We
were told that Lynn might end up with a stroke and that
the baby's life might also be threatened. Until the surgeon
actually went into the brain, he wouldn't know the full
extent of the possible damage. There was a real danger that
Lynn might lose all feeling down one side. There were
other, more chilling possibilities that we tried not to
think about.

The advice was to wait until September and the baby's
birth before performing the operation. We faced an
anxious summer. During these awful few days, the
England squad had been assembling for the first Test

against India at Edgbaston, and normally I'd have been gutted about being dropped and consigned prematurely to the scrapheap. But I never gave it a thought, not for a moment, after I was called away from the Oval that Sunday. This was going to be a time for strength from both our families.

I'd already been tested in that area earlier in the year. After we'd lost the Cape Town Test at the start of January, Lynn sat me down in my hotel room that night and told me some disturbing news about my Mum. She was due to fly out with Dad to see the cricket, but there had been some sort of delay and I was told there was nothing to worry about. In fact, they were keeping the news from me until after the Test. Mum was suffering from a brain tumour. She'd struggled with her hearing in her right ear for a few years and her doctor had sent her to an ear specialist. Judy, my sister, was about to drive my parents to the airport when the specialist rang to say that her ear was fine, but that the MRI scan had revealed a tumour on the brain. It was about the size of an apricot, but large enough to kill her unless she had urgent medical attention. She went into hospital that night. A few days later, after I'd found out about it, I talked to Mum in intensive care. She was putting a brave face on it, but I could tell she'd been scared.

Should I go home? Raymond Illingworth, having talked to Dad, thought I should, but Dad disagreed. He said, 'What can you do here? She's in the hands of medical experts, and she'd want you to stay out there as long as your mind's right. We won't get the results for a couple more weeks, and then you'll be home for a few weeks before the World Cup starts. She knows you're thinking of her and if things get worse, then come home. Just phone every day.' That night I talked to my Surrey team-mate Graham Thorpe about it, and he couldn't believe I was staying in South Africa to play in the one-day series. But Dad was the perfect person to talk to about it, because he could marry up the personal with the professional. My brother and sister were there, living close by, and so Mum wouldn't lack for family support over the next few weeks. Lynn and Andrew were with me, so that was a great consolation, to have my family to share those worrying moments with. I'd be able to phone daily and probably speak to Mum most of the time. I decided to stay on. Athers was very supportive, leaving the decision totally to me, while the lads in the tour party were respectful of my privacy and wished us well.

Time dragged in South Africa during that January, but when I got home the initial tests were optimistic. It wasn't until early June that Mum finally got the all-clear, which makes it doubly ironic that my wife then also suffered a serious brain illness. So the focus was fully on Lynn for the rest of that summer. The night before she gave birth early in September, she had an epileptic fit, which she had never experienced before, and had to be rushed to King's College Hospital as an emergency case. But Emily was born safe and sound and I was there for the birth, an overwhelming moment. I had missed Andrew's birth by a couple of minutes in 1993, as I dashed down the motorway after playing for England against Australia in a one-day international at Edgbaston. By the time I got to the ward Andrew was half-way into the world. I was greeted by Mum, in floods of tears, saying it was the most wonderful sight she'd ever seen – and she'd had three kids herself! Second time around, with all the concerns about Lynn thrown in, it was highly emotional. It had to be a Caesarean birth, because it would be two weeks early, and when Emily was brought out to me, she looked like a little doll. It was a wonderful experience.

Two weeks after Emily's birth, Lynn had a seven-hour brain operation. She stayed in for a fortnight while I took time off cricket and looked after Andrew with help from Lynn's mum and dad, who had come down from Durham. We were warned that Lynn could suffer epileptic fits for the rest of her life, and she's had a few since. The first one came a few months after the operation, when Andrew ran down the stairs to find Lynn lying on the floor, unconscious. He opened the door, ran next door to a neighbour and shouted, 'Mum's dead!' As they waited for the ambulance, Lynn gradually came round. I was very proud of my three-year-old when I heard how brave he'd been. I experienced one of Lynn's fits one day when she was upstairs with Emily and I heard her cry out. I rushed upstairs to find that she'd just gone into a fit. I got Andrew out of the room and dialled 999 for the only time in my life. Since then she's had smaller fits, but fortunately none for a couple of years now, and she'll be on daily medication for the rest of her life. But she survived, thank God, and the mutual support from both families got us through a harrowing period.

With all that going on, I somehow managed to play cricket very well for the rest of 1996. In fact, I ended up as the world's leading run-scorer in Tests for that calendar year. I'll never know if my attitude to my cricket was simplified by Lynn's illness and that of my mother, so that I just went out there with an uncluttered mind, unafraid of failure. But I've always been a very positive person anyway. Somehow I can always concentrate on my job when I'm out on the field – I can separate the personal from the professional. Perhaps I get that from Dad. He was always very focused on his job when it was time to switch on, according to Mum. When her dad died, mine was playing cricket for Surrey, but she told him to stay there. 'You've been good to him in life,' she told him. That same summer, Dad's father passed away. They were very close indeed, yet Dad played at the Oval that day as well. He's admitted that he knew his father was going through a vital operation and that it would be touch-and-go, but that from the moment he crossed the boundary rope, he homed in on playing for Surrey. By the time he came off for lunch, his dad had died. He took it badly, because they were very close, but he felt he also had to get on with his job. I think that's one characteristic I share with him.

Those two serious illnesses overrode everything to do with cricket in 1996, but I still had something to prove when I finally got back to my job. After returning from the World Cup, I'd worked very hard with Dad in the indoor nets, sorting out my balance of weight when playing back. I needed to eradicate that problem on the back foot which had led to so many below-par efforts from me in South Africa, and I did so. Early in the season I knew I was back to my best and still good enough to play for England. But would they pick me? At 33, was I past it in the selectors' eyes? If you're good enough, does it matter about your age? This was the first time such a discussion had centred around me, and it wouldn't go away for the rest of my England career. My aim now was to force my way back, and ensure I stayed in the side, by my performances.

I would need some luck, though. Raymond Illingworth was known to dig in his heels when convinced he was right – indeed, Robin Smith never played again for England after being unfairly pensioned off that summer, and he wasn't 33 till September. But Nick Knight's finger injury meant that I was called up for the second Test against India at Lord's, so the ball was now in my court. I had no doubts that I warranted a place in the side, but I had to cash in quickly on my good fortune. I was more nervous than usual on the first morning and glad to be opening again with Athers. We were put in on a seaming wicket, and Athers was out in the first over. I grafted away to get 20, which wasn't all that great a score, but I had played well. Hopefully the second innings would give me another chance. Jack Russell got a hundred in that first innings, which really pleased me because he'd been copping some criticism recently as well.

The second innings went better for me, as I guided England towards the safety of the draw, after India had led us on first innings. I made 66 before Javagal Srinath bowled me for the second time in the match. I hoped I'd done enough to justify bringing me back. I certainly felt as good as ever.

The selectors did retain me for the next Test, at Trent Bridge, and I was very disappointed to miss out on a hundred on a flat wicket. Athers and I put on 130 for the first wicket, then umpire K. T. Francis gave me out, caught at the wicket off an apparent inside edge. I didn't touch it. To his credit, the umpire apologized to me for his mistake next day and I appreciated that, even though I was still envious of my opening partner, who had gone on to make a hundred. We batsmen do tend to remember when we get sawn off, because it ends our innings, while we conveniently forget when we're lucky enough to get away with it. In the Edgbaston Test that summer, Nasser Hussain gloved one down the leg side off Srinath and got away with it early in his innings. He ended up with a century. A few years later, when he was England captain, he had some shockers given against him, but then he got a hundred in Kandy against Sri Lanka when he was out at least three times. And he survived a few in Australia in 2002–3. As long as you take the rough with the smooth, that's fine. I have no problem with a batsman standing there when he knows he's nicked it. Early in my career I made the decision not to walk, and 80 per cent of the time I've stayed there. It's an individual thing. Brian Lara always walked; Graeme Hick did so early in his England career, but not towards the end. I'd suggest that my attitude is now the norm in international cricket.

So, having scored fifties in my comeback Tests as opener, I was down at number three for the next one, at Lord's, the first of a three-Test series against Pakistan. Nick Knight was fit again, so he came back as opener. I'd love to have stayed as Athers' partner, but getting back into the team was enough for me. That was still a very fine Pakistan attack and I enjoyed the challenge. I think they respected me after my performances against them in 1992, and I was happy about the way I played the leg-spinner, Mushtaq Ahmed. I got 89 in the second innings at Lord's before gloving one from him that had turned sharply, but I'd batted positively against him and did throughout that series, in which I averaged 79. Mushy was a bigger spinner of the ball than Shane Warne and his googly was harder to pick, but he lacked the Australian's cricket brain and his control. Mushy was smaller, he had to toss it up higher and therefore he was slower. He would try to get a wicket every ball whereas Warney would set you up and work you out over a few overs. But Mushtaq Ahmed was a very fine leg-spinner, and I'd like to think that the success I had against him in the summers of '92 and '96 might be remembered when it's stated that I've been vulnerable against spin. My record against Warne is indeed below par, but I usually batted in the middle order against Australia, which meant that Warne would be on when I was just starting my innings. Batting higher up the order against Pakistan meant that I'd be already established when Mushy came on. I'd always have a better chance of playing top-quality spin if I'd got my feet moving and my balance sorted out. Most batsmen have been tentative against the great Warne when they're just starting their innings and he's waiting for you, licking his lips…

Mushy bowled a lot of overs at me in the next Test, at Leeds, but I won that particular round by scoring 170 and getting the Man of the Match award. I was back as opener, with Knight dropping down to six. It was one of my better Test hundreds, as I took the attack to the fast bowlers who obligingly gave me enough to cut, hook and pull. Everything seemed to flow naturally and I was very comfortable back in my position as England's opener. I got to my hundred by forcing one past Wasim Akram for three and my ecstatic reaction told everyone what that hundred meant to me. The press made a lot of the fact that Raymond Illingworth gave me lukewarm applause, compared to everyone else around him, but I wasn't bothered as I knew he was impressed with me. When Nick Knight got to his century the next day, I joked with Illy that he should climb on to his chair to applaud. And he did! I had no problem with the chairman of selectors wanting to ease me out, as long as I'd been given the chance to prove him wrong. And I had done. I was an automatic choice again and that was sweet. Having faced the axe, I'd scored at least a fifty in my last four Test Matches that summer.

At the Oval I made it five in a row, with 44 and 54. I was opening the batting again, but also keeping wicket. It was by now the familiar scenario – we were one down in the series, so Jack Russell was ditched to let us play five main bowlers. It didn't work and we lost heavily.

I'd kept wicket for 159 overs in Pakistan's first innings, but I still wanted to open. I was playing so well and it was still my favourite place in the order. So I faced a tremendous barrage with Athers in our second innings, as

ABOVE The Stewart family in 1970 – the year that Chelsea won the FA Cup – and Neil (left) and I are kitted out in royal blue to celebrate. Judy, my sister, hogs the camera as usual.

OPPOSITE Just one day old and Mum's wondering when I'll make a grab for those pearls!

PREVIOUS PAGE Dad wanted me to be thinking about cricket even at an early age – although I still needed to grow into one of his old bats!

TOP With Lynn on our wedding day, 28 September 1991.
ABOVE LEFT Our first child, Andrew, in May 1993.
ABOVE RIGHT Emily arrives, September 1996.

LEFT Showing off my soccer skills in my Chelsea kit in Barbados, 1994 – a time when my team got through to the FA Cup Final and I scored two hundreds in the Test match that we won.
BELOW With five-year-old Emily at a charity cricket match.
BOTTOM With Dad, then England's cricket coach, after I'd been named Man of the Match for scoring a hundred against Pakistan in a one-day international at the Oval, my home ground, in 1992.

TOP LEFT Trying to ignore the verbals from a pumped-up Desmond Haynes as we left the field during the tense final day of the Trinidad Test in 1990. Dessie did all the talking, while I just tried to blank him out!

TOP RIGHT Grappling with a snake on the tour to India, 1993. The things you do to please sponsors and press!

ABOVE Meeting the Queen, introduced by Graham Gooch, alongside the England coach, Keith Fletcher.

TOP On England duty with Graham Gooch, my first captain and the player I've admired most in my career.
ABOVE One of the most important catches of my England career: Brian Lara off Darren Gough at Lord's, 1995. Getting Lara out then was decisive in winning that Test.
OVERLEAF Celebrating my first England Test cap, Jamaica, 1990.

Wasim and Waqar came steaming in at us in the hour and a bit before the close on the fourth day. They really bombed us. There was a great photo in the papers of one that Wasim bowled me which just missed my chin as I pulled out of the shot. It was torrid stuff – proper Test cricket. They gave us the verbals, but because Athers and I knew them both so well, we knew it was all tongue-in-cheek and joked with them. They were happy to trade runs for wickets, but this time they were second best. That was a test of character for all four of us and we walked off at the close, delighted to have got through. I was 40 not out and full of adrenalin from the challenge. Later that evening, four players were the last to leave the England dressing-room and two of them were Pakistanis. Athers and I sat having a genial yarn with two great bowlers who had been county colleagues of ours and it was fun. Wasim and Waqar were great guys to play against – tough as nails and giving their all on the field, but good men off it. Occasions like that one at the Oval are highlights for me, and the main reason why I've wanted to go on playing Test cricket for so long.

The cricket that summer couldn't really have gone better for me, and winning the Sunday League in my final season as Surrey captain just topped it off. But now I had to make a difficult decision. Should I go on the England tour that winter to Zimbabwe and New Zealand as my wife recovered from a brain haemorrhage and having a baby? There were to be no visits from our families on that tour. Athers and Illy felt that we had been too distracted at Christmas and New Year in South Africa twelve months previously, and it had been decided we'd just have ourselves for company this time. They believed that it had become a farce to see the England tour party swell to almost seventy over the holiday period and that this time we should concentrate totally on our cricket. I thought that was wrong, irrespective of what had happened recently to Lynn, because I'd always been able to switch on to the cricket during the day, then enjoy my family in the evening when I came back to my hotel room. Lynn's not interested in the game at all, which suits me fine because I wouldn't want to talk about the day's events anyway. You need to switch off. During a Test match abroad, I'll have room service with my family or nip out for a quick bite, but I won't make any concessions to them being there. Lynn knows this is my job and understands that she's on holiday out there because of my success at that job. The problem for the team dynamic comes when a player wants to get out of the dressing-room sharpish at close of play to get back to the hotel, so that he can be with his family. For me, you should live the same life during a Test when your family is out there as you do when they are not. Of course we want them around, but not at the expense of failing to prepare to represent your country.

We never really dug our heels in over the family issue on that 1996–7 tour, although lots of us felt strongly about it. Darren Gough was particularly upset, and pointed out: 'Businessmen go abroad at Christmas and New Year and their families are allowed to come out, so why are we being treated differently?' I think we were too blinkered and should have made a bigger fuss.

The situation was that I'd be without Lynn, Andrew and Emily for Christmas if I went on the tour. Should I go? We talked it over long and hard, and Lynn decided that I should make myself available. It was what I did for a living and I wouldn't always be away. She said she'd get a live-in nanny to help with the kids while I was absent. She was convinced that she'd be fine medically, because I wouldn't leave until at least two months after she'd recovered from the major brain operation at Atkinson Morley Hospital. With misgivings, she persuaded me. Since then, she's admitted that she really wanted me to pull out of the tour, especially with hindsight as she had a couple of epileptic fits while I was away.

Even though I was preoccupied with my family for long periods on that tour, I again managed to compartmentalize things mentally and I played very well indeed. I needed to have a good tour to justify leaving my family. I was told very early on that the selectors had at last made a decision about the wicketkeeper's role and they'd be sticking to it, unless form or fitness dictated otherwise. I would be first-choice keeper, and bat at number three. I wanted to stay as high up the order as possible, so the compromise was fine. Jack Russell would therefore be my understudy and that must have been very hard on the man who was still the best keeper in England.

Jack was tremendously supportive, however. You would never have known how disappointed and frustrated he was, because he didn't show it. As usual he worked hard at his own game, even though he wasn't going to play, and he always helped me as we practised together. It was difficult to know what to say to Jack to keep his spirits up. I couldn't say, 'Come on, Jack, you might play, you know' when we both knew I'd have to be injured or in poor form to make that come about. It was to be a very long tour for him, and he must have been grateful that he had his painting to take his mind off things, as he slipped away to catch some wildlife on canvas.

That was the first tour on which I did as much preparation in wicketkeeping as in batting, and it showed. Previously I would focus on my batting and do what I could with the gloves, knowing that I wasn't the first-choice keeper. But now my attention to detail was trained on both disciplines. Alan Knott came out on the early part of the Zimbabwe tour to work with me and Jack and he was fantastic. Knotty had been one of my schoolboy heroes – I had his autograph more times than that of any other player. He was so thorough in his preparations with us. We'd do skills work with him on a one-to-one basis, then he'd have us working with the bowler, offering technical advice. After I'd done my batting practice, he'd say, 'Right, now you've prepared half your game, we'll go off and concentrate on the other half – and concentrate totally.' I did, and he helped me improve.

Back in England, he worked with me for a few years. Before a Test we'd sit and watch videos and then, after two days of preparation, he'd go home and sit in front of the telly all day. He'd ring me each night in the hotel and, as well as pointing out the positives, he would say something like: 'For the fourth ball of the 39th over, you could have got one more step in for that leg-side take' or remind me that I'd fumbled a ball in the 58th over, and did I remember? This after I'd kept wicket all day! He'd talk for about an hour, really enthusiastically, and after taking about fifteen minutes to say our goodbyes, we'd finally put the phone down. I always felt stimulated and energized by Knotty's supportive phone calls. He was a genius as a keeper, and Jack and I felt privileged to be able to work with him. I just wish we had a wicketkeeping coach who could go around the counties, helping with technique and preparations. Knotty lives in Cyprus, so he's out of the picture, but another great England wicketkeeper, Bob Taylor, is available. I had a couple of sessions with Bob and his advice was simple – keep it simple. He said, 'If you stand on your head and catch the ball, keep doing that. Just don't drop the ball.' The young English wicketkeepers need specialist tuition – it's a vital position in any team.

We weren't very impressive on that Zimbabwean leg of the tour, drawing the two Tests and losing the one-day series by 3-0. Our coach, David Lloyd, got most of the flak for what many thought was a bad impression left by us. David had replaced Raymond Illingworth as the man in charge of cricket preparations during our summer and I was delighted to work with him. I thought he was terrific – brimming with fresh ideas, passionate about England being the best – and he clearly had a great working relationship with Mike Atherton.

Bumble – as everyone called David Lloyd – got himself into hot water at the end of the Bulawayo Test, when his frustration at the negative tactics of Zimbabwe boiled over and he made a few injudicious remarks to some of their cricket dignitaries. I'm sure he regrets that, because there's no malice at all in Bumble. We'd done everything bar actually winning. They'd used up 101 overs on a flat pitch to make 234, then we had to get 204 in 37 overs. It was a Sunday League-style target and we went for broke. Nick Knight and I put on over a hundred and I got 73 in as many balls before top-edging a sweep. Then they went completely negative, with their leg-spinner Paul Strang bowling around the wicket into the rough and Heath Streak concentrating on the leg side. The umpires allowed Streak to get away with some blatantly negative stuff down the leg side and the scores finished level, with us six down. It was very tense at the end, with emotions running high, and Bumble was frustrated. He felt the umpires had been lenient and don't forget that he'd been a first-class umpire himself, so he knew the rules. In fact, the Zimbabweans were well within their rights, and I must admit we'd have done the same. However, Bumble told the media, 'We flippin' murdered 'em,' and although he was speaking emotionally he was quite correct. Nevertheless that sentence came back to haunt him over the next few weeks.

We prepared for the Boxing Day Test in Harare by training on Christmas day, and then stopping off on the way back to the hotel for a Kentucky Fried Chicken and chips. The joys of touring, not to mention the diet! It was a lonely time and our thoughts inevitably strayed towards home. Definitely not a good scheme by Athers and Illy! I had some more sombre news to digest at the end of a year which had brought serious illness to my family. My Surrey team-mate, Graham Kersey, was killed in a car crash in Australia. Graham had been understudy to me and you couldn't wish to meet a better bloke or team man. He joined us from Kent for the 1993 season and fitted into our dressing-room right away. He was great fun, and a fine young cricketer who would do anything for you. Hearing of his death wasn't the best preparation for a Test match.

It was a rain-affected Test, but we didn't exactly impress by being bowled out for 156. The Zimbabweans were wondering if we thought that this time we'd 'flippin' murdered 'em', and David Lloyd got some stick from the crowd. Rain spoiled a chance of a positive result but not before I got my first Test hundred as a wicketkeeper. I batted nearly six hours for my 101 not out, which is not my normal scoring rate, but the outfield was desperately slow. You'd only get two when normally it would go to the boundary and that slow rate of scoring made for boring cricket.

So I ended 1996 as the top scorer in Test cricket for that year. These things are neither here nor there but in the circumstances, taking into account what had happened to me, I felt proud. Had the selectors got it wrong in dropping me for that first Test of the summer? They hadn't trusted in me to eliminate that technical fault that had dogged me in South Africa – instead they trotted out the line that I was now too old. I was to get used to hearing that one.

They didn't understand that my technical problems were solely due to being out of the game for so long through my finger injuries. I knew exactly what I was doing wrong, but couldn't put it right. There was a great deal of satisfaction in turning in enough consistent performances in 1996 to prove that the selectors had made a mistake. And it was doubly satisfying that I'd done that while still greatly worried about the health of my wife and my mother.

When we left Zimbabwe, after being whitewashed in the one-day series, we knew we had to buck up our ideas in New Zealand. We'd been hammered in the press back home for being surly and unapproachable to the locals, and we hadn't played all that well. The new chairman of the ECB, Lord MacLaurin, had been to see us in Harare and made it quite clear what he now expected from us. He made a good start when he said he was amazed that we had to share rooms on tour. He got us single rooms when arriving in New Zealand, so that impressed us. He'd made his name with the Tesco supermarket chain and had clear views about selling the product that was the England cricket team. He said we were the cream of English cricket, and in the shop window, and we must look the part as well as play well. In press conferences, we must look smart. That was no problem to me, but the likes of Athers – who still hadn't lost his scruffy student ways – would view it differently. Lord MacLaurin appeared like a breath of fresh air and although he made some enemies during his time as head of English cricket, I had no problems with him. He gave the impression that he cared about the welfare of the players and that marked a pleasant change.

Meanwhile, David Lloyd was still under pressure. He'd been told by Lord MacLaurin to be more careful with his public comments and, on the first day of the first Test, it looked as if Bumble was going to apply that to his dressing-room. At lunch, he didn't come in to see us when we came off the pitch. The simple reason is that we had bowled like novices. The Auckland pitch was green and damp and any English seamer worth his salt would have expected to clean up in that first session. But they sprayed it around everywhere and the ball rarely landed on the cut strip. We were hopeless, and Bumble obviously thought so because he left us to stew at lunchtime. If he'd come in he would have exploded at us for our unprofessionalism. He'd done all he could to prepare us, and then we bowled like absolute beginners. We'd won the toss, stuck them in and let them get away with it. They ended up with 390 when they shouldn't have got 200.

I got 173, later hearing that this was the highest ever Test score by an England wicketkeeper. I'd joined Athers early on after Nick Knight was dismissed cheaply, and went for the bowling almost straight away. Chris Cairns disappeared over square leg for a hooked six and I felt in great nick. I almost ran out Athers going for my hundredth run and told him he was too slow! After that, I kept motoring along smoothly until Simon Doull pulled off a sharp caught-and-bowled as I drove the ball back firmly at him. Missed out again on a double hundred, but you'd take 173, wouldn't you?

I shared the Man of the Match award with Nathan Astle and I had no problems with that because he helped save the game for them with a gutsy century. Astle we knew about and rated, but we didn't bank on Danny Morrison holding us up for almost three hours. At the time he had the world record of Test ducks, and when he came in at number eleven we definitely sniffed victory. But Astle inspired him and the wicket just got flatter and flatter. We couldn't finish them off, but we had at least improved greatly over the five days since that dreadful first session.

We felt we were the better side, and we proved it in the next two Tests.

We won by an innings in Wellington and I failed – caught at slip for 52! Seriously, I was seeing the ball so early and so large that I felt I could get a hundred every time I walked to the crease, an amazing transformation from a year ago on my last tour. We then chased over 300 successfully to win at Christchurch. It was a long, tense day on a dry, wearing pitch. I hung around for two hours to make only 15, and we were indebted to Athers and John Crawley for playing crucial innings. Athers led from the front, batting almost twelve and a half hours in the match to make 94 and 118. It was great that he was instrumental in sealing the Test series victory after leading a long, hard tour. He'd been out of touch in Zimbabwe, but he bounced back by working even harder and trusting his own judgement. I occasionally pulled his leg about how well I was doing after being deemed to be past it just a few months earlier, but he took it in the right spirit.

This was a very satisfying period of my career, which saw me getting over my finger problem, regaining my confidence with the bat, coming through at Lord's when playing for my England future, keeping wicket very well on tour and making three Test hundreds. All this against the background of serious illness in my family and seeing my daughter born. It had seemed ages since Mike Atherton's phone call to me early in June, and I was proud that the Stewart clan had come through all the tribulations.

CHAPTER NINE
stewart for atherton

It all happened so swiftly during that summer of 1997. Just a couple of months after Mike Atherton and I had raced off the field, celebrating a nine-wicket hammering of the Australians in the first Test, I was on the phone to Athers pleading with him to stay on as our captain. The Aussies have a habit of overturning expectations, but this was a very swift change in fortunes. Even though Athers had had enough of the England captaincy by the end of that summer, he was persuaded by a few of us to stay on. I honestly thought he was still the best man for the job. A few months after my phone call, I'd succeeded him as England captain and he was on the line wishing me luck. As we both realized, luck was something you needed in buckets to do that job.

We had come back from New Zealand full of confidence that this time we could stretch Australia, and a 3-0 whitewash of them in the one-day series set us up nicely for the first Test at Edgbaston. That was a fantastic few days, especially for those veterans among us who'd suffered in previous Ashes series. We knew we had to get at them from the first ball and Darren Gough set the tone, fizzing one past Mark Taylor's bat. The crowd got right behind us and I can't remember a more fervent atmosphere in a home Test match. Those who were at Botham's match at Headingley in 1981 say the noise was similar then, although the crowds were bigger at Edgbaston. There's always a good atmosphere when England play there, and I love to hear a passionate roar from our fans. That may be the football-lover in me, but it's good to know that your supporters are behind you.

That Edgbaston Test was a perfect one for England. We had them 54 for 8 at lunch as they kept getting out playing shots to some top-class bowling. That was the Aussie way, a high-risk strategy that often came off, but sometimes caught them out. This time they were all out for 118 and we established a big lead, to put them under pressure in their second innings. Especially Mark Taylor, their captain. He just couldn't get a run so far on the tour, and we were targeting him in the same way that the Aussies target a vulnerable skipper. But he battled through to a tremendously gutsy hundred. I was full of respect for that innings – it was sketchy, his footwork was out of sync and he never looked truly in, but he stuck it out and gave his side something to bowl at.

Mark Taylor was one of the good guys in my time in the game. A fine, solid person who handled success well and took the occasional beating in the same manner, he was also a very good captain. Of course, he had a fine side, but he had his players' respect and seemed always to be on top of the tactics. Mark said the right things about the game and its integrity and I believe he was sincere. Some former players are trained to say the appropriate things to the media without necessarily sounding convincing, but Taylor was genuine in his beliefs. One of the best first-slip fielders I've ever seen, especially to the bowling of Shane Warne, Mark was one of the lucky ones who got out of the game while still at the top.

Despite the Aussie fight-back, we were on a roll and won inside four days. Athers and I rattled along at five an over and I hit the winning runs, with a four through extra cover off Warney. The crowd were fantastic; they couldn't believe we'd won so easily. We celebrated long and hard that Sunday night in Birmingham, as we were entitled to, because beating the Aussies was the ultimate in the nineties. The public expectation was suddenly enormous and it was great while it lasted. But we knew that Australia would come back hard at us and we talked about ensuring that we didn't live off that solitary victory. How right we were. Edgbaston proved to be the only time we won a meaningful Test against Australia in my seven Ashes series, as distinct from consolation wins towards the end, when the series had already been lost.

Glenn McGrath illustrated the difference between Edgbaston and the second Test, at Lord's. In Birmingham, he had been wayward in his line but at Lord's it was clear that he'd quickly sorted out how to bowl in England. He took 8 for 36 and we were bowled out for 77. The game was drawn due to a lot of rain, but McGrath continued to dominate us for the next few Ashes series. He has been a great bowler for them. His method is simple, a nice, easy, well-grooved bowling action that doesn't take too much out of him. With his control of pace, line and length, he had all the ingredients to be a top performer. With his high action, he'd get bounce and he moved the ball. When he first played against us in Brisbane, he wasn't the finished article, but his smooth action suggested he had the basics. Soon he was rated the number-one bowler in the world.

So why can't England turn out bowlers like McGrath, who is essentially an English-style bowler? Well, for a start, you have to work hard on variety and control. In Australia, the wickets are generally not seamer-friendly. They don't offer much help off the seam in sideways movement or uneven bounce. Also, after about 25 overs, the Kookaburra ball doesn't swing. So you need to learn to find something extra. McGrath did, by acquiring the knack of putting the ball consistently in the right place and getting just enough movement. In England we play with a big seam on the ball, and the weather usually allows it to swing or seam all over the place for long periods. The wickets are generally bowler-friendly, so there is too much encouragement for the average seamer. They can run up in county cricket and make the ball swing, seam and bounce. Then they graduate to flat Test match wickets and they're found out.

To be a top Test fast bowler you need pace, bounce and movement. If you have two of those, you've got a chance at Test level – one and you won't make it. McGrath has got all three. He may not be the quickest, but he gets pace off the wicket, and the nagging length he bowls at, combined with his height, hurries you up. McGrath was intelligent enough to groove his action as soon as he played for Australia, which enabled him to adapt it to the wickets he'd be playing on all around the world. They have biomechanics experts in Australia who study bowling actions, and he took advantage of that. McGrath's action has been the smoothest in world cricket in terms of not putting stress on his body. It came as a surprise when he missed a couple of Ashes Tests in the 2002–3 series, because he'd barely missed a game for Australia until then. Also, significantly, he'd hardly played for New South Wales after breaking into the national side. The Australians know how to look after their prized assets.

The quality of Glenn McGrath was certainly a challenge to one new batsman in the England side, and Mark Butcher came through it well at Lord's, making 87 in our second innings to get us a draw. Butch and I knew each other very well. I remember him as a youngster, playing on the outfield at the Oval with his brother, Gary, when I first joined the staff, and eventually they both became Surrey pros. I thought Butch had a good technique for Test cricket long before he got his first cap at Edgbaston. Predominantly a back-foot player, he played the short ball well and his temperament was sound. Nothing much fazed Butch. At the time of his Test debut he was going out with my sister, Judy, and they married later that year. The marriage foundered, sadly, as many do in professional cricket, a few years later. Butch really struggled on the South Africa tour in 1999–2000, when his personal life was splashed all over the tabloids back home. We had loads of private chats during that period. I didn't want my sister to go through a painful divorce, while I was a mate of Butch's. I managed to segment the personal from the professional and there was little ill-feeling with Butch about how it had all panned out. We are still good friends. Judy has remarried and is very happy. Butch is a fine batsman, with a Test match game and an extremely astute tactical brain. He is captaincy material for both Surrey and England.

Butch got more runs in the next Test at Old Trafford, but that match turned the tide for the whole summer. Mark Taylor gambled by batting first on a green, moist wicket and Steve Waugh made two hundreds in the match to justify the decision. Mind you, we all believed he was plumb out lbw first ball to Dean Headley on day one, but George Sharp reprieved him. He didn't need any more luck after that. When he got his second hundred of the match, I shook his hand and to my surprise, he said, 'Yeh, I've joined you now.' Always a great student of the game, he remembered Barbados '94. Waugh won that Test, despite Warne's nine wickets. He always bowled well at Old Trafford, but it was Waugh's relentless determination to battle through, despite a badly bruised hand, that set him apart. He's been the greatest competitor in my time, a player who sets the standard for the rest of the team. Not always stylish, but effective – and the wicket you really prize. As long as he was there, you could never think you'd beaten the Aussies.

Ian Healy was of similar mould. He had a fantastic series in 1997, organizing crucial runs from the tail, and keeping wicket brilliantly. At Old Trafford, he pulled off an amazing stumping to get Mark Butcher down the leg side off a full toss from Michael Bevan. It was so good that I had to go into their dressing-room at close of play to congratulate him. Healy was a great, battle-hardened cricketer who embodied the way Australians play cricket. A nuisance with the bat, who played boldly when the team was in trouble, as a keeper he just got better and better, and by the time he'd finished, he was even better than Jack Russell, especially standing up to the spinners. His partnership with Shane Warne was good for both of them. Jack was unlucky never to have the chance to shine in tandem with a great spinner as Healy did.

Although the series stood at 1-1, the momentum was now going Australia's way, and when we got to Headingley, our selectors played right into their hands by picking the wrong bowling line-up. Mike Atherton was no longer a selector – by choice, as he wasn't seeing enough county cricket – but he was surely entitled to take the field with the eleven he wanted. Yet the selectors opted for Gloucestershire's Mike Smith to get his first cap ahead of Andy Caddick. Athers was furious and I don't blame him. Smith was a very good county bowler who swung the ball effectively, but who would the Aussies prefer to face? Caddick had the height advantage over Smith by about nine inches so he'd be bringing the ball down from a height that would benefit him on the Headingley wicket. But Smith got the call, much to the dismay of Athers. The ball didn't swing, which was unlucky for him, and he had nothing else to offer because he lacked pace and bounce.

It's true that he had Matt Elliott dropped off him by Graham Thorpe – an absolute sitter – and then Elliott went on to make another 170 runs when they should have been 50 for 5. But Smith didn't take a wicket on a pitch of uneven bounce that would have suited Caddick. We lost by an innings, having played poorly. We were in trouble now and Athers was not overly happy. His runs had dried up, McGrath was getting him out regularly, and he didn't have the eleven he wanted. On top of all that, he'd lost the toss in all four Tests so far. Was Edgbaston really only a few weeks ago?

The selection of Adam and Ben Hollioake for Trent Bridge was a welcome one in the Surrey dressing-room. Adam had impressed in his first season as Surrey captain and he was a bold, adventurous cricketer. Comparisons were being made with Athers' body language and the feeling that he was no longer enjoying the job. In fact, he offered to resign during the Trent Bridge Test, but the selectors wouldn't have it. Half-way through the game he was forced to act against the growing press speculation and issue a statement saying that he'd see the job through, whatever that meant. But he was clearly finding it tough.

After their success against the Aussies in the one-day series in May, the Hollioake brothers were suddenly the flavour of the summer and represented the brave new world of English cricket. Ben, in particular, seemed totally unaffected by the big-time pressures. At the age of nineteen, he had batted wonderfully at Lord's twice that summer, against Australia in the one-day international, then in the Benson and Hedges Cup Final. I'd batted with him each time and was totally overshadowed by the youngster. Ben had the potential to be a Test all-rounder. He was a natural athlete in the field, timed the ball beautifully and, although his back had troubled him, his natural athleticism meant he would have sorted out his pace bowling as he got older and stronger.

I could understand why the Hollioakes were such an attraction to the selectors that summer, because we needed something to get us back into the series. They were both possible match winners and big-occasion players. They'd both learned their cricket in Australia, so wouldn't be unduly troubled by the pressures exerted by the likes of McGrath or Warne. They both battled hard but, like many new players to Test cricket, they didn't set the world alight. But I'll always wonder if Ben would have got there if he hadn't been killed in that terrible car crash in Australia when he was just 24. His natural talents were starting to shine very brightly.

I was in London when I heard that Ben had died, one Friday evening in March 2002. I'd been in the Sky TV studios, giving my thoughts on England's performance in the Test at Wellington, and I was waiting for a car to take me home when someone from Sky said, 'We've just heard some tragic, unconfirmed news concerning Ben Hollioake.' Having stupidly left my mobile at home, I spent an agonizing 45 minutes in the car. When I got home, five messages from the Surrey boys were waiting for me. I rang his best mate at the club, Ian Salisbury, and he confirmed Ben's death. It was an awful moment. I hadn't just lost a valued team-mate, but far more importantly a close friend and great bloke.

The Surrey players all flew out to Perth for the service and funeral. It was a sombre flight. We'd never again see that slow, laid-back smile of Ben's, that languid way he'd time the ball around the ground or throw down the stumps with a superb run-out. His relaxed, genial character had been very good value in the dressing-room and he was popular with everyone. I was asked by his family to speak at his funeral and it was the hardest thing I've ever had to do. My subject was Ben the cricketer and friend. The most difficult part was trying not to break down, and somehow, my voice faltering, I got there. I'd taken my example from Adam when he'd spoken the previous afternoon at the service. He's one of the toughest guys I've ever met, yet even he broke down, as you'd expect after such a tragedy. How he got through that I'll never know. It was very moving and touching and we all cried our eyes out on those two days: a tragic loss to a wonderful family and his many friends.

I felt that as a cricketer Ben was just realizing his potential when he died. Now I know the stats don't appear to reflect on his talent, but the sheer quality was in him to succeed in international cricket. Duncan Fletcher, the England coach, appreciated his huge potential and had earmarked him for the 2003 World Cup as a key all-rounder. I used to single him out in press conferences as the kind of player who needed to realize his value to the team. I was frank about how he could frustrate us, but that stemmed from valuing him so much as a player. There had been talk of him moving away from the Oval, to try to do himself justice, but he'd told me just before his death that he was staying at Surrey to give it his best shot. Michael Vaughan and Marcus Trescothick were the same age as Ben at his death when they came into the England side, with unimpressive county stats behind them, and they showed they had the right stuff. Duncan's judgement was correct there and he and I both believe that Ben could have developed into a Test batsman at number six who bowled effectively – as Andy Flintoff has done. We'll never know. More importantly, Ben Hollioake the man is still greatly missed.

That Trent Bridge Test was clearly the time for gambling

by England, because, apart from the inclusion of the Hollioake brothers, I was pushed up from number three to open as Butch had been dropped. Coincidentally, I played my best innings of the series, racing to 87. I timed the ball sweetly, and thought I was at last going to get a hundred in an Ashes series when Healy again pulled off an incredible catch. I went to drive Warne, got a thick edge, and although Healy dropped it at first, he dived behind him to his left and caught it one-handed in the leg slip area.

By the fourth day, we were looking down the barrel of another heavy defeat and it came in the evening, with a day to spare. It was a very disappointing capitulation, getting bowled out in just 48.5 overs. The final wicket summed up our brainless play on that Sunday. Graham Thorpe was the only one to sell his wicket dearly, and was looking in no trouble at all when he was joined by the last man, Devon Malcolm. The Australians, who had already claimed the extra half-hour, fancied a day off and wanted to finish it that night. So Thorpey's job was to frustrate them, protect Devon and get them back there for the fifth day. It would have hacked him off had the boot been on the other foot, and you always try to do what annoys the opposition. Unfortunately he couldn't manage this and we lost.

Thorpey's efforts in the final Test at the Oval paid off and his 62, the highest innings in the match, was instrumental in giving us something to defend. Caddick and Phil Tufnell bowled them out for 104 on a dry pitch that turned too early. The game was over by Saturday afternoon, with victory to us by 19 runs, which was unsatisfactory if you're a fan of the proper, five-day Test but wildly exciting for the partisan crowd and for the England players. Thorpey was Man of the Series for England and he had stood out for his sheer competence. He was the type of batsman you need against the Aussies.

He had a solid defence, a great range of shots when necessary, and a terrific temperament. When he first came into the Test team in 1993, he looked a natural. He scored a hundred in his first Test, against Australia, and never looked out of place. He was a top-drawer Test batsman, whom the Aussies rated. As soon as he came into the Surrey side, you could see that mental strength was his forte. That plays a huge part in a batsman's make-up at the highest level, and even though he hadn't made many runs for Surrey before he was picked for his first 'A' tour, we could all see that he'd take to international cricket.

Yet that 1997 summer was to be the last time that Graham made a significant contribution against the Australians. Injuries and some dreadful marital problems meant that he didn't feature all that much in the next three Ashes series. Now, I don't know if he'll play against them again. Graham's not in love with cricket, which he sees very much as a job, as much as I am. He can find the peripheral things like travel and hotels boring. He'd far rather be at home, playing with his kids, as all we family men would love to do. But get him on a cricket pitch, with his mind switched on, and he's your banker player. He's so good a batsman that he could get a hundred with his eyes shut at county level. He's a great mate of Nasser Hussain's and the captain bent over backwards to accommodate him on the Ashes tour of 2002–3, accepting that he was traumatized by his personal problems. I was amazed when Thorpey made himself available for Australia because I believed his mind clearly wasn't quite right. When he pulled out the following week, I thought he'd done the right thing. England have missed Graham Thorpe a great deal. He hasn't made a significant contribution since March 2001, when he batted so brilliantly on the Pakistan and Sri Lanka tour, and throughout his career he has missed too many

Tests for one reason or another. If he'd been out there consistently over the past decade, England would certainly have lost fewer Tests. He has been the genuine article as a Test batsman and I am sure he will prove to everyone that he still is for a few years yet.

While we celebrated that Oval victory – convinced that the Aussies hadn't been complacent, we were determined to give credit to our bowlers – our captain was seriously thinking about resigning. He hadn't been fooled by the narrow margin of defeat, and felt that 3-2 perhaps flattered us. I wouldn't disagree with that; they'd just got better after a sluggish start and we'd crumpled at key moments. The Oval win was a much-needed boost for England players and supporters alike, but we weren't fooled. The trick was to get Australia under pressure more consistently because, as they showed at the Oval, like any other side they could buckle under the pressure. However, Athers looked as if he'd had enough. To him, playing well for England was always the most important thing, whoever was captain, and by the Oval Test he was looking to clear his mind and get focused on the tour to the West Indies. The strains of captaincy didn't appeal, and no wonder. He'd been doing the job for four years. As you'd expect with any captain, he had got better and better with the experience gained, but he had never coveted the job – any more than I had – and he felt his value to England now lay as a batsman and a willing team-man under whoever took over.

A few days after we dispersed from the Oval, our coach David Lloyd rang me. Athers was about to resign the captaincy, he said. Would I call him and add my voice to those of Bumble and David Graveney in trying to talk him out of it? I did, willingly, telling Athers, 'Look, in my opinion you're still the best man for the job. I know you've got total respect from the rest of the players and there's also no other candidate. I can't tell you to carry on, just ask – and I know the team feel the same way.' I'd already talked to a few of the lads and I knew I was telling him the truth. Never a man to say all that much, Athers thanked me warmly for my call, but didn't commit himself. It seemed that the captaincy had become a bit of a chore, and that this concerned him: if the enjoyment was diminishing, then perhaps he wasn't doing the job properly. As I was to find out when it was my turn, the England captain feels defeat worse than anyone else – he takes it personally. Athers had led England to a lot of defeats by Australia since 1993, and he was feeling the hurt. He was wondering just what more he could do. Wouldn't a new skipper freshen things up?

In the end he was talked round by the chairman and coach and led the side to the West Indies. Perhaps the gap of three months before the tour started was a factor, because it gave Athers time to switch off, enjoy other things and recharge the batteries. I was delighted that he'd agreed to stay on, but the West Indies series proved to be his last as captain. Next time, he wasn't going to be talked out of following his instincts.

For England to lose that series in the Caribbean 3-1 flattered the West Indies. We could easily have won in Barbados if it hadn't rained on the final day, and we should have batted out the closing stages of the final Test, in Antigua, to get a draw that had appeared on the cards until Nasser Hussain and Thorpey were involved in a silly run-out. The series had started with a Test that lasted just 56 minutes before it was abandoned because the wicket was deemed too dangerous. The 9 that I scored there will end up as the best not out of my career, and it was the first time I've batted all the way through a Test! For once, I was aware of physical danger.

The day before that Test, at Sabina Park, Jamaica, we

looked at the pitch and feared the worst. The whole square had been re-laid and it was full of ridges. When we won the toss and decided to bat, everyone sat outside the dressing-room to watch how the wicket would perform. With Ambrose and Walsh on hand, it was bound to be interesting. The third ball of the match whistled past Athers' nose. I was at the other end, grinned at Athers and thought, 'Here we go, another belter to bat on!' There had been no time for the soil to bed down after it had been re-laid and it was anything but a flat surface. Soon I'd been hit on the hand and shoulder off a length, then another flew at me and whizzed over the wicketkeeper's head for four byes. Athers was caught in the gully off the shoulder of the bat and in came Mark Butcher, a late replacement because Jack Russell was ill on the morning of the match and we'd had to juggle around our batting order. This was the first ball he had faced out in the middle on tour because of a shortage of warm-up games. It pitched around leg stump and just took off to hit the middle of his bat handle and be caught at slip. Welcome to the Caribbean, Butch...

Nasser Hussain then nicked another unplayable one to slip, and by this time our physio, Wayne Morton, had been out in the middle giving treatment six times. When Graham Thorpe arrived, I told him, 'This is fun. Good luck, mate – I can't tell you about the bowling, except it's doing a lot. If you get hit, go down and we'll get the physio out again.' Not very reassuring, I admit, but by now I was keeping an eye on the two umpires and dropping heavy hints. Steve Bucknor, on his home island, was in a dodgy position because he'd get some grief from the crowd if he was a party to the match being abandoned, so I looked to Venkat for some guidance – 'This isn't too clever, is it?' – and he agreed. Walsh and Ambrose were concerned, asking if I was OK every time they hit me. That showed how unreal it had become. I said to Bucknor, 'Mate, you've been around a bit – you can't tell me this is right.' Unfortunately I received no reply – just a blank look.

When Thorpey was hit on the hand and getting treatment, I called Athers out and said, 'I don't mind a challenge but this is ridiculous.' Athers was in full agreement and spoke to the West Indies captain, Brian Lara, who was also under the cosh, having taken over from Walsh, who was a legend in Jamaica, his home island. But the umpires then called in the match referee, Barry Jarman, and thankfully he abandoned the game. So I batted undefeated through a Test match! I was hit on the body almost as many times as I hit the ball. It was tragic for the Jamaican public, for the game of cricket and for those England supporters who, having saved their well-earned money, had flown out to watch a Test and saw just one hour's play. But that wicket was unfit for any level of cricket, and I'm convinced that our tall fast bowlers would have been just as dangerous as Walsh and Ambrose.

To compensate, we ended up playing two Tests in Trinidad, and they were close contests, both won by three wickets, with one victory to either side. They were tense, hard-fought matches played on sporting pitches where the ball seamed about and kept low. Gus Fraser profited from the uneven bounce to take 8 for 53, and that underlined what a great pro he was. Ashley Cowan of Essex had come out as the young fast bowler and had a great chance of playing in the Tests ahead of Gus, as you'd expect – but Gus wouldn't give in without a fight. Gus had the responsibility of working with the other bowlers and did that very well, but Cowan appeared to have no interest in finding out what you need to do to become an international cricketer. He didn't seem bothered about doing the hard work, and Gus out-bowled him on the tour and deservedly stayed in the side. Ashley Cowan still hasn't played a Test match, yet he couldn't have had a better mentor on that tour than Gus Fraser.

I played well in those two Tests in Trinidad, scoring three fifties and a 44, and twice getting us off to important starts with Athers. Walsh and Ambrose really stretched us in the second game, bowling 71 overs out of 108 in the second innings on a pitch of uneven bounce. They gave us absolutely nothing, and Athers and I grafted to put on 129 in four hours to set up the victory. We made it home to square the series, thanks to the calmness of Butcher and Headley, but those two West Indian bowlers were a great challenge. That's why I was so pleased to do well again out there, scoring more runs than any other batsman on either side, and averaging 45. Every run had to be earned against those two guys. On the previous tour, in 1994, I'd worked out a method of dealing with the low bounce by batting fractionally outside leg stump. I stayed leg-side because I wanted to get at the ball. If I were to keep my usual leg-stump guard, there'd be a chance that when playing back and across, I'd be lbw with the ball keeping low. So I trusted myself to get the bat at the ball from standing just outside leg stump instead of trying to play around my front pad. I then continued to use the conventional method of going back and across to the fast bowlers, but I wouldn't be as far across my stumps as normal. I had to rely on a sharp eye, but it worked on both tours.

Losing the toss and batting last in the next Test at Guyana was an important factor in our heavy defeat, but I didn't help by dropping Shivnarine Chanderpaul at slip as soon as he came in on the first day. He went on to get a hundred. The pitch broke up after day one, and Ambrose and Walsh did it again. The major consolation for England was the mature way that Mark Ramprakash played in both innings. He was at last in the side after a frustrating wait, and he vindicated his selection in great style by making 154 in the drawn Barbados Test. I thought at the time that Ramps had finally arrived as a Test batsman.

It was a quality hundred, made when England were in trouble, having lost early wickets and with Graham Thorpe off with a bad back. Thorpey returned eventually, they added over 200 together, and Ramps looked a high-class act. When I think back on that innings, I wonder – how did he manage to score only two Test hundreds? He was probably the most technically gifted England batsman of my time. I first saw him when he was seventeen, playing for Middlesex in a pre-season game at the Oval, and I was struck by the assurance with which this lad played our fast bowlers. I looked out for him after that and wasn't at all surprised at his maturity in the 1991 Test series against West Indies. He batted for long periods throughout, never looked uncomfortable and it was always a surprise when he was out. I was certain that he'd enjoy a long and productive England career, because he had the lot.

With Ramps, it may have been the mental side of his game that let him down, because his many disappointments had nothing to do with ability. He was given chances, but each time he came back after being dropped, the pressure on him to perform grew. Then it's the age-old question: can the individual deal with it? Don't look any further than going out there to score runs. Don't worry about whether you feel loved and respected in the dressing-room – forget the peripherals: show everyone your natural talents. It didn't help that he was shunted up and down the batting order. When I became England captain, I stuck by him because I was such a fan. He needed to feel there'd be continuity of selection, that we had faith in him. When he wasn't picked to go to South Africa in

1999–2000, I felt that was a major knockback for him. They picked Michael Vaughan, Chris Adams, Mark Butcher and Darren Maddy ahead of him, and the reason for that, I assume, was the selectors looking at temperament rather than talent.

Ramps can show emotion when he gets out and I have no problem with that. He was fined after the Lord's Test in 1998 when he disagreed with Darryl Hair's decision to give him out, caught behind off Allan Donald. He told the umpire, 'You're messing with players' careers, Darryl,' and although he was in the wrong to say it, that showed how much he cared and how desperate he was for success. I felt he could have made a fresh start in South Africa under Duncan Fletcher and Nasser Hussain. After all, Nasser has been a hothead at times in his England career when decisions have gone against him. Ramps isn't the only one to get wound up. We haven't been blessed with so much talent in the England set-up that we can afford to blow hot and cold over a player of his ability.

I've often wished, seeing him so relaxed in the Surrey dressing-room, that he could go out in the same frame of mind and bat like that for England. We are close friends and he has often talked to me about the frustrations he's felt at failing to replicate his thought patterns in county cricket when he gets on to the international stage. In the end, it's the individual who has to do it. It's such a shame. He's a very popular bloke, charming and polite when he's out in public, and great fun to have around in the dressing-room when it's raining. The impersonations he does in benefit matches are superb. He'll do Bob Willis, Abdul Qadir, Curtly Ambrose and Courtney Walsh bowling, and me and Brian Lara batting. They come easily to him. So does batting. If Ramps and Graeme Hick had managed to get their mental approach to batting right, we would have been a more successful side. They are the two most natural talents from my England career who I wish had been more successful.

The fourth day of the final Test, in Antigua, was Mike Atherton's thirtieth birthday, but he didn't have much to celebrate. He was done again by Ambrose, for the sixth time in the series, as we began the uphill struggle to avoid an innings defeat. We should have made it, but were bowled out the following day. As the West Indies players celebrated their 3-1 series victory, running triumphantly around the boundary edge waving the Wisden Trophy, we sat shell-shocked in our dressing-room. We ought to have batted it out for a boring draw, but Nasser's run-out had been decisive and the tail was then exposed to Walsh. I had wondered what Athers was discussing during his frequent chats with Bob Bennett, our manager, and David Lloyd during that final day, but wouldn't presume to intrude on their private conversations. It was soon clear what they'd been talking about. Before Athers went off to do his media duties, he asked for some quiet in the dressing-room. He then told us that he had resigned. He believed he had done all he possibly could in the job, but didn't want to carry on any more. After thanking us for our efforts, he left. The dressing-room was deathly quiet for ages. We all felt responsible. He had dealt with so much over 52 Tests and four and a half years without complaint. Now he wasn't to be denied. It was particularly hard for established players like Jack Russell, Gus Fraser and me who had been at his side for most of the past decade. Gus, a close friend, sat for ages with a towel over his head, in tears. It was the end of an era. No one had led England in more Tests or been better at leading from the front. We hadn't won enough Tests consistently to encourage Athers to believe that better times lay ahead. It was often one step forward, but two steps back – especially against Australia. I'm sure he was troubled by the back injury which continually gave him pain – although he would never let on about it. He was Iron Mike to us. Athers would have been aggrieved by averaging just 18 in this last series and only 23 in the previous one against Australia, and his pride in performance would have demanded that he sorted out his batting and fitness. Something had to give if he wanted to go on playing for England, and that proved to be the captaincy.

It was a shock, even though we knew that he'd had to be persuaded to stay on just six months ago. Athers kept the hurt and frustrations of the job to himself, but he was very proud to have led England so many times. We had an idea about how he must have been feeling and I said to the boys, 'Listen, over the next 24–36 hours, he's going to need our support and any comfort we can give him. We've got to be there for him, as he was for us many times.' He stayed on for the one-day series, but didn't play a game as Adam Hollioake captained the team. Athers did his twelfth-man duties with good humour and seemed more relaxed and comfortable with his decision.

So the speculation started about Athers' successor. As I understood it, there were only two contenders, me and Nasser Hussain. Nasser had taken over from me as vice-captain in Zimbabwe and New Zealand, and had been doing the job in the Caribbean. I had no problems with that. Nasser hadn't changed much from the character straight out of university who toured the Caribbean with us in 1990. He spoke his mind to anyone in the squad, and that was fine by me. The problem came when less sensitive souls were upset by his straight talking. But he didn't bear grudges and within half an hour he'd forgotten all about the reason why he'd spoken so frankly. Nasser always talked cricket, and had a good feel for the game. By the time of Athers' resignation, he was a good Test batsman and an automatic choice. That, to me, was the crucial point. Whoever took over from Athers had to be worth his place in the side. We weren't good enough to carry a player so that he could be the captain.

As the speculation mounted over the next month I just kept my head down and got on with the job of preparing myself for the season. I wouldn't make any public comment about my chances, restricting myself to praising Athers for his contribution to English cricket. No way was I going to get involved in any sort of electioneering in the press. The important aim for me was still getting into the England side that summer, and for me and the team to be playing well. I didn't even talk to Dad about it. I had the same attitude as in 1993, when the captaincy was last up for grabs – I'd accept it if offered the honour. You don't turn down the offer of the England captaincy, I felt, but you don't actively seek it. I did feel that I was more suited to it now, five years on, because I had greater experience and was now an established international cricketer, but that was as far as it went.

I was invited to the House of Lords for lunch with Lord MacLaurin and the chairman of selectors, David Graveney. The ECB chairman expressed his views on the captain's responsibility to sell the game and project the right image and, at the same time, lead England to success. We had a good chat in which I expressed my opinions about the job and how I would tackle it if invited to take on the challenge.

On 5 May 1998 I was presented to the media at Lord's as England's new captain for the six Tests that summer, along with Adam Hollioake, who was to lead the one-day team, continuing on from the Caribbean series. My tenure would last almost exactly twelve months and ironically it would be our poor one-day efforts in the World Cup that would lose me the Test captaincy.

CHAPTER TEN

captain of england

It began with a phone call as I drove home from the House of Lords and ended thirteen months later with a call on my mobile at Glasgow Airport. Each time the caller was David Graveney, the chairman of selectors – first with the good news that I was the new England captain, appointed for a twelve-month period, then that I'd been replaced. In those thirteen months I went through all sorts of fluctuating emotions, ranging from patriotic and personal pride to frustration with some ECB officials, and ending with a slightly cynical view of the way I'd been treated.

The highlight for me was winning the Leeds Test against South Africa, and with it the series. Not since we beat the Australians in the summer of '85 had we come out on top in a five-Test series, and the reaction from the crowd that Monday morning at Headingley was fantastic. I was particularly pleased at the way we had fought back over the previous month to stay in the series and inch our way to victory at Trent Bridge and Leeds. After losing badly at Lord's, we had again played poorly over the first three days at Old Trafford. They are never slow to show their feelings up there, and at the close of play on the Saturday night, we were booed. It hurt me as captain, but I have to say that we deserved that reaction. We had bowled unimaginatively on a slow pitch as they racked up a huge score, then batted badly after tea. We were eight down at close of play, with the follow-on almost a certainty and another defeat likely.

I had thought about what to say before the start of Sunday's play at Old Trafford, and I gave it to the boys straight and sharp. We hadn't given our best and I told them we weren't just playing for ourselves but for the whole of Britain. We were in danger of letting down the entire country. For me, it was important to lead from the front and I count my 164 in the second innings as one of my better knocks for England. I batted for more than seven hours, and Athers and I set the right example by adding more than 200. Allan Donald got me out, caught hooking, and Athers went the same way. It may have looked reckless, but we both got hundreds of runs with that shot in our Test careers. For some reason, nicking a wide one to slip never seems as big a talking point as holing out on the hook. One looks like the sucker punch, the other not. We'd both batted with controlled aggression, and that defiance was followed by our bowlers when they had to bat it out for the draw against Donald, who was magnificent, pushing himself to the limits as the other South African bowlers were almost at a standstill.

Darren Gough, Angus Fraser and Robert Croft stood there and took all that Donald could muster up. Croft, in particular, was superb. Glenn McGrath had showed him to be fallible to the short ball the year before, but he wouldn't buckle. We all sat on the balcony, willing Croft and Gus through the final overs, and then Donald summoned up one final over at Fraser. He had a big appeal for a close lbw turned down, and Gus survived – and so did we. I ran on to the outfield to embrace our two batsmen, and I suppose it may have looked a bit much that I was so thrilled at getting away with a draw when we'd played so badly in the first three days. But it did feel good, and the South Africans were shattered at the end, while we celebrated as if we'd won. I just felt that our defiance might have turned the series our way that final evening at Old Trafford. Dad's words about staying in the game came back to me: we might easily have lost, but we lived to fight another day. We could build on that great spirit shown over the past two days. And we did.

We won the final two Tests, taking the series 2-1, and the enthusiasm that swept through the country was gratifying and very significant. We knew that it was up to us to provide excitement and a winning team to our supporters and to sports fans who weren't necessarily regular cricket watchers. Football's World Cup that summer had occupied many sports fans' attention, even though England had gone out to Argentina on penalties, and in the gap between that tournament and the start of the Premiership season, Test cricket came roaring back into the public's affections. Even after the English football season started in mid-August, cricket still claimed a lot of media exposure. The goodwill was there and it was up to the England players to build on that. There was enough drama and excitement in those last two Tests to satisfy anybody who craved that extra something from sport, and I look back on those weeks as one of the most satisfying periods of my England career.

The South Africans felt that most of the key umpiring decisions went against them in those two dramatic Tests, but I don't agree. Of course, Mike Atherton should have been given out, caught behind off Donald at Trent Bridge, and that might have altered the result, but Merv Kitchen's decision led to the best passage of play I've ever seen, as a great fast bowler tore into a top batsman, with no holds barred. The most memorable thing for me, apart from that fantastic, full-on duel between Athers and Donald, was the sight of them having a beer in the England dressing-room the next day, as Donald was big enough to congratulate

Athers and the rest of us on a vital win. Donald was massively respected down the years by the England boys for many reasons, and his generosity of spirit off the field was one of them. The way he conducted himself at Trent Bridge in '98 helped remind me of why we play the game

At Leeds, the umpire Javed Akhtar had a poor match, but I believe his decisions didn't favour one side in particular. They thought Makhaya Ntini was unlucky to be given out lbw to lose the match by 23 runs, but I didn't see it that way at all. I'd have been desperately disappointed if that decision hadn't gone our way – it just looked stone dead. Hansie Cronje and Gerry Liebenberg thought they were hard done by when given out in their second innings as the tension rose, but what about the ones that we copped? Nasser Hussain might have been unlucky to be adjudged caught behind, Andrew Flintoff padded one to short leg and was given out – and so it goes on. Earlier in the series, it went against us. At Lord's, Mark Ramprakash and I were on the wrong end of decisions on appeals for catches by their wicketkeeper, but you just have to take it. Ramps was rightly disciplined for speaking out of turn to the umpire who sent him on his way. The South Africans should have followed the lead of Donald, swallowed hard and reflected on where they lost the series.

The atmosphere at Headingley on the final morning of the series was fantastic. They needed 34 to win we wanted two wickets. I'd used my experience the night before to get us off the pitch before they claimed the extra half-hour, and got away with it. I wondered how significant that might prove. Shaun Pollock was batting well, and our fast bowlers were on their knees. Gus Fraser, who had gone in the back, was hardly able to move. We needed to get off because there were cheap runs to be had against our tired attack. The South Africans had been too slow in deciding whether to take the extra half-hour. I noticed their twelfth man, Paul Adams, on the boundary edge carrying a fresh pair of batting gloves for Pollock, and I guessed that he was bringing out a message to tell the batters to claim the extra half-hour. So when the last scheduled over was bowled, and the batters started to walk off, I whipped off the bails sharpish and handed them over to the umpire. The umpires asked what I wanted to do, and I said straight away, 'We'll go off.' Adams had got out there too late, and I understand their captain, Hansie Cronje, was furious that he'd taken so long. The rules state that the batsmen out in the middle represent their captain and that it needs only one captain to claim the extra time. If the umpires believe a result is possible that night, then the extra half-hour can be taken. Staying out there was South Africa's best chance of victory, with the light good and our bowlers knackered.

Admission was free the next morning and the Yorkshire public, spotting a bargain, rolled up in their thousands. It could all have been over inside two balls, but the action lasted half an hour in front of about 10,000 delirious spectators. We were really fired up by the atmosphere before the start, aware that the South Africans had missed a trick the night before by not staying out. It was left to young Matthew Wood to find the right words to send us out of the traps. Woody, a Barnsley lad, had been our twelfth man during the last few days and he'd been brilliant. He was making his way in the Yorkshire side as a batter and enthusiasm poured out of him. It was clearly a memorable experience for Woody. As we warmed up on the outfield, with David Lloyd and Wayne Morton putting us through our exercises, I was conscious that we needed something extra to send us over the top at eleven o'clock. Bumble and I were talked out – we'd been coming up with the usual stuff for the previous four mornings – and I wanted something different from somebody. I could see that Woody was relishing the atmosphere on his home ground, so I said, 'Right, Woody, we've done all our talking, so it's over to you, mate. Your speech is going to win or lose us this game!' He wasn't fazed at all. After calling for quiet, he pointed over to the South Africans on the other side of the ground, and, in a broad Yorkshire accent, said to the group of experienced England players, 'Look at that lot over there. Go and spoil their day and win us the game.' Perfect – all we needed. We couldn't wait to get at them.

It was desperately tense. Pollock was the danger man and we had to prise open the other end. Eventually, after half an hour of taut cricket, Gus had Donald caught by me off a feather of a nick. Then Darren Gough, ever the showman, finished it off next over, trapping Ntini lbw. Typical Gough – his best Test figures, in front of his home crowd. Time to spray the champagne, drink in the fervour of the crowd and float on adrenalin for hours. I gave it the FA Cup Final impression big-time, brandishing the Cornhill Trophy to the supporters and yelling my head off. We allowed the TV cameras into our dressing-room, proud to share our pleasure with the nation. I was delighted to see Athers back in time to share the celebrations. He'd gone to hospital with a mysterious stomach complaint and got back to the ground just as the last South African wicket fell. It was a sweet moment for him. Athers had had so much to do with our Trent Bridge victory, had helped me start the fight-back at Old Trafford and had been tremendously supportive to me generally since resigning as captain.

We were heroes, whereas only six weeks earlier, at Old Trafford, we'd been booed off the field. What pleased me most of all was the resilience and heart we'd shown to claw our way back into the series. We kept hearing how strong-minded the South Africans were, how the competitive spirit in them was second only to Australia's, yet they were the ones who had buckled. Hansie Cronje looked absolutely shell-shocked that Monday morning, as the reality of the defeat sank in. For us the feelgood factor was brilliant. If we could show that sort of character against the Australians in a few months' time, anything was possible.

Within three weeks, however, the bubble had burst and I was far from happy about it. We were due to play Sri Lanka at the Oval, and when we turned up two days earlier to look at the wicket, I was astonished to see that it was dry and bare. It would offer nothing to our fast bowlers and delight their off-spinner, Muttiah Muralitheran. He could turn the ball on anything and he'd be in his element on what looked like a typical wicket from Colombo. David Lloyd and I were furious. We were rightly not allowed input on the preparation of the wicket, but the groundstaff would surely have been aware that pace and bounce was preferable for us, and ideally some sideways movement for our seam bowlers. That pitch was perfect for the Sri Lankans. We wouldn't be able to ruffle them with fast, short-pitched bowling, their stroke-makers would be able to stand and deliver without bothering about the ball moving around, and Murali would have a field day. He took sixteen wickets in the match and we lost by ten wickets after scoring 445 in the first innings. What a letdown. Our team was on a high, the country was at last talking about cricket rather than football, and we were up against a side that we'd been expected to beat. Yet we handed the match to them by preparing that dry pitch. No other country on the Test circuit would hand such an advantage to a touring side. The marketing people at the ECB would be pleased that the game went into the fifth day, but winning Test matches also brings the crowds in.

Anything that we had gained by our great fight-back against South Africa was knocked out of us at the Oval in just a few days.

David Lloyd, our coach, allowed his frustrations to get the better of him when he questioned the legality of Muralitheran's action. Some said that was just sour grapes, but ever since we had seen Murali in Sri Lanka in 1993, we had wondered about how he got such turn. He'd been born with a deformity of the elbow joint and it was certainly a unique action. However, an ICC committee with many illustrious former players had examined him in great detail and he had been cleared. As far as I was concerned, it was more important to deny him a wicket that suited him perfectly than to go on about his action. He wouldn't now be asked to change it, after picking up more than two hundred Test wickets. But I would still defend Bumble to the hilt over his remarks. He is an honest, passionate man, and was totally devoted to his players and to the best interests of English cricket. If he thought Murali was getting an unfair advantage, he was entitled to say so.

Bumble believed in speaking his mind and I had no problems with that. He upset those in power who thought that England should be whiter than white, but Bumble knew about the real world in cricket. He wanted things to be fair and above board and that's why the players loved him. He was terrific as coach when I worked with him – very progressive, dynamic, fizzing with ideas. I was dismayed when the ECB disciplined him publicly over his remarks about Murali. He was given a final warning, and no doubt his public comments in Zimbabwe in 1996–7 were also taken into account. But why make that final warning public? Couldn't it have been handled privately?

Instead we were going to Australia, to face the best team in the world, with a cloud hanging over our coach. Graham

Gooch was to be the manager, with extra responsibilities for dealing with the media. Bumble was going there under pressure to be diplomatic, rather than his natural, open, bubbly self. He was, in effect, muzzled. It was to prove a hard tour for him. At times he was emotionally drained and it all came to a head at Hobart Airport just before Christmas. The day before, we had been thrashed by an Australian 'A' team. I had the match off and Mike Atherton was in charge. For reasons best known to himself, he decided against batting out time and declared, giving them a run chase on the flattest of pitches. They cantered home, scoring around six an over while our bowlers struggled to get anything from the wicket. It was humiliating and the worst possible preparation for the fourth Test, due to start at Melbourne in a few days' time. At tea, Bumble came into the dressing-room fuming, and told the players, 'It's all right for you, but my job's on the line. Thanks very much.' Next morning, at the airport, he told me he was packing it in. 'What's the point?' he said, 'I've done all I can.' He was very flat, totally unlike his usual self, as low as I've ever seen him. Graham Gooch and I worked hard at getting his spirits up over the next few days.

At Sydney, at the end of that Ashes tour, I made a point of saying in my speech at the awards ceremony that I was looking forward to continuing to work with David Lloyd. That was a deliberate vote of confidence from the captain. He had been tremendous. Lots of things like videos, sophisticated fitness training and central contracts – which are now seen as essential tools of the trade – had been pushed by Bumble. He was very hot on continuity of selection and wanted to create a more supportive sense of harmony in the team, so that the players weren't continually looking over their shoulders, concerned that the selectors were chopping and changing the side.

We lost the Ashes series 3-1 for three reasons. Australia again proved to be the best side in the world, while we suffered too many injuries and dropped too many catches. The captain losing the toss in all five Tests didn't help either. I was told it was the first time this had happened in a five-Test Ashes series in Australia. Always nice to make history. Losing out on the toss meant we faced major disadvantages in two Tests – when they batted first in the stifling heat at Adelaide, then on a turning pitch in Sydney. But no excuses otherwise. We probably would have lost the first Test, in Brisbane, if a spectacular thunderstorm hadn't washed away the last three hours on the final day. On the other hand a crucial run-out decision that went against us in Sydney had a significant bearing on that result.

Taking a chance on Graham Thorpe's fitness rebounded on us, just as it did with Darren Gough four years later. In both cases, the risk was justified because they were key players. Thorpe had been our best player in the last Ashes series, in 1997, but his dodgy back only lasted out for one Test and he went home. His experience, calmness and left-handed batting would have been a godsend against the leg-spin of Stuart McGill, who took 27 wickets in the series. Athers also struggled with his back, which affected his batting against the relentless Glenn McGrath, so we rarely got a good start at the top of the order.

Losing the third Test in Adelaide, to go 2-0 down in the series, meant that we couldn't win back the Ashes. I was absolutely gutted, and when asked in the press conference what I had to say to the people back home, I wasn't at my most fluent, offering my apologies but probably sounding less than convincing. But I was sorry, more than the public realized. I'd had genuine hopes that we would win that series. Shane Warne's absence apart from the final Test due to a shoulder operation was a big factor in my pre-tour optimism and I felt we'd picked the right squad, with experienced, reliable players who would give everything to the team. But yet again the quality of the Australians was obvious. There was always someone to make runs when they were needed or, in the case of McGill, to step into the hole left by the absence of a leading bowler. We were still trying to catch up, and this was my fifth losing Ashes series in a row.

Yet we'll always have Melbourne to remember. That was as tense a Test match as I can remember. After the first day was washed out, there was enough drama spread over the next three days to keep everybody enthralled and underline yet again the appeal of Test cricket. For me, it was an unforgettable game. We won by 12 runs, and at last I scored my first Test century against Australia. And it came in my favourite position as opener. We had to reshuffle our final eleven at the last minute because Alex Tudor had a hip injury. It was decided to play four fast bowlers, bring in Warren Hegg to keep wicket and hopefully stiffen the lower-order batting, move in Mark Butcher to bat at number three and move me up to my favourite position.

We were in trouble straight away, losing Athers and Butch for ducks to leave us on 4 for 2. I needed some luck and got it when I edged Damian Fleming through the slip cordon to get off the mark, but then I flowed along, playing as well as I can. Mark Ramprakash batted very well at the other end, and we both played as the Australians do when they've lost early wickets – confidently. I reeled off boundaries, driving the ball better than at any stage of the tour, and when I got to my hundred with an all-run four, I celebrated more animatedly than usual. I took off my helmet, waved my bat to every corner of that vast MCG and kissed the three lions on my shirt. Getting a hundred at last as captain in an Ashes Test meant so much to me. Having learned a lot about the game in Australia during my apprentice years also added to my sense of pride and pleasure. Justin Langer came up to me after the game and said, 'You're mad if you don't open for England now for the rest of your career, and all our boys think the same.' Having played against Justin many times in my Perth days, I knew he was being serious, but there remained the old problem of my best role for the side. I'd never make excuses for my poor batting stats against Australia, but the need to keep wicket is relevant here. This was only the sixth Test against Australia in which I'd played purely as a batsman and only the fourth in which I'd opened the innings.

We surprised all Australians by continuing to compete hard throughout those three days. They needed only 175 to win and started off confidently as usual. Perhaps they got over-confident; perhaps it was just that we battled gamely and kept picking them off. What I do know is that we were shattered mentally when it was all over, once the adrenalin of victory had worn off. It was a ridiculously long day – almost eight hours out in the middle. The final session alone lasted more than four hours! The rain of previous days meant long periods had to be made up under new regulations, and we needed to show plenty of stamina. Darren Gough was fast and hostile, and Dean Headley was quite fantastic. It was the day of his cricketing life as he reeled off the overs, never slackening his pace. Deano was the type of person I'd wanted in the England side, someone who would never give up and would also support the other bowlers enthusiastically in the field. And he never looked for excuses, always backed himself. He thoroughly deserved to be named Man of the Match.

The spark we needed to pressurize the Aussies was Mark Ramprakash's astonishing catch at square leg to dismiss Langer. They only needed another 70 to win, with eight wickets in hand, when Ramps took off athletically to take the catch inches from the ground. He sprung up instantly, celebrating with all of us, whooping and hollering. Just what we needed. I'd told the lads before we went out that the Aussies had a history of choking on a run chase when it seemed a formality. They'd bottled it against us at the Oval the year before and in Adelaide on the previous tour. And we all knew about their collapses against Bob Willis and Ian Botham in that amazing summer of '81. It was our chance to be heroes, I told them, and we must give everything.

We worked our way through the batting, but there was still Steve Waugh at one end. He'd scored a typical hundred in the first innings and as long as he was there, they had to be favourites. We had to knock them over when he wasn't on strike. Waugh didn't subscribe to the philosophy that you have to protect the tail, believing that if you respect your batting partner and let him take some of the bowling, he will gain extra confidence and play above himself. So Waugh wasn't going to farm the bowling in those dramatic final overs. That suited us.

They needed just 14 to win, with three wickets left, when Waugh claimed the extra half-hour. I tried it on, as I had at Headingley a few months earlier, but this time didn't get away with it. Our bowlers were out on their feet and Waugh knew that. When it came to the scheduled close, I picked up the bails, handed them to the umpire Darryl Harper and made as if to walk off. But Harper knew what I was up to, had a chat with Steve Bucknor at the other end, and then spoke to Waugh. We had to stay on. I'm glad we did so, because we then cleaned up the tail.

Immediately, Nicholson nicked a catch to Hegg off Deano, and then Waugh had all the problems. He took a single off the first ball of Darren Gough's over, leaving Stuart McGill exposed. His first ball saw him yorked with an inswinger, then, two balls later, Glenn McGrath was cleaned up with another fast inswinger. Goughie, ever the man for the big occasion, had done it for us when the chips were down. We grabbed the stumps and celebrated a fantastic win. I went over to commiserate with Steve Waugh, and he was absolutely hacked off with losing. His massive disappointment pleased me greatly. It was the evidence I needed in case anyone suggested that the Aussies weren't too fussed about the result, having already retained the Ashes. Australians don't like losing at any time in international sport. Waugh wanted to make the series score 3-0 at Melbourne, not 2-1.

It had been an amazing turnaround. It was only a week since the shambles in Hobart, with the bowlers performing dreadfully, David Lloyd seemingly at the end of his tether, and the whole tour in danger of ending disastrously with us losing the series 4-0. Now Bumble was running around the outfield of the MCG, hugging every England player he could find, then spraying champagne over all of us. He deserved that wonderful moment, for all the hard work and passion he brought to the England job.

So we had a chance of squaring the series by winning in Sydney. My favourite cricket ground after Lord's – the crowd is almost on top of you at the SCG and it's an old-fashioned ground, unlike the modern stadia that you mostly get in Australia. The first day of that final Test had everything. The Waugh twins batted brilliantly, then Goughie took a hat-trick near the close and we bowled them out for 322. That meant we ended the day on a high after it looked as if they were going to bat us out of the game, with the pitch bound to turn for McGill and the recalled Warne. Goughie's success – achieved with the perfect swinging yorker to bowl Colin Miller – was a belated reward for his magnificent bowling on the tour. He never gave up, bowled fast and intelligently, staying fit, and had cruel luck with dropped catches. He took 21 wickets in the series, but deserved at least 30. The Australian crowds loved him, because he gave the impression that he was enjoying himself and couldn't wait to bowl fast at anyone. I think this was Goughie's finest series for England.

We trailed by 102 on first innings, as McGill turned the ball sharply. But I honestly believe we still could have won if an umpiring decision had gone our way – or more precisely, if the TV facilities had been available to help the third umpire come to the correct conclusion. They were 60 for 2 when Michael Slater was caught short by a direct hit from Dean Headley on to the stumps at the non-striker's end. You could tell from Slater's reaction that he knew he hadn't made it as he slapped his gloves in annoyance and kept on running towards the pavilion. But he stopped when umpire Steve Dunne referred the decision to the third umpire, Simon Taufel. Unfortunately for us, the TV cameras that Taufel relied on weren't precise enough on the moment that the stumps were broken. Peter Such, the bowler, was obscuring the wicket from one side, and there wasn't another camera available from the other side to confirm that Slater was out. So he got the benefit of the doubt, which is fair enough – that's in the laws of the game. But if you are going to rely on TV replays, there should be fixed cameras on either side of the wicket, level with the line. The technology is there, so why not make sure that it's used professionally? There would be a better chance of getting the right decision. We had been equally unlucky during the Adelaide Test, when Mike Atherton was given out, caught low down at slip by Mark Taylor. Neither Athers nor Taylor was sure it had carried, but the wicketkeeper Ian Healy was certain it had. The third umpire, Paul Angley, made up his mind in just a couple of seconds, which was quite ridiculous. The numerous TV replays showed that there was evidence that the ball might have bounced before Taylor caught it, and there was sufficient doubt for Athers to be reprieved, as Slater was in Sydney. We felt so incensed by the decision of the inexperienced Angley that our manager, Graham Gooch, sent an official letter to the match referee, John Reid. In my match report, I made some observations about the role of the third umpire and how TV can help him make up his mind, but also confuse him.

However, Slater was given not out, and after that he started to play fabulously, playing some great shots. Following his reprieve on 35 he went on to make 123 out of a total of 184 all out. If he'd gone when we thought, we would only have had to chase about 180, rather than the required 287. We were getting on top when Deano's throw hit the stumps, and I believe we would have bowled them out cheaply. A target of almost 300 on a worn pitch against McGill and Warne was too much, and we lost by 98 runs.

The Ashes had stayed with Australia again, but now it was time to get that disappointment out of our system and prepare for the World Cup, which was due to start in England in just four months' time. We needed to get into one-day mode quickly, and we got some hard work in when we stayed on in Australia for the triangular series against two top one-day sides, Australia and the World Cup holders, Sri Lanka. We reached finals, having played well early on, then had some careless days, but Australia finally beat us 2-0. Most of our matches against Sri Lanka went our way, but one that didn't, in Adelaide, and was the worst I've ever played in. If I had to pick the one game of cricket that I enjoyed least of all in my career, then it would be England v. Sri Lanka at the Adelaide Oval on 23 January 1999. The facts are that they beat us by one wicket with two balls to spare, chasing 303. It sounds like a great game, but I assure you it was dreadful to play in.

The first flashpoint came when Muralitheran was called for throwing by umpire Ross Emerson. The Australian umpires had suspected Murali's action for years and Darryl Hair had called him in a Test match, but Murali stayed in the game because it was felt that his action, although freakish, was legal. That caused dismay in Australia, where hostile crowds tended to back up vocally the doubts of Darryl Hair and a few other umpires who wouldn't put their heads above the parapet. But Emerson would. I knew him from my days of grade cricket in Perth and, a fortnight before Adelaide, he told me he would call Murali the first time he stood in the same game as him.

At our team meeting on the morning of the match, someone asked what would happen if Murali was done by Emerson. David Graveney, who was acting as our tour manager, said we should just get on with the game. We would have loved to, except that the Sri Lankans downed tools when it happened. Graeme Hick and Nick Knight had to stand on the outfield in the intense heat for about fifteen minutes while the Sri Lankan captain, Arjuna Ranatunga, had a fierce finger-wagging session with the umpires, then took his players off to the boundary edge to talk to his tour officials. They made a huge fuss, and had various mobile phone conversations with executives in Colombo, while our two batsmen stood there, waiting to resume the match. Ranatunga was clever enough to ensure that they didn't go off the field, because the umpires would then have surely awarded us the match. When we resumed, it was clear that the umpires were going to be severely pressurized by Sri Lanka's captain.

Murali switched ends to bowl at Emerson's end to make sure he wouldn't call him from square leg and he also asked the umpire to stand up to the stumps, so that he wouldn't have a good enough sight of his arm to continue no-balling him. Ranatunga bullied Emerson, demanding he stood close to the stumps, and this particularly incensed David Lloyd, who as a former first-class umpire, knew the appropriate regulation. He read out the law to us, which stated: 'The umpires shall stand where they can best see any act upon which their decision may be required.' By now it was all getting out of hand, and we were fuming at the way the umpires were being hassled.

When they batted, the atmosphere between the two sides deteriorated even further. Ranatunga was a past master at obstructing the fielders or keeper when the throw was coming in. He always seemed to be in the way, looking for overthrows. Then, as they got closer to our score, Goughie was impeded by Mahanama as he was about to gather the ball and throw at the stumps. Goughie was raging, convinced that he'd been obstructed, and the giant TV replay screen at the ground confirmed that. Out of frustration, Goughie mimed a head-butt at Mahanama. I never thought he'd actually go through with that, but it just demonstrates how incensed he was. Then, at the end of the over, I brushed shoulders with Mahanama, because neither of us would give way as I walked down to the other end. His reaction was totally ridiculous. He jumped around, flapping his arms as if I had tried to strangle him. Compared to what he'd done to Goughie a few balls earlier, it was laughable. Even a mild bloke like Graeme Hick was getting wound up now, and their batsmen were receiving the full verbal treatment from us.

Ironically, it was Murali who won the match, slicing the ball over point. We were very down in the dressing-room, and not just because we had lost. We knew that the game of cricket had suffered through some of the day's disgraceful scenes. We hadn't been angels ourselves, but we'd been dragged into it by the Sri Lankans. Just to inflame matters even more, their players then trooped into our dressing-room to shake our hands. When we'd beaten them earlier in the tournament, they didn't want to know and none of them would shake hands with us. Now they did want to do it because they'd won. I said to their manager, Ranjit Fernando, 'Just be consistent. If you want to shake our hands, just make sure you do it after every game, not just when you win.' We couldn't wait for them to clear off that night.

I'd been so angry at Ranatunga's behaviour all day that I told him what I thought of him while he was batting. Unfortunately the TV microphone picked up my words and I also cocked up what I wanted to say. I said, 'Your behaviour today has been appalling for a county country captain.' I'd stuttered at the wrong moment and for some reason pulled out the word 'county' from somewhere, but he got the point. He should have been suspended for his part in that awful game, but he got away with it. The ICC series referee, Peter Van der Merwe, had warned earlier that he dealt in suspensions, not fines, but his hands were tied by an army of Ranatunga's lawyers. A few days later, I spent a frustrating afternoon and early evening at the disciplinary hearing in Perth, when Ranatunga was given a suspended sentence of six matches and fined 75 per cent of his match fee, the maximum permissible. I understood that if Ranatunga had actually been banned, his lawyers would have contested it in court the following morning. The series referee had no chance against these legal heavyweights.

I was exonerated as England's captain for my part in that awful match, but I voluntarily issued a statement accepting my responsibilities. It's true that some of our actions when we fielded must have looked bad. When I saw the video, I wasn't proud, but it was about time we stood up for ourselves. You have to mix it with the opposition when they're trying it on.

So, instead of copping a deserved ban, Ranatunga was tossing the coin with me the next day at the WACA. When he came out to bat, I went forward to shake his hand, but that was done purely for cosmetic reasons. I wasn't wishing him well. Actually, I quite like Ranatunga and I have a sneaking respect for the way he led his team and stood up to the opposition. He got under the skin of the Aussie players, and he's the only cricketer who's ever wound me up on the field with his antics – like stopping to tie his shoelaces or changing his gloves when we're trying to bowl our full fifty overs in the allotted time. He was a past master at irritating an opponent, yet after he'd retired I had some genial chats with him when I saw him in Sri Lanka in 2001 and in South Africa during the 2003 World Cup.

One thing that spat at Adelaide had confirmed – we'd really be up for our first match in the World Cup four months later. It would be against Sri Lanka. But first we had to get our preparations right. And they weren't going at all to plan.

Looking back on it, the way we prepared for that World Cup would make a textbook lesson in how not to do it. At the start of April, we spent a week training in Lahore, then went to Sharjah for a triangular one-day tournament, also featuring India and Pakistan. I just couldn't see the point of that, and I thought so before we lost three of our four games. The conditions in Lahore and Sharjah were totally dissimilar to what we would encounter in England in May, where instead of being dry and dusty it would almost certainly be dampish with green wickets. After all, we English cricketers know a bit about how it is back home in the first month of the season! Why go and prepare in the desert? We should have gone to Lanzarote for fitness training, a place where we had recently prepared for winter tours, then got home as soon as possible to re-acquaint ourselves with conditions that ought to have favoured us more than any other side. We needed a break after being in Australia for almost four months, and then to bond as a team unit after the break. I wasn't consulted about this, as the decisions had been taken long before I was made captain.

When we did return to England, we had to practise in Canterbury. This was wrong, and I say this without any disrespect to those at Kent County Cricket Club who did their very best for us. David Lloyd and I wanted to be at Leicester, where they have the best net facilities in the country, but India got the use of Leicester instead of us. I'm sure that pleased the local Asian community, but can you tell me any other host country staging the World Cup that would have bent over backwards so obviously to give an advantage to a visiting side? I thought back to the amount of travelling we'd had to do in the two previous World Cups, while any possible advantage always went the way of those staging the tournament. I saw nothing at all wrong with that in '92 and '96, so why were England now not getting those extra little perks that could mean so much?

I also didn't get the exact squad I wanted for the World Cup. Bumble and I both wanted Chris Lewis, but we were told by David Graveney that was out of the question. Now I know that Lewis had been a wild card, that he had famously been late one morning at an Oval Test, blaming it on a punctured tyre, and that many believed he wouldn't fit into the team culture. But the captain and coach both felt they could handle him and get the best out of him. We'd sat him down in Melbourne over the previous Christmas and told him what we wanted from him. He'd been playing grade cricket out there, and he was very receptive to what we said we expected. Bumble felt he'd got all the right answers to the tough questions that we'd put to him, and as far as we were concerned he was in. But we came up against a brick wall. I'm not saying that Lewis was an automatic choice, but I saw him as a three-in-one cricketer. He was capable of brilliance. A natural athlete, Lewis was a wonderful fielder, a bowler who could reverse-swing the ball, and a dangerous batter. I never went overboard about him; in fact I think he was overrated because he looked so good. He wasn't technically sound with bat or ball, but in the first fifteen overs, with the field up, he was dangerous with the white ball. He would also save us runs in the field and inspire the others. We weren't such a good one-day side that we could do without Chris Lewis, but we were told categorically that we couldn't have him.

Then there was the pay dispute with the ECB over the players' contracts for the World Cup, in which I got involved in long negotiations with Simon Pack, the ECB's International Teams Director. Simon had a very distinguished career in the Army and he was fascinating to talk to about his career. He was actually very good company, when we didn't have to talk cricket with him. That was the problem. In the Army, when you're told to jump, you answer, 'How high?' – but that doesn't work in sport and Simon couldn't see that. When we were first introduced to him at training camp in Lanzarote, he addressed the squad. He ended up saying that we would 'r.v. at 9 a.m. tomorrow'. We wondered who this 'r.v.' was until someone pointed out that it was Army shorthand for 'rendezvous'. The working relationship he had with the players was never very close.

Simon lacked the experience to deal with cricket issues. Our first outline discussion about the World Cup contracts came at the worst possible time for me – the afternoon before the start of the Ashes series in Brisbane in November 1998. Anyone with any awareness of international sport should realize that this is a difficult time for a captain, because he has so much on his plate, but Simon insisted on the meeting. It took place in my hotel room, lasted two hours and didn't go at all well. I had a problem with the £200,000 on offer to the squad for winning the World Cup. This may sound a lot, but there were fifteen players to account for and it bore no relation to what we might possibly achieve for the game of cricket in England. I pointed out to Simon that it was the same amount that we got for winning the 1998 Test series against South Africa, but that victory in this would carry far more prestige. I said, 'You saw the public response to us beating South Africa. Imagine building on that goodwill by winning the World Cup. Can you imagine what it would do for the game in general, for kids and for the sponsors? We're worth more than £200,000 if we do that.' He said there was only so much in the pot to play with it, but he didn't grasp the point. I told him we needed to discuss it more, but then returned to thinking about winning back the Ashes.

I didn't see Simon Pack again until the spring of '99 at a photo shoot at Lord's to publicize the World Cup. I told him that I still wasn't happy, and that the players would be talking about it in Lahore, as we prepared for Sharjah. After playing a day/night match out there, we had a meeting with Tim Lamb, the ECB Chief Executive, and David Acfield, Chairman of the Advisory Committee. Not the best time for a meeting of this importance, as the players had been representing our country until a couple of hours earlier, and it lasted till 1.30 in the morning, but we had to lump it. The boys expressed their views strongly – I remember Graeme Hick being particularly vocal – and it got rather heated and personal. Negotiations didn't break down, because they never got started. It was a case of 'take it or leave it' and soon the whole thing became 'them against us'. That's how it stayed.

The management tactics were sadly typical of those in many industrial disputes. Despite all our meetings, the ECB just ran down the clock because they knew that no player would go on strike. Gus Fraser, Neil Fairbrother and I represented the players in various discussions with the ECB, but we got nowhere. We were basically paid the usual one-day international rate despite being on tour in our own country, and we never got them to budge from that £200,000 win bonus offer. Our contracts for the World Cup arrived ridiculously late – when we'd got to Canterbury for training early in May – and we were lambs to the slaughter. The management waited for us to buckle and we did, signing the contracts in Canterbury.

Once we'd agreed in a team meeting that no one would walk out of the World Cup, whatever we were offered, we didn't stand a chance. It would be different now. Richard Bevan of the Professional Cricketers' Association, who showed his steel to the ECB over the Zimbabwe Affair during the 2003 World Cup, would certainly have driven a harder bargain for us. That would have enabled me to take a back seat.

That pay dispute never affected our relationship in the dressing-room or how we played in the World Cup. We went out early because we didn't play well enough. But I am convinced that the issue definitely had a bearing on whether I stayed on as captain or not. After the harsh words spoken in those pay discussions, I needed an impressive tournament to stay in the job.

We crashed out early because we lost badly at the Oval against South Africa, batted too slowly in beating Zimbabwe, then lost at Edgbaston to India. Finding our-selves out of the·tournament before the official World Cup song was released was the final embarrassment. It was my mistake to put South Africa in after winning the toss. I thought, after consulting a few of my players, that they'd prefer to chase, so I felt we should pressurize them straight away. But then we were bowled out for 103 inside 42 overs, to lose by 122 runs, and that did our run rate no good at all.

Then we took too long to finish off Zimbabwe at Trent Bridge. We only needed 168, but Nasser Hussain, Graham Thorpe and Neil Fairbrother had an extended net out in the middle and we took 38.3 overs to get those runs. Bumble and I were at fault in the strategy. We were just looking to win games at that stage, when we ought to have looked at the wider issues and factored in the possibility of upsets in the other games in our group. The shock we hadn't bargained for came when Zimbabwe beat South Africa at Chelmsford. That meant that we simply had to beat India at Edgbaston. Sadly, in a game spread over two days due to a thunderstorm, we lost by 63 runs. All of a sudden, we were out of the World Cup.

I think the fates were against us in that Edgbaston game. The Indian batsmen played and missed regularly against the swinging ball in humid conditions, yet survived, and then we nicked everything against their seamers when the pitch was juiced up for them after the downpour. Worse, Graham Thorpe got a shocking decision from umpire Javed Akhtar that knocked us sideways. Javagal Srinath, operating around the wicket to the left-hander, got an lbw decision when the ball was clearly going down the leg side. Thorpey was a proven match-winner in tight situations like this one, and after that baffling decision we faded away.

The scene in the dressing-room was a funereal one of tears and regrets. As captain, I felt the humiliation keenly and I had to switch to automatic pilot for my various media responsibilities, parrying the inevitable questions about my future as England captain. I said I'd be happy to stay on, but going out of the World Cup so early was the story, not me. It was already the end for David Lloyd as coach of England. It had been announced six weeks before the competition started that he wouldn't be re-engaged – but why make it public then? I felt that should have been kept under wraps and that Bumble didn't deserve to be treated that way after all he'd done for England. When I got back to the mournful dressing-room, I discovered that the lads from Lancashire and Essex had already been contacted by their counties to ensure that they'd be playing for them in one-day county matches over the next few days. Couldn't they have waited a little longer to let them get over this huge disappointment? At least Surrey treated Adam Hollioake, Graham Thorpe and me with a little more understanding and left us alone. All that made me wonder about the grasp of priorities some counties have. I can't see England's footballers being treated in the same way after they'd been eliminated from the World Cup.

The drive home from Edgbaston seemed to take ages as I tossed all the factors around in my mind. We hadn't been sharp enough in improving our run rate; that Zimbabwe victory over South Africa wasn't in the script; and we'd been unlucky against India. The ECB had worked the media well against us, portraying us as greedy in our negotiations over bonuses, and as a result I got the feeling that the public wasn't totally behind us. I was still annoyed at the amateurish and irrelevant aspects of our build-up, wondering just what those games in Sharjah had done for us when we faced the ball jagging around on a damp wicket at Edgbaston. But the bottom line was that we should have gone further. Heads were almost certain to roll as a result – probably the captain's.

I was realistic about the speculation that was bound to start. All the steers and whispers coming out of Lord's later on hinted that my days as captain were numbered, and I was expecting the call to come from David Graveney. He did in fact ring me twice, first to say he was still undecided, then to tell me he was coming to see me in person. He drove from Bristol to Cheam one morning, stayed an hour, yet didn't give me a concrete decision. When Grav left, I was none the wiser, but I was impressed that he showed that he cared. Perhaps he was looking for a sign from me that I was prepared for the chop and might even volunteer for it.

Three weeks after our defeat at Edgbaston, I got the fateful call from Grav informing me that my reign as captain was over. He was very tactful and considerate, confirming that I'd be in the side for the first Test at Edgbaston against New Zealand, although it wasn't clear whether I'd be keeping wicket. I thought the whole thing had dragged on far too long. What is a fact is that I'd lost the Test captaincy off the back of failure in a one-day competition and that seemed illogical. After phoning Nasser Hussain, the new captain, to offer my congratulations and full support, I gave him the same advice that Athers had given me the year before – do the job your own way. You have to have no regrets about how you went about the job when it's all over. We had a very constructive conversation about the rest of the summer, and there was no trouble or embarrassment between us. Cricketers are like that: they don't fall out over such things, because it's all out of their hands.

I wasn't surprised by the decision to sack me. I could

understand that they needed a change after our abject performance in the World Cup, and I knew enough about sport to be aware that it's usually the captain or manager who takes the rap. I'd been appointed one-day captain in succession to Adam Hollioake for the triangular series late in the summer of 1998 after Adam had done the job earlier on against South Africa. So I was now in charge of both Test and one-day teams until the end of the World Cup. In June 1999 I lost both posts, even though our Test performances against the two best sides in the world had been fair. By beating South Africa at home, we won a five-Test series in England for the first time since 1985, and the euphoria and national pride on that August day was unforgettable. English cricketing success was now firmly dominating the sports media at last and even football had take a back seat for a week. Then we went to Australia, where we lost 3-1, but if a key run-out decision had gone our way, I believe we'd have won the last Test in Sydney to draw the series. Unfortunately, ifs and buts add up to nothing. In any case, we had done marvellously well to fight back and win the Melbourne Test and thus keep the series alive, going into the last Test. But I was still eased out of the Test captaincy, even though my failure was clearly not as a leader in the long form of the game, but in the World Cup.

When Mike Atherton led us to a shambolic failure in the 1996 World Cup, he didn't lose the England captaincy, even though he'd lost the previous Test series as well, against South Africa. I thought it was right to stick with Athers, but it was therefore surely inconsistent to drop me for another World Cup failure.

I'll never know if I was fated to be just a fill-in captain when I got the job in 1998. I was 35, after all, so perhaps the influential people who made the decision believed I wouldn't be around very long as a player in any event. I suspect all of them would have been amazed to see me still playing for England after I passed forty! Looking back on it all now, I can see that my image suited the aspirations of Lord MacLaurin as he tried to revive the standing of English cricket. He had made it clear in the previous year what he expected from England's cricketers on duty in the public eye, and he reiterated that when I was interviewed by him at the House of Lords in April 1998. I was known to be the smartest and tidiest of the players, and unashamedly patriotic. Image seemed to be so important all of a sudden, which amused Athers, to whom it didn't matter in the slightest if the captain had a stubble or was intolerant of the media. All he felt the image of English cricket needed was for us to win a few more matches, and he was right. Winning is the vital ingredient. Was I just a stop-gap?

I believe one of the reasons I was replaced was that I became too closely associated with the players' dispute over money as we prepared for the World Cup. The big wheels in the ECB came to see me as the shop steward, rather too vocal in my desire to stand up for my players. David Graveney had a quiet word with me about it as we lurched towards deadlock, just a few weeks before the tournament started. Grav was wearing two hats – as the head of our union, the Professional Cricketers' Association, and as chairman of our selectors – and as such, he would be privy to the views of a lot of people who could affect careers. Grav has always shown his support for me, and I know that he meant well when he warned me that my stance might tell against me later if things didn't go well on the field, but I wasn't going to back down in fighting for what the players deserved from the ECB. I had various disagreements during the months of negotiations with Simon Pack, the ECB's International Teams Director, which eventually became just a stand-off. Simon had been appointed to the job by Lord MacLaurin, even though he knew very little about cricket or cricketers. Simon's approach to the pay dispute was, shall we say, rather old-fashioned and entrenched on behalf of the management. I wouldn't change any actions of mine during those frustrating and fruitless negotiations. I was part of a three-man deputation, along with Gus Fraser and Neil Fairbrother, that tried to broker a compromise with the ECB, and even though we failed, I feel it was right for the captain to be on that panel. You have to fight for your players, as they look to the captain for a lead.

As for my captaincy, I wasn't really in the job long enough to stamp my style on the team and make a big enough impact. It was important to me to inject more toughness and steel into the side and make it more obvious that we would fight all the way. I've never had any doubts about the pride and passion the guys feel in playing for England, but I wanted us to wear our hearts on our sleeves more. I wanted the National Anthem played at the start of each England game, but the authorities said that wasn't feasible. No one ever gave me a good reason. Before England teams play rugby or soccer, the players sing the anthem, so why should we miss out? It all adds to the pride and pleasure you feel, and I'm sure a cricket crowd would respect the two anthems being played. Perhaps spending so many years in Australia has made me value my country even more, but I do feel it's politically correct in England not to make a fuss about shouting from the rooftops our pride in our nationality. Good luck to the Irish, Scots and Welsh in the enthusiastic way they celebrate their national days – I just wish St George's Day got as good a show. I do feel annoyed when England sportsmen don't all sing the National Anthem, nerves notwithstanding. If you're all in it together, you should be pumping out the volume for England, and be proud of it.

For me it was a case of being realistic in how I went about the nuts and bolts of the job. Captaincy is largely concerned with trying to get the right people in at the right time. You can only do as well as the quality of players that are available. It is tempting to say that anyone could have led the great West Indies teams of the seventies and the eighties, and the recent Australians. Dad's advice to me was: 'You've got to stay in the game – if your bowlers are conceding six an over, then you're out of it.' I was keen on my bowlers building up pressure by churning out maiden overs, because as a batsman I wanted to score freely and didn't like getting tied down. So bowlers like Fraser, Walsh, Ambrose, McGrath and Warne were my ideal men. Unfortunately, only one of them was English!

When I was England captain I went for never-say-die bowlers, guys who had fire in their bellies and didn't look for excuses. Bowlers like Gus, Dean Headley and Dominic Cork. I never picked Phil Tufnell or Andy Caddick during that time, because I had doubts over their temperament. With hindsight I admit that Caddick proved me wrong, but at the time I felt he turned it on in fits and starts and didn't impose himself on a match as he should have done with his ability. Since he came back into the side he has been outstanding. In the Caribbean in 1998 he reacted badly when our coach, David Lloyd, said in public that he ought to have bowled better in conditions that favoured him during our narrow defeat in Trinidad. Caddy will never admit it, but I think a year out of the England side helped develop him into a top-class England bowler with greater consistency and, more importantly, mental toughness. Nasser Hussain got the best out of him, whereas I might not have done so. In any case, I don't believe that any of the fast bowlers who went to Australia ahead of Caddick let me down.

At no stage did I feel the burdens of captaincy. Lynn and I had talked it over and we agreed that we would not be pushing our family into the limelight. There'd be no photo-shoots in glossy magazines. Life would go on happily as normal, without the need to make money out of the job. Lynn's lack of interest in cricket was a big plus; she was proud of the fact that I was England captain, but wouldn't let it affect life at home. I refused all offers to do an exclusive column for a newspaper, because I felt strongly that the England captain's thoughts should be available, within reason, to every paper. There was a limit to what the captain should say in any event – and my offerings at press conferences were never gems of enlightenment – but I was determined that no paper was going to get the inside track from me. As I discovered, there were enough leaks flying around without the media needing any steers from me.

The playing demands didn't weigh me down either. By then I was very experienced, and knew my own game inside out and how to prepare myself, physically and mentally. Keeping wicket, batting at number four and captaining the side all added to the challenge. I hadn't coveted the job at any stage, but no one can ever say I didn't give it my all, and with immense pride.

Now my aim was to remain an England player. I'd done my best, and it had been an honour, but the priority at the end of June 1999 was to get over my disappointment and prolong my England career. After all, my career ambition had always been playing successfully for my country, not captaining it.

CHAPTER ELEVEN

back in the ranks

I wanted to make an impact as soon as possible for the rest of my Test career when I turned up at Edgbaston for the first Test against New Zealand. I'd passed my 36th birthday and I knew that many felt it was time I was pensioned off, as Nasser Hussain started to build a team that he wished to go forward with. Fortunately Nasser wanted me in that side, and after Edgbaston proved to be the worst Test match of my career, he was good enough to take me to one side and tell me that I was in the team for the next Test at Lord's. I appreciated that. There was no doubt in my mind that I could still operate at the highest level, but I knew that I needed to prove it.

I was now back in my preferred position, opening the batting with Athers, while Chris Read took over as wicketkeeper. I had no idea if that was the shape of things to come in the minds of the selectors, because by the fourth Test Chris had been dropped and I was back keeping wicket. Chris had struggled making the adjustment, despite his undoubted talent. I just think he was too young, and that set him back a couple of years. Not many 20-year-olds make a significant impact in Test cricket and continue to do so.

Nassser got it exactly right in the build-up to Edgbaston. On the Tuesday, he led a team meeting well, thanking me for my captaincy over the past year, then going on to say in his forthright manner that he'd be doing the job his way from now on. He stamped his authority on the squad right away, and that's been the hallmark of his captaincy ever since. You knew where you stood with Nasser. He was very supportive of me at Edgbaston and I was at my most diplomatic when the press asked me if I felt I'd been made a scapegoat for our World Cup failure. I said it was up to them if they wanted to use that word.

Yet a few days later, I was well aware that I was now on trial. At Edgbaston, I scored one and nought, dropped a regulation slip catch and got nowhere near another that I picked up late and should have snaffled. I had no idea why I'd had such a bad match, although it was suggested in the media that my eyes had gone. That was rubbish. There were no problems with my concentration either, it was just one of those things – although I could have done with a better performance in my first Test as just a player again.

So Lord's was a challenge for me. Although my confidence was lower than it normally is on the eve of a Test, I knew I had to deliver. My form hadn't been all that great for a while, beginning with that one-day series in Australia, and all I could think of was that I was lacking rhythm in my batting. My mind slipped back to 1996, when I was also playing for my place at Lord's, after Raymond Illingworth had dropped a major hint that my time had passed. I had responded in the right manner three years ago, and did so again now. My fifty in the first innings wasn't all that fluent, as I just hung on in there while we struggled to build a decent score, but my 35 in the second innings was more like my old self. I felt vindicated in my belief that I hadn't lost that spark and drive you need to survive in the Test arena. A professional sportsman with powerful self-belief expects to raise his game when challenged – to perform when the chips are down. I knew that mistakes I made at Edgbaston as a 36-year-old would have been tolerated more easily if I had been ten years younger, but I still believed I had the hunger and know-how to justify my place.

I batted even better at Old Trafford in the next Test, making 83 not out in the second innings. Mark Butcher opened with Athers and captained England for the first time after Nass had broken a finger at Lord's. I had no worries about that, as I knew I wouldn't be asked to hold the reins for one Test. My time had passed and I was very comfortable playing under Butch. I also noted with sympathy that he didn't enjoy the job very much, because he wasn't given the team he wanted. Butch wanted two spinners but he was outvoted. I think that Old Trafford experience was an eye-opener for Butch, as he believes the captain should have the eleven he wants.

For the last Test at the Oval, we were back in our familiar routine. I was given the wicketkeeper's gloves again as we played another bowler. So I'd opened in the first two Tests, batted at number three at Old Trafford and now at five at the Oval. Our tail was too long, and our front-line batsmen kept getting themselves out with ill-judged strokes. It was a poor team performance, and New Zealand deserved to beat us and take the series. Nasser was booed by some spectators as he was interviewed during the awards ceremony, and that was not pleasant to hear if you cared about the reputation of the England team. Athers and I could identify with Nass at that stage, because we had both suffered dreadful England performances like this one and then carried the can in public. It comes with the territory, but you have to experience the stick before you can relate to someone else in your team copping it.

It had been a dreadful summer for English cricket. One cricket magazine worked out that we were now the worst in the world, which I thought absolute nonsense, but it made a good debating topic for a time after the Oval. We had crashed out early in the World Cup, and seen our captain replaced and his successor struggle to make an impression. Two selectors, Graham Gooch and Mike Gatting, also lost their jobs, and we had a vacuum in coaching once David Lloyd left us in May. Duncan Fletcher had been appointed to the job, but was seeing out his time with Glamorgan and played no part in our matches that summer. On top of all that, we lost a series that we really ought to have won – and would have won if we'd played to our potential against a good, spirited New Zealand that lacked the quality that we had, yet somehow didn't display consistently.

I assumed I was still part of the England scene at the end of that 1999 summer. I felt I'd done enough after the bad match at Edgbaston, so my selection for the tour to South Africa seemed assured to me. The night before the squad was announced, however, I got a phone call that worried me. It was from a cricket journalist who'd been at the NatWest Cup Final at Lord's that weekend, and he said all the chat was that I wasn't going to get picked for the tour. I was now concerned for my England future. If I wasn't going to South Africa, that would have to be due to my age, and there would be no comeback for me.

I spent a fretful night at home, and when David Graveney rang in the morning I was ready for a frank exchange of views. In fact he wrongfooted me by saying that I was going on the Test match part of the tour, but Chris Read would be the keeper for the one-dayers. I wouldn't even be used as a batsman. I was surprised at that. Grav said the selectors were looking to build the squad for the next World Cup. But that was four years away, the last one having been only three months ago! I disagreed with Grav and told him so, but at least they still saw me as a Test player, which was the most important thing. So it looked as if I was no longer a one-day player, and was certain to miss out on the next World Cup. When I managed to prove those selectors wrong by making it to South Africa on merit for the 2003 World Cup, I remembered that conversation in September 1999 with a certain amount of satisfaction.

I'm almost certain that the selectors had one hand tied behind their backs when they picked those squads for South Africa. The call from the media after our abject summer had been for youth under our new captain. The new broom had to sweep away the dead wood. The selectors had to make it look as though they were planning for the future. I'm all for that, but when you're losing, you have to plan for now. The inclusion of Mark Ramprakash and Graeme Hick would have strengthened the squad, and I think I subsequently proved that I was still an integral part of the one-day side.

I set myself a few targets after that decision by the selectors in September 1999. One of my aims would be the 2003 World Cup, when I would be just one month short of my fortieth birthday. I would do everything to prove them wrong. More immediate was the lure of a hundred Test matches, and I calculated that I could reach that total in the following summer of 2000 if I stayed in the side. Old Trafford against the West Indies would be the relevant Test match. Both these targets were achievable aims, something I could realistically go for. I was deadly serious about playing in the next World Cup. Both aims I kept to myself, but they were the sort of challenges I liked for extra motivation.

A visit to me by the new England coach gave me solid reason to set myself those goals. Duncan Fletcher came to see me to talk through his vision for the upcoming tour and how he saw the future, and I was very impressed. Having had a successful business career, Duncan brought a new dimension into the management of England cricket sides. He was keen on establishing a committee, where selected players of varying ages would give him and the captain feedback about decisions taken on the tour and what could be improved. Duncan said he wouldn't put me on the committee, because he wanted other players to take on extra responsibility, but he would be seeking me out regularly to hear my private views. He also confirmed how important senior players like Nass, Athers and myself were, and he gave the impression that he didn't buy into the idea that youth was the answer to our current problems. He talked clearly and well, obviously having thought a lot about the job since he'd been appointed.

I was greatly encouraged by that chat. Duncan and Nasser were to form a very good team and Nasser would be the first to admit that he's been very fortunate to work with a coach as good as Duncan Fletcher. They blended well together, complementing each other with differing qualities: Nasser the fiery one, not afraid of being confrontational with any of his players, always ready to speak honestly and openly; Duncan more phlegmatic, biding his time before he speaks. Duncan is a very thorough man, with great tactical knowledge, and he came into the job with no baggage, having been associated only with Glamorgan in our cricket structure. Because he was over fifty, that gave him a sense of detachment from us and an automatic respect. He'd been a success in his business career, and was obviously a bright bloke, but he never talked down to any player. His calmness was in contrast to Nasser's passionate ways, but that added up to a workable and impressive package. Duncan studies other sports deeply – he's a huge fan of the golfer Tiger Woods – and he brings whatever he can from elsewhere into his job. He's taken everyone's game forward, including mine, underlining the fact that you can never stop learning.

I was hugely impressed by his contribution to his first England tour, in South Africa. His fielding drills were excellent and imaginative, and he imposed discipline in a firm, fair manner, without any fuss. He treated the senior players like Athers and me with just the right amount of respect and curiosity. He would ask me why I batted in my own particular manner, why I played back and across and stood quite deep in my crease and that got me talking about my game. He would never impose his views, but would suggest things, just to try to get you thinking. He was very hot on staying in the game, competing hard against such strong opposition.

Duncan seemed to know instinctively when my game was in good order. He'd wait for the right moment and just say something like 'well done' as he passed me. Even a senior player needs praise from someone he rates, and I was no different. When I got myself out on the hook in the Cape Town Test, having played so well to get into the forties, he waited for a few days before having a quite word. I said that forties mean nothing if you then throw it away, but Duncan told me, 'Yes, but you're a very good hooker and puller. That one was on you too quickly, so just make sure the execution is right.' We knew I'd got it wrong in Cape Town, but he handled it constructively and intelligently.

When Duncan Fletcher accepted the England job, I had reservations only on a matter of principle. As a proud Englishman, I thought that we had enough coaching talent in our own country. I was wrong. I knew he was good, but didn't realize how good till I toured with him. He has been an outstanding coach for us and he has certainly helped improve my game. When we had our spat in September 2001 over my non-availability for the Indian tour, we both said a few harsh things in the heat of the moment. But I'm glad that it was all eventually smoothed over. That was the only time that Duncan and I weren't on the same wavelength, and I still have enormous respect and affection for him.

That South Africa tour was long and hard. Our batting was too inexperienced, with only Michael Vaughan of the younger batsmen coming through to promise greater things. Athers, Nasser and I were told we had to take on greater responsibility as senior batsmen and I think we all did well, although not so at the first time of asking in the Johannesburg Test. At one stage we were 2 for 4, with the three seniors all out for nought! That Test was a lottery – win the toss, bowl on a damp pitch and win the Test. We were blown away for 122 in the first innings, and after that we could only aim for stubborn defiance. We managed that, but the wicket got more uneven and Shaun Pollock and Allan Donald took nineteen of our twenty wickets. I played my shots to make 86 in the second innings, ending up caught at cover. I'd have loved a century, but felt it was worth the risk to counter-attack.

At Durban, I played one of my most fluent innings for England, making 95 on a slow wicket, where it was difficult to time the ball. I was really pleased at the way I adapted because it was a grafter's pitch and the draw was inevitable after a couple of days. That innings in the last Test of December 1999 meant I had become the leading run-scorer in Test cricket in the nineties. I had absolutely no idea I was anywhere near the record until our statistician, Malcolm Ashton, told me about it after I was out, plumb lbw to Nantie Hayward. That 95 got me past Mark Waugh. I was very pleased, because it indicated consistency over a long career. Some statistics are more relevant than others.

We ended up losing the Test series 2-1, with our successful run chase in the final Test at Centurion Park giving us a consolation. That eventually turned out to be one of the matches over which Hansie Cronje had deceitful dealings with bookmakers, but we all felt at the time that he'd made a great declaration in the wider interests of cricket. Of course, he wouldn't have dreamed of doing that if the series depended on Centurion Park, but we still had to work very hard for that victory, and Cronje and his team gave us absolutely nothing in the field as we chased 249, to win by just two wickets. It was basically now a one-day game and we just got home. I hit the ball very well for my 73, and in my partnership with Michael Vaughan I saw at first hand the qualities that eventually made him a world-class batsman. He'd struggled so far on the tour, lacking the command and fluency that was so impressive a couple of years later, but this 69 of his was a gem.

So Vaughan was definitely one for the future, but apart from him our best performers on that tour were the seniors. If we'd had more batting experience, we would have got closer. I felt I'd done myself justice as the side's all-rounder, keeping wicket well and averaging 42 with the bat. Duncan Fletcher clearly believed so, because as I prepared to go home soon after the Centurion Park Test, he told me I should be staying for the one-day series. I, of course, agreed with him, but the selectors had made their decision to go for youth and build for a tournament that was three years away. I'd be looking to regain my place in the one-day team as soon as I could. You didn't have to be a rocket scientist to get the hint that the selectors felt I was finished as a one-day player, but at no stage did I believe I deserved to be on the scrapheap after South Africa.

I hardly watched the one-day series when I went home, so I can't comment on how Chris Read did as my replacement. I went on holiday, re-charged the batteries and got myself up for the new season. I still felt I was England's best all-rounder and that if they were picking the one-day side on merit, then I should be in, even though I had just celebrated my 37th birthday. Duncan Fletcher had hinted to me in South Africa that he'd had nothing to do with my omission, and I got the impression from him that he was somewhat concerned about change for the sake of change. If the door was still slightly ajar, I'd be doing everything I could to kick it open. Whenever I did well in those first weeks of the 2000 season – especially after my 97 not out that won us the Benson and Hedges quarter-final against Yorkshire – I was happy to feed the line to the media that I hoped the selectors had been watching. I may not give all that much away, but there are times when a hint or two to the cameras and notebooks can be helpful.

That summer of 2000 contained a couple of ironies for me. Not only did I get back into the England one-day side, but I ended up as captain of both that and the Test team – just a year after I'd been finished in the job. Nasser Hussain's broken thumb, picked up in the first Test against the West Indies, led to my being offered the job of stand-in captain for the next Test at Lord's. I was perfectly happy to help out, but when Nasser's injury was slow to heal I found myself also doing it for half the Triangular Series involving England, Zimbabwe and the West Indies. We ended up winning the trophy, I was named Man of the Series, and as Nasser and I posed happily with the trophy on the balcony at Lord's, I could reflect on the satisfaction of proving my point to the selectors. I was really happy with the way I had played – even though in my first three innings I was out for 12, bizarrely. After scoring two hundreds in a row, I made 97 in the final and was very annoyed to get out, chasing a wide one from Heath Streak.

In that fortnight, I suddenly started to see the ball like a football. Nasser said I was in the zone, like Tiger Woods when he's burning up the golf course, and I didn't want to lose that feeling. My feet were moving superbly, I was seeing the ball very early, and confidence just oozed out of me. It was one of those periods that all pros get from time to time if they're lucky – and you just hope you can cash in. I'd made a good 74 not out against the West Indies on an excellent pitch up in Durham, then 101 at Edgbaston against Zimbabwe, then the West Indies suffered again at Trent Bridge when I scored 100 not out. By the time I got to Lord's for the final against Zimbabwe, I was playing as well as I could. I do regret not getting three hundreds in a row, but an average of 81 for the series wasn't bad! I also kept wicket to the high standards I set myself. When I bat well, I also tend to keep wicket well. I had a point to prove too: that I was still good enough for the one-dayers. I wanted the selectors to look at the bigger picture, at performances not age. Changes in such key areas as opening bowlers and batsmen and the wicketkeeper should be made gradually and when the time is right, not just to please the media who are clamouring for youth and someone new to write about. By this point the World Cup didn't look quite so far away for me. That was now my target.

The summer of 2000 just got better and better for both me and the England team. It was a bowler-friendly Test series against the West Indies, with the pitches aiding some high-class fast bowlers such as Walsh, Ambrose, Gough and Caddick. As a result we had some short Test matches, in which the batsmen struggled, but that also led to some riveting, dramatic cricket. The summer ended with England beating the West Indies in a series for the first time since 1969. Some of our lads hadn't even been born then, which shows how dominant the West Indies had been for so long.

The turning point in the series was our desperately close victory at Lord's by two wickets. We'd gone one down at Edgbaston, when they had bowled with greater discipline on a wicket of uneven bounce and we lost by an innings inside three days. Same old story, many thought, and with Walsh and Ambrose still so outstanding, they had a strong case. But Fletcher and Hussain had been working hard at our team spirit and durability and I could see that we were now a harder team to beat than just a year earlier when we'd lost to New Zealand. At Lord's it all came together.

When we bowled them out for 54 in their second innings, you could see the self-belief surging through our dressing-room. Andy Caddick crystallized it in his own performance. Caddick's spell of bowling that brought him 5 for 16 was the best I've ever kept to by an England bowler. He had good pace, steep bounce and he didn't waste a single ball. He was fantastic that day. He was so outstanding that he almost made a rod for his own back, because by showing his true quality he set a new standard for himself. Since coming back into the England side in South Africa under Nasser and Duncan, he's been top drawer, and also a more mature character than in his early days, when he would rub people up the wrong way without realizing it. His outstanding performances helped to relax him, and he fitted more easily into the dressing-room. He and Gough were brilliant in that series against the West Indies.

So, after the bowlers had got us back in with a chance, now it was up to the batters. But a target of 188 was a big request against Walsh and Ambrose. The pitch was bouncy, the ball seamed around in overcast conditions, and it was going to be very hard work. That Lord's Saturday was one of the better days of Test cricket I can remember. For long periods, we barely scored a run against two great bowlers with massive pride who would give us nothing. Atherton and Vaughan, at that stage very similar in style as batsmen, were terrific in adding over 90, but then they both got out. I slapped a couple of boundaries, then fell lbw, trying to ease the tension by playing positively. At 160 for 8, with 27 still needed, they were favourites. Darren Gough came in to join Dominic Cork, who was playing his first Test for more than eighteen months. Cork loves playing at Lord's and the situation brought the best out of him, as he used his adrenalin and competitive instinct to get after the bowlers. But Goughy was the revelation. When he first came into the England team, he could clearly bat, but then the short ball sorted him out and his batting suffered. On this occasion, however, he stood firmly behind the line and gave sensible support to his great mate.

As they built their decisive partnership, we were in a desperate state in the dressing-room. Poor Matthew Hoggard, playing his first Test, was padded up in the doorway, with his helmet and gloves on, dreading having to bat. I was sitting out on the balcony with Nasser, Athers and Fletch, and even the coach's usual calmness deserted him as we inched towards 188. We were just as nervous as the crowd and when Cork pulled a six off Franklyn Rose, we were out of our seats shouting our heads off. Then we'd sit down for the next ball, thinking, 'What's going to happen this ball?' We were just fans with England sweaters on during that last hour. When Cork hit the winning runs off Walsh we were ecstatic, and I stole a sideways look at the relieved Hoggy. He was very grateful to take off that helmet!

In all the euphoria, I had to have some sneaking sympathy for Ambrose and Walsh. They were simply magnificent. Ambrose took 1 for 22 off 22 overs and he was reduced to philosophical smiles as he beat the bat time and again. On another day, he'd have taken 7 for 15. To get those runs against those two marvellous bowlers was a tribute to the leadership of Hussain and Fletcher. We could easily have lost, and that would have given them a 2-0 lead with three Tests to go. The knowledgeable Lord's crowd appreciated that, and the stillness during play on that Saturday was remarkable. When a single was scored after so many maiden overs, the cheers made you realize what this all meant to the supporters. It was one of the great Test match days of my career – cricket at its very best.

If the Lord's crowd was impressively quiet, the one up at Old Trafford a fortnight later was ecstatic. The reception I got on that Friday after reaching my century was the best I've ever received, and I suppose only the one that Steve Waugh got from his home crowd when he achieved his hundred against us in Sydney 2003 comes close to it. The way the Old Trafford crowd greeted me is something I'll never forget and it's one of the reasons why it is one of my favourite grounds. I could understand the warmth of that ovation if it had been for their own Mike Atherton, but for a Surrey batsman?

By coincidence, Athers and I both won our hundredth caps in that Old Trafford Test. We were both very proud, although Athers was more reticent than me about showing it in public. You don't reach a hundred Test appearances without being able to play and it was a nice gesture by the ECB to give us each an England cap with '100' underneath the three lions. We were both given a cut-glass decanter by the ECB and Lancashire CCC and I received telegrams from several county clubs. Yet there was nothing from my own county, Surrey, and that disappointed me. They later admitted it was an oversight. At least they got it right two years later, when the great Sachin Tendulkar was honoured by Surrey when he reached a hundred Tests at the Oval in 2002.

Anyway, I enjoyed the kind words and attention from the cricket world and I was particularly proud to be part of a historic photograph that was taken before the start of the second day's play. Athers and I stood beside the other England players who had reached the landmark of a hundred Tests. Sadly, Sir Colin Cowdrey was too ill to be there, but the rest were alongside us – Ian Botham, Graham

Gooch, David Gower and Geoffrey Boycott. A select group of top players, and it was terrific to be in that company. Next time an England player reaches that milestone, I'll be delighted to stand alongside him for the photograph, and I expect he'll be as thrilled as I was that day.

I hoped I'd be able to celebrate that achievement in style on the field, but I never thought it would happen so spectacularly. I came in when we were in trouble at 17 for 3 and I was out of the traps almost immediately. Because of my excellent form in the recent one-day series, I had no inhibitions. A stiff wind was blowing from one end and neither Ambrose or Walsh fancied it, so they weren't operating in tandem. Yet I wouldn't have bothered who I faced that day. Everything was right – footwork, timing, stroke selection. I just raced to my hundred in three hours, and then I received this amazing ovation. I started by raising my bat to all quarters of the ground – with a particular flourish to the area where Mum and Dad were sitting – and then waited for the applause to die down. But it didn't. At one stage, I started to wonder whether someone like a streaker had come on to the outfield, because I couldn't understand why the ovation was so prolonged. I didn't know what to do, other than keep acknowledging it with my bat. It went on for two minutes, which is a long time when the bowler's waiting to send down the next delivery! Mum and Dad told me later that they were equally amazed, and I admit I was very emotional during it. The warmth and appreciation from the Old Trafford crowd meant such a lot to me, and the West Indies boys were very gracious as well. They've always been very appreciative of me when I do well against them – perhaps it's the positive way I bat. Even Curtly and Courtney, those two great silent starers!

To cap it all, that Friday, 4 August, was the hundredth birthday of the Queen Mother. Now I've never hidden my admiration for the Royal Family, so for a patriotic Englishman like myself, this was a fairytale day. I'd never met the Queen Mother, but it was a good line for the media that night, and I happily played along. It was an outstanding day for me. I'd played as well as I possibly could, we were on the way to an important lead, and I'd celebrated a landmark in my Test career in a fitting way. I didn't sleep very well that night, with the adrenalin flowing as I played my innings over in my brain. My aim the next day was to get a big one, to build on my 105 not out. And would I play as well again? I'll never know. I nicked one to the keeper off Ambrose second ball next morning. Typical of sport – you can never take anything for granted. So I got another standing ovation for facing two balls and not getting a run!

Rain washed away some meaningful time over the next three days, so the Old Trafford Test was left drawn, the only one that series to go the full distance. The next, at Leeds, was in sharp contrast. It was all over just after five o'clock on the second day, with England winning by an innings. It was fantastic if you were an England player or supporter, but Test cricket should last at least until the fourth afternoon, if the wicket is satisfactory. You want the players to be tested out in conditions that are fair to both bowlers and batters. Ironically, this particular Headingley wicket wasn't as erratic as others I've played on up there. This was just one of those matches where the batsmen nick everything and the bowlers get it in the right place consistently. It was a freak that a batsman of Brian Lara's quality should be out lbw twice, padding up without playing a shot. We had high-class fast bowlers on each side getting remarkable sideways movement on a wicket of indifferent bounce. Caddick took four wickets in an over and I was so excited that I ran to him, celebrating what I thought was a hat-trick!

The Yorkshire folk in the crowd weren't even bothered

that they had no cricket to watch on the final three days, because they had the success of their own players to celebrate, with a stack of wickets for Craig White and Darren Gough, while Michael Vaughan got the Man of the Match award for his 76. That was a fine innings in the context of the match, but it says a lot for the quality of batting on show that a knock of 76 was so influential in a Test match. The recent trend, established by the Australians, had been towards faster scoring and shorter Tests, and although it was good that there were fewer boring draws, there has to be a balance. You don't always want the fast-forward button to be pressed in Test cricket. I was delighted that we'd won so comprehensively and quickly at Headingley, but still hoped it was a one-off in terms of the stature of Test matches.

The paying customers certainly got better value for money in the final Test, at the Oval, and that last day was memorable for all lovers of English cricket. Interest from the public had really built up after Headingley as our great fightback since Lord's gathered momentum. We started the last day at the Oval as favourites, but it was far from clear-cut. It could go either way. They needed another 341 to win, with all their wickets in hand, but Brian Lara could get them close if he played as well as we all knew he could. The match situation clearly caught the public imagination, because the Oval was packed out before the start of play. Surrey CCC had marketed the Test very intelligently, and on that last day children were admitted free of charge. Then the club opened up the unused executive boxes and a few hundred lucky fans got a great view of the play. About five thousand supporters were turned away, and while some went to pubs to watch the action on TV, thousands more gathered on Clapham Common to watch it on a giant screen, courtesy of Channel Four. It was like

People's Sunday during the Wimbledon Tennis Championships, when the ordinary punter gets priority over the corporate hospitality people and the atmosphere is fantastic. We just lapped it up. Playing in front of a full, patriotic house with victory in sight is what it's all about when playing for your country, and we greatly appreciated the support we got that day. It showed the vast amount of goodwill there is for the England cricket team if we could just deliver results more consistently.

It was the first time we'd had a full house on the final day of an Oval Test since we'd won back the Ashes in 1953, and I can only imagine what that must have been like for those eleven England players. I just hope I'm around long enough to see that happen again at the Oval, because it was a tremendous experience to beat the West Indies on that sunny afternoon in September, 47 years later. Now I appreciate that they were not the force they had once been, that they relied too much on their senior players, but we had played superbly since Corky and Goughy had inched us home at Lord's. Our respect for Walsh and Ambrose had only increased during this series and to mark their final appearances in a Test in England we gave them a guard of honour as they came out to bat for the last time. It was Nasser's idea, and full credit to him for that. Even in the hard world of Test cricket there should still be room to acknowledge the feats of great opposition players. Our admiration for those two guys was obvious in that gesture, and it was wonderful to hear the capacity crowd applaud them so warmly. Any runs you chiselled out against Walsh and Ambrose were hard earned, and playing against them summed up Test cricket to me.

All of a sudden, Test cricket in England was on a high. Just a year earlier, at the Oval, Nasser Hussain had been booed by some spectators after we'd lost the series to New

ABOVE Meeting Nelson Mandela alongside Devon Malcolm and Mike Atherton in South Africa, 1995.

TOP LEFT A rare occasion when father and son were photographed while working together.

TOP RIGHT Old Trafford, 2000, against the West Indies – and I celebrate my hundredth Test with a century, one of my most fluent innings in Test cricket. Everything slotted into place that day.

ABOVE One of my proudest moments, captaining Surrey to the Sunday League title at Cardiff, 1996.

TOP One of my favourite strokes – the hook – this one against Australia.
ABOVE Headingley, 1998 – and we had narrowly beaten South Africa to
take the series 2-1 under my captaincy.

TOP LEFT A distraction of an unusual sort while batting during the one-day international against the West Indies at Durham in 2000. I hope he collected on the bet!

TOP RIGHT Guesting on *A Question of Sport* with Ally McCoist (centre) and Jamie Redknapp.

TOP CENTRE A proud moment for Mike Atherton and me as we both celebrated our hundredth Tests in the same game against the West Indies at Old Trafford in 2000.

ABOVE Receiving yet another memento from that occasion – a commemorative set of pictures.

LEFT Reaching the landmark of a century in that Test – the historic nature of that game and the fact that I had played so well explain why my celebrations were a little over the top by my usual standards!

OPPOSITE Taking another blow from the bowlers during a torrid 58 minutes in the Jamaican Test, 1998.

TOP A crucial stumping to dismiss Kumar Sangakkara in the Kandy Test in Sri Lanka, 2001. We went on to win the game – albeit narrowly – after this. Graeme Hick and Marcus Trescothick share my delight.

ABOVE LEFT Nasser Hussain and I shared captaincy duties during the 2000 Nat West one-day series and here we brandish the trophy after winning the final at Lord's.

ABOVE RIGHT Hoping for a rare mistake by Steve Waugh – the toughest bowler I've faced in international cricket.

OPPOSITE My son Andrew seems almost as pleased as me to receive the MBE at Buckingham Palace in 1998.

TOP LEFT My last one-day match for England in the World Cup at Port Elizabeth, March 2003 – Craig White has run out Brett Lee with a direct hit. But Australia won by two wickets and ended our hopes of going any further.

TOP RIGHT Over and out – my last Test innings comes to a close.

ABOVE The perfect finish to a most enjoyable career. Steve Harmison and Andrew Flintoff carry me round the Oval on a victory lap of honour after our win over South Africa.

Zealand. Now he was a hero. But the squad was improving in all areas. Graham Thorpe had returned, as gritty and efficient as ever, while Marcus Trescothick had made an immediate impression as our new opener. I'd batted with him on his debut at Old Trafford, and although I was delighted to be crashing the ball about, I did notice Tresco's uncomplicated, sensible technique. Temperamentally, he looked a natural Test batsman, unflustered, quietly confident, in awe of nobody and relaxed. I have to go back to Graham Thorpe's hundred on his Test debut against the 1993 Australians to think of an England batsman who looked as assured as Marcus as soon as he came into the side. A major feather in the cap of the coach, who had spotted him making a very good century down at Taunton against Glamorgan. Fletch filed that one away and he'd talked about Marcus when we were in South Africa. I knew little about him, but Duncan had spotted something and got him into the side when Nick Knight was injured for the Triangular Series in the summer. His judgement was handsomely vindicated. The same applied as regards Michael Vaughan, who continued to make impressive progress in his calm, phlegmatic way.

Duncan was lucky that his first summer as coach coincided with the long-awaited introduction of central contracts. From now on a group of England players would play for their counties when the coach decided, not the county. This was designed to ensure that players turning up for Test matches would be fit, rested and ready to turn it on. In the past we'd travel all over the country in between Test appearances and we probably weren't physically or mentally right. You didn't realize that had been the case until you pitched up at a Test once central contracts had started. Now there were fewer niggles and we could work at our technical skills, rather than have prolonged treatment on the physio's couch. That had to lead to better results, and it was no fluke that our fast bowlers stayed fitter under central contracts than before. England used only seventeen players in that West Indies series, the lowest figure in a long home series since 1987. It was something that David Lloyd had gone on about when he was England coach and the progress under Fletch proved his point. I understand that county members have misgivings about their England players barely playing for them any more, but wouldn't they like us to have a successful national side and win back the Ashes? Judging by the crowd at the Oval on the day we clinched the series against the West Indies, I reckon most cricket lovers around the counties will eventually see the bigger picture.

Duncan Fletcher's coaching expertise had a great deal to do with us continuing our winning run after that triumphant series against the West Indies. A few months later, we had beaten both Pakistan and Sri Lanka on their home pitches, which had been unfamiliar to us. It was one of the most impressive team performances I'd been part of as an England player, and what made it doubly satisfying was that we were rewarded for hard work and tactical planning. The key to our planning was Fletch's insight into how to play spin out there. Recently, we hadn't been the best international side at combating spin, especially away from home, and so we weren't fancied to win in either Pakistan or Sri Lanka, especially as each of them had a world-class spinner. But we kept our nerve on turning pitches and eventually wore them down.

When we got to Pakistan, Fletch's attention to detail was immediately impressive. He made sure we faced lots of local spinners whenever we had a net and we'd rough up the surface with our spikes to simulate match conditions, with the ball turning sharply. We'd throw a spinning ball at the next batsman due to get a net, so that he could attune himself to the turn. Because there's not a lot to do socially in Pakistan, we had lots of time to study videos and talk about techniques against the turning ball. Mike Atherton relished this new challenge. Athers wasn't just expert against fast, hostile bowling down the years, he was also a very accomplished player of spin. In the Pakistan series, he gave a regular masterclass against the spinners, with precise, confident footwork, soft hands in defence and exact punishment of the loose ball. His immense powers of concentration meant that he wouldn't be bothered by the accuracy of the spinners or the menacing close fielders. He batted for nearly 23 hours in the three Test matches and he was in his element.

Graham Thorpe was also outstanding. Because he's a short man, he could rock back quickly on to the back foot if necessary, and his excellent footwork meant he was rarely out of position. Being a left-hander, he disrupted the line of the spinners, and he was totally focused on the job on both tours. Focusing has often been Thorpey's problem. He never really enjoyed being away from home on long tours, but this time he'd clearly benefited from staying at home when we were in South Africa the previous winter. When he was with us in Pakistan and Sri Lanka, he was hungry for success and a terrific team man. He returned a world-class batsman. The way he just batted and batted for his hundred in the first Test at Lahore was fantastic. They played four spinners, knowing that the ball would turn, but Thorpey just ground them down into frustration. He had hit only one boundary when he got to his century, but that didn't matter. The patience he showed against the turning ball demonstrated to the rest of us what was possible.

Thorpey and I had some useful input to give to the rest of the squad about our Surrey team-mate, Saqlain

Mushtaq. We knew him as a great bowler, with a 'mystery ball' that left the right-hander late and got him many catches at silly point and slip, but we also knew that he could be mastered. I'd kept wicket to him many times at Surrey and was familiar with the speciality delivery of his that had picked up so many wickets as the ball drifted away, often causing a leading edge. It appeared to be an off-break, and the batsman would play for it, but, as I told the lads, when he bowls it he gives it more air than he does with a regulation off-break. He took eight wickets in our first innings in the Lahore Test, but he had to bowl 74 overs to do so. This meant that we had an extended net against him and managed to familiarize ourselves with his subtle varieties. Craig White played him aggressively, sweeping him particularly confidently, while some of the others just occupied the crease, watching him closely. He wasn't the same threat for the rest of the series, and in fact Saqlain has been played better by batsmen around the world since then. The TV coverage has been particularly useful to help batsmen negate Saqlain.

Although my figures don't suggest it, I thought I played the spinners well in Pakistan. Having never played out there in a Test, and just one in Sri Lanka, I was bound to find those two tours a challenge to me against spin. Duncan Fletcher knew that I looked vulnerable against spin when I batted in the middle order, whereas when I was in the first three I'd be established when the spinner came on and I'd look to dominate. When you bat at number five or six, you're invariably the one who's tentative at the start because the spinner is already settled and into his spell. You're always a little tense early on, and I had a tendency to go hard at the ball, bringing the close fielders a few catches. That was certainly my undoing in India and Sri Lanka in 1993, and I was disappointed because I used to play the spinners well when I batted for Surrey in the eighties. I remember John Emburey telling me once that he liked the way I played him, going down the pitch and trying to hit him over the top – mind you, Embers often profited from my rashness in those days as I holed out to deep mid-wicket or long-on! Embers once said to Dad when they were together on England duty, 'One player I hate bowling to is your nipper – he hits me all over the place,' and that confidence used to be my hallmark against spin. When I got my 91 in the Sydney Test on the 1990–1 tour, I hit the spinners over the top without any hesitation, but the experience in India and Sri Lanka did affect my confidence against high-class spinners.

I knew that Pakistan and Sri Lanka would be a major challenge for me and I worked hard at my technique against spin with Dad before I left England. I wanted to groove myself into playing straighter and ensure that my hands were softer in playing defensively. Then Duncan Fletcher built on that when we got to Pakistan. He talked about the idea of 'pressing'. Basically that entails getting your momentum and balance right, so that you don't go at the ball so hard. Duncan suggested I should make a slight press forward when the ball's about to be delivered, but still be balanced enough to play off the back foot. The bowler might see me coming forward and drop it short, but I must be in a position where I can profit off the back foot if he drags it down. The essence is that you don't commit yourself too early, so that you have time to play off front or back foot. And play defensively with soft hands. If you're in the right position, you can stun the ball defensively dead in front of you, rather than keep the close fielders interested either side of the wicket.

Fletch was very good for me in re-educating myself against spin. He had clearly looked closely at my game, analysing where I wasn't particularly confident against spin, and come up with a technical suggestion. He never said, 'This is what you should do,' but merely suggested an alternative method in a calm, thoughtful manner. He was spot-on. He helped me to feel more in control at the crease, knowing what I'm doing, rather than just hoping. Soon all the lads were batting the same way, even the tail-enders. We played the sweep more confidently, working on the angle of the bat when it hits the ball, preventing it being in the air too long. Since that tour, I believe the England players have played spin as well as any other group of Test players. I know that several overseas batsmen are outstanding, but I'm not sure that any squad is better than us collectively. The Australians do struggle at times against the turning ball – as they did at the Oval in 1997 against Phil Tufnell – and they don't have to bat against Stuart MacGill and Shane Warne. Duncan Fletcher's coaching skills have been greatly valued by the England players, and I believe he's the best coach I've ever worked with. His all-round knowledge is outstanding, his man-management is excellent and he rarely has to raise his voice because he is so respected. When Duncan speaks about the game, you listen, no matter how experienced you are.

The determination that Fletch and Nasser had gradually instilled into our team ethic was best illustrated in that great win at Karachi that won us the Pakistan series. They'd kept telling us to hang on in there throughout the series, that there'd be a chance to win at some stage and that we must be ready to take it. It came when Pakistan played some rash shots as we pressurized them in the field with disciplined bowling and brilliant fielding. We were left to get 176 to win in a minimum of 44 overs, but delaying tactics by the captain, Moin Khan, ensured that we wouldn't have as many as that. I don't blame Moin for slowing the game down once he knew that he couldn't win. We would have done the same, dropping heavy hints to the umpires that the fielders couldn't see the ball in the dark. Steve Bucknor, the senior umpire, was outstanding, telling Moin that if he'd bowled his overs at a faster rate, the game would have been over by then. It was so dark that it reminded me of my club days, when we'd play fifteen eight-ball overs each side in the evening and the game would end with the car headlights on in the outfield! We got there in the 42nd over, with Thorpe playing brilliantly. He was so strong mentally, refusing to be fazed by the chattering around him by the fielders and Moin Khan's gamesmanship. It was right that Nasser was in there with him at the end, because his leadership was becoming a major factor in our improved performances. Our series win in Pakistan owed little to flair but everything to effect-iveness, discipline and terrific team morale. For that, the captain and coach deserve great credit.

If the Pakistan success was impressive, our victory in Sri Lanka was twice as sweet. It was a tremendous performance to win the series 2-1 after going one down in the first Test in Galle. On turning wickets, with Muralitheran expected to dominate, we could have gone down by 3-0 after losing that first Test, especially in the kind of humid, hot conditions that even had the locals complaining. Our fitness trainer, Nigel Stockhill, was very influential at the start of the tour in February. After Pakistan we had been home for a month, but you can't really simulate Sri Lankan conditions in England in January! I trained indoors, running for stamina, doing short sprints for explosiveness and gym work for strength, but I knew that the heat and humidity would be draining when we got out there. Nigel worked us very hard in that first week in Colombo, and although I gave him more earache than anybody, I knew how important it was for us to be confident that we could get through hard days without our performances suffering. It's not just about bowling, batting and catching in Sri Lanka: you simply must be fit enough to concentrate. Nigel made sure we could do that, and he played a big part in our success.

Not that we looked like the winners after the first Test. We lost the toss, fielded for the best part of two days in draining humidity and lost by an innings. The umpiring was diabolical, the worst I've ever seen in my Test career. Umpires Jayaprakash and Manuel had just eight Test appearances between them and they simply weren't up to the job. The atmosphere was passionate, the appeals were numerous and both sets of players behaved badly at times, but I put that down to weak umpiring. The players lost confidence in them and we were close to anarchy. My lbw decision in the first innings was the worst I've received in Test cricket. Sanath Jayasuriya pitched one about eight inches outside my leg stump and I was dumbfounded to be given out. It was so laughable that I didn't show dissent – it was unbelievable. Afterwards, five players were fined or given suspended sentences by the match referee for misbehaviour, and the fact that the sole England player was Graeme Hick confirms the incompetence of the umpiring. Hicky is the least difficult of players, and rarely lets his emotions spill over, but he was furious to be given out caught behind in the first innings when he got nowhere near it. When Graeme Hick gets done for being disgruntled, you know that there's a problem.

The umpiring was almost as bad in the next Test, at Kandy. This time Hicky got his own back. I was batting with him when he hit one straight back to Murali for a blatant caught and bowled. But Hicky decided to stand his ground and, to general astonishment, he got away with it. The umpire involved, B. C. Cooray, had a shocking match. Nasser grafted his way to a hundred and, by our estimation in the dressing-room, he was out four times. Jayasuriya was caught superbly by Thorpe at slip, except it was a 'bump ball'. Even we were a little embarrassed at that one. Soon after that dreadful decision, Athers had a set-to with their excitable wicketkeeper, Kumar Sangakkara. That was a hangover from Galle, when Sangakkara had claimed a catch that didn't carry and got the verdict. In Kandy, Athers took one at slip, but signalled straight away that it didn't carry and the batsman was reprieved. But then, after Jayasuriya was out, Sangakkara called Athers a cheat. He wasn't having that, and the two were at loggerheads, wagging fingers, before the umpire stepped in. Everything seemed set to boil over, and the heat and the fantastic support from our noisy fans all served to stoke up the fire.

Some of our players reckoned that the umpires made fifteen major errors in that Kandy Test, and even though the majority of them favoured us this time, it was disturbing. I believe there's a direct connection between umpiring incompetence and misbehaviour by players. If you umpire in a composed manner, the odd mistake is accepted far more easily. But if the umpire gives a 'make-up' decision, to compensate for an earlier mistake, he's just making a second error and that leads to frustration by the players. So the fielding side then appeals for everything and tempers rise. Umpiring is the hardest job in world cricket at the moment. Ten years ago umpires' decisions weren't analysed as minutely as they are now by the various TV cameras. It's correct not to show the replays in slow motion to the crowd, because they'll boo and heckle if the umpire's got it wrong and the players out in the middle will also react badly. The ICC should sit down with the international panel of umpires and ask them what sort of TV coverage of their decisions they want, and how far it should be extended to help them make their job easier. Don't ask the players for their opinions on dismissals, because we can't be expected to be reliable witnesses, as we're playing for our careers out there.

I judge an umpire by his decision-making and how he deals with the players. Some get better, others deteriorate under the pressure. For me, David Shepherd has been the best umpire over a long period. He makes good decisions, is honest enough to admit when he's got it wrong and never thinks he's bigger than the game itself. Neil Mallender is one for the future because his manner with the players is good and he just exudes competence in a quiet, capable manner. The Sri Lankan Asoka de Silva impressed me enormously when he stood in the third Test at Colombo in 2001. That game could easily have got out of hand after Galle and Kandy, but he made all the right decisions. It was only his second Test as an umpire, but having only recently retired as a first-class cricketer, he was firmly in touch with the modern game and nothing seemed to affect him.

I've never umpired and have no desire to, because it's a very difficult job. The umpire has to be very strong when pressurized by top bowlers, and there are times when the batsman knows the umpire has got it horribly wrong. I believed I was wrongly given out by Peter Willey in the Oval Test of 2001. Shane Warne bowled me one, my bat brushed my pad and I was given out caught behind, to become Warne's 400th Test victim. I swear blind I didn't nick or glove it. I stood there for 2.4 seconds, looking up at the sky in my disappointment before walking off. Andy Caddick came in and was given out lbw in the same over. He was equally unhappy and stood there for seven seconds before trudging away. Yet I was the one hauled up before the match referee that night and done for dissent!

I walked into that meeting furious that I was there in the first place. Duncan Fletcher, Nasser Hussain and Peter Willey were all in there. The referee, Talat Ali, told me right away that I was being fined £1000 for dissent. I asked him if anything I said would alter his decision, and when he said 'No', I piled into him and Willey. I think Nass and Fletch got two sentences out in the next half-hour! I told the match referee what I thought of him, then turned to Peter Willey. I said he was weak, and pointed out that Warney had been on at him over a few decisions that had gone our way and he hadn't picked him up. 'Bloody typical,' I said. 'The first time an England player shows disappointment he gets hammered, but you're not strong enough to take on one of the best bowlers the world's ever seen. That says a lot about you.' I continued going for the jugular: 'As a cricketer, I respected you as one of the toughest and hardest I ever saw, but as an umpire, you're weak.' We were eyeball-to-eyeball and he said, 'That's quite a strong statement,' and I told him, 'Yeh, and I ******* mean it.' I didn't see the point in holding back, so I put my point of view very forcefully, with a fair amount of industrial language thrown in. I had no desire to see Andy Caddick get dragged into all this, but it seemed bizarre that I was the only one to be singled out for a dissent charge. In hindsight I was wrong to talk to Peter Willey as I did, and should have shown him the respect he was due.

In the end, it worked out for me, because I didn't have to pay the fine. By telling me right away that I was being done, Talat Ali had failed to follow the proper procedure. He should have listened first to what I and the England management had to say before giving his judgement, so I didn't need to search for my wallet at the end of that Test. But I felt there was an important point to make. England players are expected by our administrators to be whiter than white and behave according to some nice, old-fashioned, public-school standard, yet we're always being told we should play more like the Australians. Meanwhile, Merv Hughes and Shane Warne have abused umpires all over the world down the years and usually got away with it. I couldn't believe the stick Terry Alderman kept giving Peter McConnell in my first Ashes series when his decisions displeased the bowler. An England player would have the book thrown at him in such a situation. All I ask for is a level playing field and the best chance of us winning. Players must always respect the game and those who have to umpire, but it isn't fair to give us a hard time when we approach the game in a battle-hardened way.

The umpiring errors in that Sri Lankan series would have thrown us off course if it hadn't been for the new fighting spirit instilled in us by Nass and Fletch. In both Kandy and Colombo, we had to dig deep in the fourth innings, facing the kind of targets that we'd fallen short of in the past. Turning the series round with victories by three wickets and then by four wickets was a triumph of willpower above everything else. The way we dealt with Muralitheran showed how far we had come. He'd gone through us like a dose of salts on previous encounters – the Oval in '98 was still fresh in our memory – and yet this time we thwarted him. In this series his wickets came every 101 balls, whereas his previous average at home had been 59 balls. We set out to be very patient and frustrate him even if we didn't score off him.

It was harder to work out where we could score off him. There'd be little for the right-handers outside-stump, unless it was a long hop or full-toss – and you'd wait a long time for that from Murali. The key was to realize there'd be long periods when we wouldn't score off him, so the priority was to block him out and look to score at the other end. Commonsense played a part. It would be daft to cut him, because he turns it so sharply that there was always the danger of bottom-edging the ball on to the stumps. The big, booming off-drives were just not on, because he was likely to bowl you through the gate, as the ball turned in at the right-hander. The sweep and the pull were business shots on the leg side if Murali dropped it short. If you played the slog sweep at him early on, he'd put a man out, but at least that opened up another area on the leg side and you could just push him for a single. It was a game of patience. Luckily we always felt that we could score at the other end, and that worked for us.

It was a huge achievement to win in Sri Lanka, as good as winning in Barbados in '94 after being bowled out for 46 in the previous Test in Trinidad. We were now the most improved Test side in the world and had won the last four series in a row. That hadn't happened for England since Mike Brearley's day more than twenty years ago. Discipline had been a key factor, as well as the willingness of the players to take on board Duncan Fletcher's imaginative coaching ideas. There seemed to be a point in everything he did, and Nasser always credited him for our revival. I had been stimulated by Fletch and found it very satisfying that I could adapt my approach to the spinners after being so long in the game. Certainly I wanted to learn new tricks and I was a willing listener. He took me on to a different level in one-day cricket after that tour. In the one-day internationals in the summer of 2002, I found myself down at number eight at times, which was quite a change after opening for so long. But Fletch helped me broaden my outlook in my approach to the final overs. He encouraged me to keep my left leg out of the way in order to get at the yorker, one of the stock deliveries you face in the closing overs. The trick is to have the feet in the right position, otherwise you go too far across and can't get at the ball. So I hit boundaries when we needed them, and my 38 not out at Leeds that helped us beat Sri Lanka gave me as much satisfaction as any one-day innings for England, because I played differently from the way I'd played in the past. Fletch had a big hand in helping me to adapt – at an age when many thought I shouldn't still be playing.

CHAPTER TWELVE
under suspicion

I was sitting on my bed, watching television, in my room at the Pearl Intercontinental Hotel in Rawalpindi when the phone rang. It was 31 October 2000, and for me that call in Pakistan marked the beginning of a process that saw my name dragged into the mire of cricket corruption. It would be another eight months before I was cleared – an agonizing period during which innuendos swarmed around me, everything I stood for in the game was questioned, and my family was put under the sort of pressure that we'd only read about. That sort of thing happened to disgraced politicians or wild rock stars, we thought, not to a supportive family, proud that one of theirs had played a long time for England.

I thought the phone call was from one of the lads, who were organizing a night out – a rare thing on that Pakistan tour. There's not a great deal to do there socially when you're playing cricket, so a wild night out at the High Commissioner's Social Club – featuring darts, a game of pool and a plate of chicken and chips – certainly appealed. Touring can be very glamorous! But on the line was a female producer from the Indian satellite television station, Star Sports. She said I had been named in a report that was due to be published, stating that I had been accused of taking money from an Indian bookmaker. Did I have any comment to make?

I had absolutely no idea what she was talking about,

told her so in a polite manner and hung up. I was baffled, but didn't really think anything more about it. There was nothing at all to connect me with that allegation. I knew that India's Central Bureau of Investigation (CBI) was due to publish its report into corruption in the game, because it was all over the local papers. Cricketers are no different from any group of people – we like a gossip – and we'd been wondering who would be named. It was common knowledge that betting on cricket was all the rage on the subcontinent, and that many bookies were involved, but it never occurred to us that an England player would be mixed up in it. Least of all me.

As I lay on my bed, sifting through my recollection of that short telephone call, I realized that I ought to tell the management about it. So I popped down to Phil Neales' room, and had a word with him and Andrew Walpole, our media relations manager. Andrew told me to refer all further calls to him. He and Phil were perfectly relaxed about it all, and I then concentrated my mind on what colour T-shirt I'd be wearing for the big darts match. These are the considerations that weigh heavily on your mind when you're filling time between matches on tour…

The night was enjoyable, with the usual banter and cheery chats with ex-pats eager for any news from back home. Earlier, one of our travelling English reporters, Richard Hobson of *The Times*, had rung me to tell me what was being said about me in the CBI report. I was grateful because I don't think he was after a story at that stage; it was more a case of letting me know in case I was going to be ambushed by some of the local journalists. Richard said that an Indian bookie called M. K. Gupte had alleged that I had taken £5,000 from him during our tour of India in 1993, in exchange for information about our likely team for the next Test, the state of our morale and my opinion of how the pitch was likely to play. I'd apparently drawn the line at trying to fix a match. I thanked Richard for his help and reiterated that there was absolutely nothing in all of this.

I thought it best, though, to call my family and let them know what was going on, just in case anyone hassled them back home. Lynn was perfectly calm about it all, as a mother would be when she's looking after two kids on her own, but my parents were far from happy. As someone who had been involved in professional sport for almost all his life, Dad was furious that the Stewart name was being dragged into wild allegations from a bookmaker in India. As it happens, his father had been a bookie, but it didn't seem a good idea at the time to make a joke about it! I reassured Mum and Dad that nothing would come of any of it, and that it would be forgotten after a couple of days. I was still unaware, as I went to bed that night, that so many in the media were getting very excited. I was about to experience one of the worst weeks of my life.

Our next match, against the Patrons' eleven, was starting the following day, but I was due a rest and wasn't going to the ground. A day of relaxing by the pool with my book was the plan. That morning, however, I had another call from the Indian media that was very disturbing. It was a newspaper reporter and he was very abrupt and rude. He began by saying, 'I suppose you don't want to talk about it now that you've taken the money.' I couldn't believe his attitude and told him to speak to Andrew Walpole, wondering if there were going to be any more calls like that one. I went to see Andrew and he advised me to put a bar on calls to my room, because this was now building up into a big story. He'd be getting the press cuttings from back home later in the day, but it appeared that I was now generating a lot of interest.

So as I sat by the pool, my mind started to focus on all of this. Of course, I realize now how naïve I must have been during the previous 24 hours. The fact that I knew it was all a load of rubbish didn't automatically mean that I couldn't be under suspicion. My mind went back to a conversation I'd had with a *News of the World* reporter fourteen months earlier, at Lord's. Surrey were playing Middlesex, and as I came off at the tea interval on the Saturday afternoon, I was given the reporter's card and told it was a matter of great urgency. I had a quick word with him and we agreed to meet at close of play. He then told me that a bookie was alleging that Chris Lewis, Alan Mullally and I had been offered a lot of money to under-perform in that summer's Old Trafford Test against New Zealand. I said I knew absolutely nothing about it and asked him to put me on to his news editor, to ensure his paper wasn't going out on a limb for no reason at all. I then spoke to Tim Lamb, the ECB's chief executive, and he was very reassuring. 'Don't worry about that, Alec,' he said. 'We know about this, but we're not concerned. Forget it.' The paper ran the story the next day, but they phrased it sufficiently cleverly to make sure they did not implicate any of us.

The allegations were unbelievably stupid. For a start, Lewis didn't play in a Test all summer, Mullally was dropped for Old Trafford in favour of a spinner, and I scored 83 not out, hardly an under-performing effort from me. In the year 2000, however, cricket corruption was a hot topic, and reporters were sniffing around for all sorts of connections. Since April, Hansie Cronje's reputation had been destroyed by his admission of various offences that were astonishing to all of us who had played against him, and now it was open season on the game.

After all these years, I'm still amazed at what Cronje got

up to. England had been involved unknowingly in one of his scams, at the Centurion Park Test in January. It was a game badly affected by rain and when we arrived on the final morning we fully expected a dull draw. But Hansie, who had already won the series, was keen to make a game of it. After some negotiations, he offered Nasser a target and we went for it. Michael Vaughan and I both made half-centuries and we got home with two wickets to spare in the final over. It was a great day's play and, as Hansie said afterwards, the game of cricket was the winner. Imagine our astonishment a few weeks later, when he admitted taking money and a leather jacket for his wife from a Johannesburg bookie, in exchange for ensuring that there wouldn't be a draw on the final day. All of us knew him as a tough competitor, who was proud to be leading South Africa, and we thought he would be the very last player to get involved with bookies.

There was worse to come. Cronje also admitted that he'd tried to bribe some of his players to under-perform in one-day internationals and that on one occasion he offered the whole team cash to throw a one-day international. This was amazing, and it was no surprise that he was banned from cricket for life.

The bookie now making allegations against me, M. K. Gupte, was the one who drew Cronje in for several years, and his influence had spread. The former Indian captain Mohammad Azharuddin eventually admitted being involved in fixing one-day internationals, and he too was banned for life. Gupte had fingered him to the Indian police and CBI. He also got involved with the Pakistan batsman Salim Malik, and the Indian players Ajay Jadeja, Ajay Sharma and Manoj Prabhakar. According to the CBI report, Prabhakar had introduced me to Gupte in India on that 1993 tour and it was then that I took the money.

As I sat on my own by the hotel pool, I tried to figure out how these accusations about me had emerged. I barely knew Manoj Prabhakar to talk to, even though he had played in all three Tests, so I would have remembered a rare conversation with him that had led to an introduction to a bookmaker. As for meeting Gupte somewhere on that tour, it might have happened, but certainly not in the context of his allegations. Over there international cricketers are treated in the way that top footballers or rock stars are in England these days. When you walk through a hotel lobby, you are besieged by autograph-hunters and fans who just want their photos taken alongside you. They are highly excitable, they clearly love their cricket and I like to think I'm one of the better England players when it comes to being obliging for the cameras and those desperate for my autograph. We would have gone to various official functions and I know I talked cricket to anyone who met me, because that is safe ground when you come from different cultures. I'm always happy to talk about the game to anyone who is polite and interested and certainly I would have mentioned how we were coping on the tour and the topics of players and pitch conditions would no doubt have cropped up. When you're introduced to someone, you don't always catch their name, especially an unfamiliar Indian name. You shake hands, say all the right things because you're on duty, and then move on.

So I might have met M. K. Gupte fleetingly on that tour, because you have hundreds of brief conversations with local cricket fanatics amid all the mayhem involved in being an England cricketer in the public eye. I certainly didn't recall meeting someone who said he was a bookmaker. More to the point, I think I might have remembered someone handing over £5,000 to me. Anyone who knows me will know that I am a touch careful with my money! Not even in the early nineties, however, when rumours about bookies and cricketers were unknown to me, would I have considered taking money even for harmless information about the pitch. All that information is readily available via the media the day before a game, so why wouldn't the bookies just tap into all that, rather than hassle a player? I now realized that such initial contact is just what draws the player into the bookmaker's web, after which the risk of blackmail makes the cricketer vulnerable and he gets further embroiled. All that came out during the King Commission inquiry into Cronje's activities in the summer of 2000, but I knew nothing about such matters seven years earlier when I first toured India.

All of this was running through my mind when Andrew Walpole returned from the ground to tell me that he'd fixed up a conference call with the ECB at Lord's. He'd seen the press cuttings from home and they were going big on the story. It couldn't be ignored any longer. On the line from Rawalpindi to London, we talked with Tim Lamb, Lord MacLaurin, the chairman of the ECB, and David Graveney, the chairman of selectors and also the head of our players' union. Janet Fisher, the ECB administration manager, was on hand to take notes. After I'd answered key questions they were all very supportive of me. Lord MacLaurin asked me whether I'd ever met Gupte, whether I had taken money from him or anyone else, and whether I could shed any light at all on the allegations in the CBI report. I was able to answer 'no' to everything, but I could understand why they were so concerned. In the wake of the Cronje revelations, Lord MacLaurin had been very strong in his public statements about corruption in the game. He'd even said that Pakistan's Wasim Akram, who had been accused of match-fixing, shouldn't be playing in the upcoming Test series against us because he was under a cloud. That caused a fuss when we arrived in Pakistan, and obviously English cricket had to be seen to be incorruptible. Especially a current, high-profile player like me. At last, I was waking up to the implications of all this. I needed help from people who were more sophisticated than me in such areas, and I was grateful to have the ECB's support and backing in that conference call.

I wasn't reassured for long, however. I called home and it sounded as if my family were having a nightmare. My son Andrew had been snapped by a press photographer going into school, and Lynn was understandably upset by that. Did the press think Andrew's father was a criminal? They were knocking on my door, putting pressure on Lynn, while my parents were getting the same treatment at their home. Dad was so angry at the slurs that he decided to go on the offensive and went on the radio and television to denounce the way that we were all being treated.

The English press cuttings contained various profiles about me, written by people whom I had never met. They had just trawled through the cuttings library, then put a spin on things and threw mud at me. That old standby, the anonymous quote, was used extensively – whether it was 'a former team-mate', 'an England source', 'an insider at Lord's' or 'a friend of the family'. I was an easy target, 'Guilty Till Proved Innocent' – all on the word of an Indian bookmaker I'd never heard of until a day ago. How could I get the pressure off my family? Why should my seven-year-old have to face cameras in his face on the way to the school playground? It was even suggested to me that perhaps Lynn and the kids should move out of our home until all this blew over, but that just infuriated me. We had nothing to hide, so nothing should be allowed to turn any of us into fugitives or recluses.

But that night I had to be a prisoner in my hotel room.

Andrew had drafted an initial statement from the ECB that said very little apart from reiterating their support for me, but when he went down to the hotel lobby to hand it out, he was almost submerged by the frantic media gathering. The statement was snatched out of his hands by excitable reporters, and when he came back to see me, we agreed that it wouldn't be a very good idea to go downstairs for a bite to eat. Even though I wanted to demonstrate that I wasn't rattled or behaving like a guilty man.

One of my best friends, Rehan Alikhan, who used to play with me at Surrey, now lived in Karachi and we had already arranged to meet up in Rawalpindi. So he and Graham Thorpe came in, and we had some room service and reminisced about former days at the Oval. I was a bit subdued, though. Nasser Hussain and Mike Atherton popped in to tell me about the day's cricket and to offer any support I needed and a few of the other boys did the same. A couple of reporters from English tabloid newspapers knocked on my door, offering me a platform to protest my innocence but I wasn't going to do that. The advice I'd received had been to stay quiet for the moment while ECB officials took responsibility.

The vision of Andrew getting photographed kept coming back to me, and that forced my hand. I was going to face the press. I went to see Andrew Walpole at around eleven o'clock that night and told him that I had to shift the focus away from my family. The story was Alec Stewart, not the Stewart family. I had nothing to tell the media, except that I was completely innocent, but if it filled the airwaves on TV and radio and padded out the newspaper speculation then that would be at least a development which would take the pressure off those at home. It was bad enough to be away from my wife and kids for winter after winter; they didn't deserve this.

Playing for England had meant everything to me, and I was distraught that anyone would think my pride and commitment would be compromised by a bookie. There had been many sacrifices in my family life to prolong my England career, and here I was, at the age of 37, holed up in a Pakistan hotel, powerless to do anything as my name was being blackened.

I barely slept that night, fully aware that whenever that press conference was called, I would be out of my depth. How could I prove my innocence? It was his word against mine – and it was being pointed out that Gupte had a good strike rate with his accusations, his fingering of Azharuddin and Cronje having led to admissions from both of them. Therefore no smoke without fire?

During the next day, I spent two hours with Andrew Walpole and Phil Neale, going over what I should say in the press conference. It was going to be held that night in the hotel, and Andrew made it clear to me that there was enormous worldwide interest. It would be broadcast live on both BBC Radio Five Live and Sky News TV back home, while the media in India and Pakistan couldn't get enough of the story. No pressure on me, then! Andrew and Phil had thought about all the various questions that would be thrown at me and they seemed to have most things covered. Andrew had talked in depth with the ECB that morning, and they now accepted that I was not going to be talked out of doing the press conference. I suppose they could have pointed to a clause in my tour contract and banned me from making public comment, but they were soon aware that I wasn't going to be silenced. My career and reputation were at stake. This wasn't the time for a non-committal statement handed out in the hotel lobby. There'd been enough of all that the night before.

At six-thirty that evening, I took a deep breath and,

accompanied by Andrew Walpole, walked into the press conference. I was way out of my league and very nervous. Basically, I knew I had nothing to say, other than a flat denial of the allegations, but I owed it to my family to go through the ordeal. They needed and deserved some peace. I'd had plenty of experience of press conferences where I'd faced questions about my batting, or about a game when I'd been England captain, but nothing had prepared me for this. A bank of cameras, snapping away, and row upon row of sceptical reporters. The questions were as loaded as I expected, but I had no problem with that. I just wanted to get over my conviction that I was completely innocent and that the ECB were supporting me. Early on, I had to field a blunt question going to the heart of the matter – 'It's your word against his, isn't it, Alec?' – and it was also put to me that there was never any smoke without fire. Fair enough. I had nothing to hide, and we just went round and round the houses. I was biting my tongue throughout, playing it deadpan when I really wanted to lash out at a legal system which allows you to be accused without any sort of comeback. It wouldn't have been allowed in England but clearly anyone was fair game under the Indian legal system. Some journalists later said they couldn't understand why I wasn't more aggressive in the press conference, and that I would have been more credible if I'd been more emotional. Well, that's not my personal style for a start; I've never been one to give much away to the media. Also, I didn't have the necessary wide vocabulary to express my true emotions, even if I'd wanted to, and I'd had no training in, or experience of, such a situation. It was the most unfamiliar territory I'd ever been in during my career, and I wonder how those press detractors themselves would have fared in that particular shooting gallery? I suspect there might have been a stutter or two, a tense sip of water and some gulping of air when a sentence wasn't coming out the way they wanted. Human fallibility it's called.

I felt I was only thrown by one question near the end. I was asked by an English tabloid reporter if I'd take a lie detector test. I was taken aback, because the implication was that everything I'd just said was suspicious and that I was still in the dock. I'd protested my innocence for more than half an hour, with all the emotional pressure of knowing that my remarks were going out live around the world, so I was thrown by the implication. We've heard all you've got to say, Alec – now let's prove it scientifically with a lie detector. That annoyed me and I nearly rose to the bait and lost my composure. I stumbled out an answer along the lines of 'are they reliable?' as if I had any idea at all, but I sniffed a tabloid stunt there. I had visions of one of the photographers turning up with a reporter brandishing a lie detector next day in the hotel lobby. I felt all that was a slur, and out of order. Were they looking for the headline – 'Stewart Says Yes to Lie Detector'?

The key word I kept stressing in the press conference was 'knowingly'. This was on the advice of Andrew Walpole and it was very sound indeed. Otherwise, if I had indeed somehow met Mr Gupte, even for thirty seconds, on that 1993 tour, and a photograph of the encounter had emerged from somewhere, my credibility would have been in tatters. Even though I carried on denying categorically that I had received any money from anyone, I'd have been compromised by proof that we'd talked even briefly at some stage. So it was very sensible to add the word 'knowingly' when saying that we hadn't met. To this day I am not aware that Mr Gupte ever came into my company or talked to me on the phone. As I've already said, however, I cannot be 100 per cent certain, owing to the nature of touring India as an international cricketer. Your time is rarely your own out there.

I knew that all sorts of games were now under the microscope after the shocking revelations in that year. One match I played in for Surrey must have looked very dodgy in retrospect, even though it was a 'clean game'. It was a Benson and Hedges Cup match at the Oval, and I still don't know how Lancashire beat us. Graham Thorpe and I were batting together and we needed only another 30 or so to win. But Peter Martin bowled tremendously to get Lancashire back in it, and we lost eight wickets for about 15 runs. We couldn't believe we had batted so badly. If that game had taken place after the Cronje affair, people would have been asking questions about money changing hands. Yet it was just one of those inexplicable collapses that happen occasionally in team games.

By now, however, there were so many one-day internationals being played around the world that clearly there was more scope for corruption than I'd ever imagined before I had got sucked into suspicion. That's why I made it clear in the press conference that when I returned to England I would cooperate fully with the Anti-Corruption Unit (ACU), a body set up a few months earlier to report directly to the ICC about any shady activities. It was headed by Sir Paul Condon – later Lord Condon – who had been the Metropolitan Police Commissioner, and he had a great deal of police expertise at his disposal. I looked forward to having my name cleared by the ACU very soon after I got home. That proved to be a major disappointment to me. It would take Sir Paul until the following July before I was exonerated.

Eventually, the media frenzy did settle down, both at home and in Pakistan. It appeared that offering myself up to a press conference had drawn the sting, so that it was now a case of whom do you believe and let's see what the ACU can unearth. I went back to my cricket and, after missing the Rawalpindi match, was pleased to make 59 on my return a few days later in Peshawar. Batting against tricky spinners was something I could handle rather better than questions about a bookmaker who claimed he knew me well enough to hand over a lot of money. Nasser Hussain told me later that I was quieter than he'd ever known me for a period of about ten days, but he understood why. Sleep was elusive as I kept racking my brains to come up with anything that had slipped my mind which would help to clear my name. After a time, the usual banter from the lads cheered me up. 'Stewie, there's a brown paper bag over there – is that yours?' or 'Lend us a few quid, you can afford it now!' I knew they were completely on my side and it was good to have them taking the mickey again. Dressing-room humour can keep you sane when you're pre-occupied with serious matters.

For the rest of that tour I was able to focus mentally on my cricket, but at the back of mind there was always the nagging worry about just how I was going to go about proving my innocence. I kept wicket well in the Test series, and there was no significance to my run of low scores, leaving me with a highest score of just 29. In my quieter moments, I did brood about Mr Gupte's allegations, and I had to work hard at switching on my concentration on the field of play. But I got through it, and the dramatic victory in the dark at Karachi that won us the series on the last day of the tour was a great boost. As I flew home that night with my jubilant team-mates, I was preparing myself to meet Sir Paul Condon.

Christmas and its various complications got in the way of those plans, but we finally met up on 11 January. I'd had a session the day before with Gerrard Tyrrell, a lawyer who'd worked with England players over contracts and our bonuses pool. Gerrard had worked with the Professional

Cricketers' Association and I had always been very impressed with him. I was even prepared to overlook the fact that he supported Tottenham Hotspur! The ACU had advised me to bring along a lawyer, so Gerrard did most of the talking the following day when we met Sir Paul at his office, near Buckingham Palace. Sir Paul was very pleasant, efficient and the whole thing lasted less than an hour. It was like a scene from *The Bill*, minus the bullying, as I answered questions into a microphone and the legal assistant typed out my answers. The questioning was done by two former Scotland Yard officers and they didn't ask me anything different from what I'd had thrown at me in the press conference at Rawalpindi or by the ECB officials. But it was all very professional and Gerrard made it perfectly clear that I would be cooperating fully in the hope that I would be officially cleared as soon as possible. I'd even hand over my financial records. Gerrard asked what evidence Sir Paul had about my involvement, saying that he was concerned about the implication that I was guilty from day one, while Sir Paul said this was going to be the biggest investigation of its type ever. His aides would go anywhere to establish the truth and a lot of money would be spent on the investigation. Gerrard underlined that I was due to leave with England to go to Sri Lanka at the end of January, returning in two months' time. We hoped it would be sorted out as a matter of urgency, but made it clear that we'd be available again for another meeting by the start of April. We parted on courteous terms, and there was no hint of dissatisfaction with us from any of the ACU officials. Sir Paul said that he'd get back to Gerrard as soon as his aides reported back to him and I asked that my lawyer would be kept in the picture while I was away in Sri Lanka. So far, no problem.

I didn't let the issue bother me at all during the Sri

Lanka tour, as I had been impressed by what I had seen from the ACU, and I was now aware of Sir Paul Condon's reputation. Because I was innocent, I fully expected it all to be a formality, done and dusted within a few weeks of my return. But it dragged on. I didn't play my first game of the season for Surrey until 5 May, but Gerrard never got a call from the ACU, even though I was available throughout the month of April. On 10 May, Gerrard wrote to Sir Paul, asking what was going on, and reiterating that we were still waiting for another meeting and that a list of questions he had put to Sir Paul at the end of January had still not been answered. A month passed without word from the ACU. On 7 June, Sir Paul contacted Gerrard, acknowledging that I wanted a meeting, that one of his people would be in touch, but still not answering any of the January questions. Finally, on 17 June, a story appeared in the *Mail on Sunday* that looked very damaging to me. It said that Sir Paul had become exasperated at my delaying tactics, my inability to suggest a date when we could meet for further investigations. The implication was clear – I was being uncooperative towards Sir Paul, obstructing his investigations by being elusive. I was in Leeds that Sunday morning, preparing to captain England against Pakistan in a one-day international. I certainly didn't need this as I prepared for the game. I was very, very unhappy at the innuendo. At no time had we been given a date, even though we had stressed in January that we'd be there if it was humanly possible. It was hardly my fault that I'd been away since then for two months, representing my country.

I wondered at the motives behind that story. Perhaps it had been planted by the ACU because Sir Paul hadn't been unearthing a great deal since being appointed to the post the previous summer? It was an expensive exercise, I understand, and it may be that he was taking some heat from the ICC, who were concerned about the game's image being tarnished by all these allegations that were taking a great deal of time and effort to investigate. I was bitterly upset that my name was still being dragged into all this, when I'd been happy to co-operate with Sir Paul right from the start. It seemed to me I was a pawn in a much bigger game.

In fact, Gerrard Tyrrell spoke to one of Sir Paul's aides who had been at our January meeting. Mr Geoff Rees didn't deny that the ICC and the ACU had been informing the press that I had been uncooperative. Gerrard was furious at these tactics and wrote an angry letter to the ACU on 18 June, outlining the sequence of events since January and totally refuting the innuendos in the press. A copy was sent to Tim Lamb and Lord MacLaurin at Lord's. The following day, Gerrard was contacted by the ACU to arrange an urgent meeting.

So at least that *Mail on Sunday* article, and the angry reaction from my lawyer, managed to fast-track a meeting with Sir Paul. On 26 June, at Sir Paul's request, I brought all my bank statements for the previous eight years to show that nothing had gone into my account in 1993 that may have been suspicious. I also brought my mortage statements for that same period. We weren't challenged with anything that was fresh in that meeting and I answered the same questions as I had in January all over again. Eventually I told Sir Paul I wanted to say something on the record. I acknowledged that he had a difficult job to do, but I was very disappointed that this had dragged on for eight months. I wanted to know when my name was going to be cleared and also why that leak from his unit had appeared in the *Mail on Sunday*. He said he'd been under pressure, and I then pointed out that I was aware of such a feeling too. We'd agreed to keep our dealings out of the press, so reading about his frustration in a national newspaper on the day I was due to captain England might be deemed to be putting me under further pressure. I spoke in a firm, polite manner, not wanting to appear disrespectful to someone of Sir Paul's stature. He said 'fair point', and added that he needed to investigate fully and efficiently. I had no problems at all with that, but when would it all be over? He said he'd be in touch, we shook hands, and that was it. I felt I'd made my point that I was very unimpressed to be the subject of newspaper innuendo.

Things moved swiftly after that frank exchange. On Wednesday 12 July, I was again in Leeds, playing for Surrey against Yorkshire. The Yorkshire Chief Executive, Chris Hassell, came to our dressing-room to tell me that I needed to ring urgently Gerard Elias, the chairman of the ECB's disciplinary committee. I went and sat round the back, in the rugby stand, and at last heard the words I'd been waiting for over the last eight months. Gerard said I'd been cleared by the ACU, that the matter was done and dusted. I felt a huge sense of relief and vindication. Anger also. I'd been the subject of nods and winks in the newspapers, and my family had been unfairly treated. But it was over. I felt very emotional, sitting there on my own in the Headingley rugby stand. Only my family had any real awareness of what it had been like since Rawalpindi. I called Lynn, then Mum and Dad. They'd been there for me, at a time when I really needed my loved ones.

I was looking forward to the press conference I was determined to give at close of play. I hadn't forgotten the nervous, dry-mouthed effort I'd given in Rawalpindi and looked forward to showing just how much relief I was feeling. All questions would be fully answered, without worrying what the lawyers would make of it. Yet there were only six reporters present for my press conference at

Headingley, and they were the ones covering the cricket match. None of the newshounds who had packed out the conference in Rawalpindi, or who had knocked on Lynn's door and bravely tracked Andrew down as he went to school. Seven-year-olds are easier to deal with, I suppose, than a vindicated cricketer, pumped up and ready to deliver both barrels of anger and frustration. It was a huge story when it broke at the start of November, but an anti-climax in July when I was cleared. But isn't that a news story? There'd have been a hell of a lot more reporters that night in Leeds if it had emerged that I was bang to rights, according to Sir Paul Condon. I was disappointed that my exoneration didn't get many column inches the next day in the same papers that had devoted pages to the word of an Indian bookmaker eight months earlier. But I suppose that's the nature of news and we have to live with the unfairness of it all.

At least the ACU did a thorough job in taking so long to clear me. I suppose I should feel even more vindicated, because the process of investigation clearly explored all avenues. The British public was tremendous during that period. I had hundreds of letters of support and only two against – both in the same handwriting and from the same postal area. The first said 'you should donate that £5,000 to charity', and the second was just sheer abuse. The fantastic support I did get through the post meant an enormous amount to me. I also can't fault the ECB, either. They had to be seen to take the accusations seriously, but they never wavered on my behalf, leaving the ACU to investigate while still allowing me to be picked for England. So they stuck by the principles of fair play, judging me innocent unless I was proved guilty. I was devastated to be the only English player placed under suspicion during a period when the rumour industry worked overtime – not that I would wish any of that on one of my colleagues. But I was out on a limb and it got very lonely and frustrating at times.

As for Mr Gupte, he failed to meet the ACU's deadline and provided no evidence to them to back up his allegations about me and several others. It's true that he landed some successful hits – notably Cronje and Azharuddin – but he failed to implicate Brian Lara, Aravinda de Silva, Arjuna Ranatunga, Martin Crowe or me. We all had to endure the innuendos until we were cleared some time later. It is true that Gupte's evidence helped to expose corruption in cricket, but the wild accusations he made in return for leniency took in too many innocent cricketers. In the end he did not have a very high success rate, despite being hailed as a hero by many who share my distaste for corruption in cricket.

I suffered from Mr Gupte's overworked imagination, and I suppose it's always going to be a footnote to my career. I hope not, but I can't do anything about it. I can only trust that those hundreds of supportive letters I received during my eight-month ordeal are the true reflection of how the public view the way I've conducted myself in cricket.

CHAPTER THIRTEEN

my career on the line

By the end of the 2001 Ashes series, I had to face up to the genuine prospect that my whole England career was over. And the reason: for the first time in my twelve years as an England cricketer I had put my family life before my cricket. Add to this a chronic problem with both my elbows, allegations against me from an illegal bookmaker in India and finally some indifferent communication from the England selectors, and it meant that after 122 Test matches, that might be it. As you can imagine, I was anything but happy with the situation.

That series against Australia was the most one-sided I had played in for England, as they outplayed us in all departments. Though I'm not proud to admit it, the overall score-line of 4-1 in their favour was certainly a fair reflection of the quality of the cricket played by both sides. As well as Mark Butcher played at Headingley to win the game for us single-handedly after a generous declaration from stand-in captain Adam Gilchrist, deputizing for the injured Steve Waugh, the gulf between the two sides had grown from the previous series in 1998–9.

Following on from that welcome win there were rumours circulating in the media that both Darren Gough and I were making ourselves unavailable for the winter tour to pre-Christmas India but would be available for the New Zealand leg in the New Year. Where the rumours began I couldn't tell you, but in my case they were correct.

Unfortunately there was also a story coming from the ECB offices that unless players made themselves available for both legs of the winter itinerary they wouldn't be considered for selection.

I knew that both Darren and I would face some hard questioning from the England selectors and the media about our winter intentions during the Oval Test, but as far as I was concerned a telephone discussion that I had with David Graveney in mid-season, concerning my winter commitments, meant that my position in the squad for New Zealand was safe. How wrong could I have been? The following few days were some of the more emotional and difficult times that I had experienced at that stage of my England career.

I believe that some personal and professional background is needed here before I recount this exceptionally frustrating period. Each winter since 1989 I had been selected to tour with England, and I had felt proud and honoured to represent my country. After marrying Lynn in 1991 and then becoming a father to Andrew in 1993 and Emily in 1996, I had grown more and more aware as each tour passed that as a husband and father I should be spending more quality time at home with my family. I know that you can never put back what you lose as an absentee father, and there are times when a straightforward task like the morning school run can seem like a treat. The number of days I was spending at home per calendar year on account of my chosen profession was a concern to me. At no time would I swap my job for another, and I've always believed in the saying that 'you're a long time retired', but family must come first at times. I believed that touring that winter had to be addressed if I wanted to continue playing in the future, which I most certainly did.

A year ago I had considered making myself unavailable

for the 2000–1 winter tours to Pakistan and Sri Lanka. By then I had already toured for eleven consecutive winters with England, and the initial itinerary for that one once again added up to a straight four months away, including the Christmas/New Year period. Many of the senior players due to be involved on the tour were far from happy over the scheduling, but fortunately, before any players even put their views, the ECB along with the host countries used common sense and split the tours. This of course meant that the festive period would be spent at home with loved ones.

When the itinerary came out for the 2001–2 winter tour it showed that the team would be arriving home from India on the afternoon of Christmas Eve, returning there two weeks later and finally reaching home again after the New Zealand leg in the first week of April. Having studied this and given it plenty of thought, I decided to make myself unavailable for the India leg of the tour, so that I could devote some proper time to my family in the lead-up to Christmas – one of the very few that I would have spent at home with them. I hope that anyone with their own kids would agree that the period before Christmas is a great time to enjoy their company as the excitement builds towards the big day.

There were two other factors that contributed to my request to the selectors. The situation with my chronic elbow injuries – an acute form of tennis elbow – meant that there was a good chance that I wouldn't be fit anyway. For the last eighteen months the problems that started during a Benson and Hedges quarter-final at Headingley had got progressively worse. During that time I had five cortisone injections in each elbow which helped me to manage this condition and allowed me to keep playing. The closest I got to missing a Test match was before the Karachi game in the final Test against Pakistan, when the pain relief I received from the injections had worn off, and even throwing the ball underarm back to the bowler, let alone picking up a bat, was a real problem. Some very strong pain-killers and, I guess, mental strength just got me through as we all enjoyed that memorable series-clinching win. Throughout this period the medical advice was that an operation on both elbows would be needed to rectify the situation. The problem for us was finding a window in a busy cricket calendar.

The third reason for missing the India leg was the allegations voiced by Mr Gupte the year before. The fact that I had been totally exonerated by the Anti-Corruption Unit earlier in the summer did not necessarily mean that the media would allow it to be a hassle-free tour either for me or for my family back home, and I wasn't prepared to risk putting everyone through that again.

I must stress that this was the least important of the three reasons for not touring India, but it was still relevant. The family reasons came first, followed by my huge concern with my elbows and whether I'd be fit anyway, and lastly the illegal bookmaker. The combination of the three made me feel that I was fully justified in asking the selectors for a little understanding. This was the only time I'd asked for a special favour from them throughout my international career. Having always done everything that's ever been asked of me by the selectors – from giving up my favoured opener's berth to keep wicket for the balance of the side, to batting anywhere in the order, including number seven, and not moaned about it once – I felt entitled to make the request.

I appreciated a phone call from David Graveney, a man I've always had a good relationship with, in late July between the second and third Ashes Tests to discuss my winter plans. I explained to him the predicament I was in regarding the need to spend more time at home, and he was also fully aware of my elbow problems. David took all this on board and acknowledged that I was very much available for the Test matches in New Zealand. I was fully aware that the one-day series there followed on immediately from the Indian one-dayers and that it would be unfair on the keeper in possession of the one-day gloves if I came back half-way through.

Following the third Test about a fortnight later Grav asked me again about my winter commitments and whether I'd given it any more thought. I re-emphasized my position regarding the family side of things and reiterated my availability for the New Zealand Test series. When Grav suggested that it would be easier all round if we put my unavailability for India down to my elbow problems, I was more than happy to toe the party line if it meant less hassle for him from the media. I was aware that Darren Gough was making similar noises to me and that, with Michael Atherton due to announce his retirement at the end of the Ashes series, the selectors would have some difficult decisions to make. They would be facing a tour of India without three very experienced, key players. However, from the two phone calls I'd already had with Grav I felt that my situation was being looked at sympathetically and that there would be no problem.

How wrong I was. Following our Mark Butcher-led defeat of Australia at Headingley and a few celebrations in the dressing-rooms, I asked Grav, our chairman of selectors, if everything had been confirmed regarding my winter. He surprisingly suggested I speak to Duncan Fletcher, our team coach, about it, and I tried to, but in the aftermath of a Test match win, Duncan understandably suggested that now was not the right time. I believed that dealing with the chairman on such a matter had been the correct way to go about things, but following the Headingley win I was starting to get bad vibes about the whole matter. The two civilized chats that I'd had with Grav earlier in the summer now seemed to be a thing of the past.

Later that week we assembled at the Oval for the final Test, and by now the media had picked up on the possible problems arising over Gough and me not going to India. I was particularly disappointed with the spin-doctoring coming from the ECB to the media, painting the two of us in a rather unfavourable, unpatriotic light. With the tour party due to be named at the end of the Oval Test, it was important to me that the issue was resolved very quickly once and for all. Unfortunately I was beginning to think that this could be my last Test match for England.

The first three days of the match saw many meetings held in the coach's dressing-room, which is next door to the players' one. I'm sure that many were not only about tour selection but also about selection policy, and the fact that the ECB media relations manager was a frequent visitor meant that a statement would soon be forthcoming. By the Saturday evening I felt it was time that I let the public know the reasons for my unprecedented request to have time off from my England touring duties, as I was far from sure that the statements that would certainly be coming out from the ECB would do justice to my side. My *Sunday Times* column the next day gave me the perfect opportunity to express my point of view. I therefore finished off the article with the news that I was looking forward to enjoying the festive period with my family and then going to New Zealand, a place where I'd had success as an England player on previous tours. I most certainly didn't want the English public thinking that I was turning my back on their cricket team.

I have to admit that I've never been one to express my views in public too often, but it seemed to me that the goalposts were clearly being shifted since my conversations with Grav, and that the selectors were now moving towards wanting a commitment to the whole winter's touring. There were to be no concessions.

By eight-thirty on the morning of Sunday 26 August, day four of the final Test, I realized that any chance of my request being granted had disappeared. I had arrived in the England dressing-room to find the other early birds, Nasser and Athers, already there. From the sarcastic and ill-timed comment that Nasser greeted me with, it was obvious that he'd read my *Sunday Times* column. Nasser and I go back a long time and enjoy each other's company and humour, but on this occasion I expressed myself strongly and colourfully in telling him how poorly I felt this whole situation had been handled. It was short and sweet but to the point.

After our pre-match preparation and before the day's play began, a statement was issued by the ECB to the effect that any players being selected for the winter touring parties had to be available for all of the Test and one-day series. This effectively ruled out Gough and me unless we changed our minds – something that I wasn't prepared to do.

By the Monday afternoon we had suffered another heavy defeat at the hands of an excellent Australian team. It was also time to pay tribute to Michael Atherton, a former captain of England, and a terrific player who was highly respected both by his own team and the opposition. The standing ovation he received from the appreciative Oval crowd as he walked from the field, after his final innings had been ended by Glenn McGrath, was fully deserved. For the previous eleven years he had been a truly supportive team-mate and it was sad to see him finish. I was wondering if this might also by the last time I'd be involved as an England player.

We were all staying up in London that night, for a farewell dinner in honour of Athers. I was a little late getting back to the hotel, having stayed in the dressing-rooms to have a drink and a chat with the Aussie boys, something I've always tried to do with each opposing team. Play it hard and fair on the field, but enjoy each other's company off it. As I drove back to the team hotel I doubted if I would ever be playing for England again, and following a forty-minute meeting after my arrival I was even more sceptical. When I returned to my hotel room David Graveney rang to ask me up to his room. I walked in to find that Duncan Fletcher and Nasser Hussain were also there. After I had been offered a cup of tea and a few initial pleasantries had been exchanged between four people who all had a mutual respect for one another, there was half an hour or so in which some forthright opinions were expressed. The three selectors all gave me their views on the selection policy and how they interpreted my own situation, fully aware of my unhappiness with the way everything had been dealt with. I gave them my thoughts on the whole state of affairs, and particularly my strong feeling that the goalposts had been moved since the earlier conversations I'd had with the chairman, and that I'd been badly let down by them. I pointed out that in all my time with England I'd always done what had been asked of me, and yet the very first time I'd asked for something in return I'd come up against a brick wall.

Emotions were running high on both sides, and some strong and choice words were exchanged. They kept going on about setting an undesirable precedent, and their concern that everyone would look to pick and choose their tours if I was given the India one off. I heard what they were saying, but argued that my circumstances were exceptional given that I'd toured for the previous eleven years, and reminded them of 1993, when Graham Gooch didn't go on to Sri Lanka after the India tour. Why not treat each case on its merits? My honesty didn't work in my favour. If I'd been more cynical, I could have made myself available for India and then withdrawn with just a week or so to go, citing the results of the scan on my elbows. It was likely that any operation I needed would keep me out of cricket for three months, but enable me to be fit for the New Zealand leg in January. However, that's not my way. It was obvious that they were adamant about their decision and therefore there was no point in carrying on the meeting. I got up from my chair and shook hands with them all. I felt like storming out of the room and slamming the door behind me, but I was determined not to. I wished them the very best of luck on the tour and left, somehow managing to keep my dignity and hold my emotions in check.

Eight months or so later, when I was fully reintegrated into the England fold, Nasser told me that this was the first time he'd ever seen me really standing up for my rights and being totally passionate in my views. It was the time to be strong, as I could see my England career going down the drain because of what I believe was a failure of communication between the three most influential members of the selection panel. Were my two phone calls with Grav earlier in the summer relayed back to Duncan and Nasser? I don't know. I was bitterly disappointed with it all, especially as they are people who at various times of my career have played an important role.

I returned to my room, showered and got ready for Athers' farewell dinner. I owed it to him to attend and show him the respect he so richly deserved. It was a good evening, during which various stories and events of Athers' career were amusingly recounted, and it was enjoyed by all, including me, even though I was slightly subdued.

As I drove home the following morning I tried to work out whether it was some omission on my part that had possibly finished me as an international player. Should I have spoken with Duncan and Nasser at a similar time as I had to Grav in mid-summer? I believed that dealing with the chairman of selectors was the correct way. Later in the year, following the 11 September attack in the USA, Robert Croft and Andrew Caddick pulled out of the India tour before Christmas, pleading personal safety issues and family concerns, but were allowed to tour afterwards, and it has been suggested by people sympathetic to me that the ECB were showing double standards. I personally don't go along with that, as I respected the two players' views, but at least those in charge showed flexibility.

It felt good, in September 2001, to be able to look forward to a Christmas period with my family, but there was a worrying question on my mind – would the selectors ever pick me again?

CHAPTER FOURTEEN

back in favour–again!

As events turned out, I wouldn't have been able to play on any of the England tours in the winter of 2001–2, because my elbow problem proved far more serious than I had imagined. I wasn't fit enough to pick up a cricket bat until the first week in March, by which time the Test series in New Zealand was just beginning. And by then James Foster, my replacement as the number one keeper on the tour, was beginning to impress. Things didn't look particularly good as far as my Test place was concerned.

I had the operation in October, and the next fortnight was a nightmare. I must be the worst patient in the world, as my wife often confirmed during that period! My arms were set in plaster casts at an angle – say, twenty to four on a clock – for that fortnight, and I couldn't do very much myself. I could just about clean my teeth, lift a fork to my mouth and a couple of other basic requirements, but that was about it. I must have been a real pain, especially when I kept asking Lynn to get rid of a stray nasal hair, or put the right amount of gel on my hair and then comb it to my exacting standards! Playing cricket for England seemed a long way away during that difficult time.

The consolation was that I got the plaster off within a fortnight, compared with the usual month, but I knew I was a few months away from even contemplating playing cricket. The scan had shown up considerable tendon and ligament damage and the elbows were torn and ripped.

Basically, if they hadn't been sorted out quickly, the surgeon suggested that my career could be finished. Years of keeping wicket and batting had taken their toll. I hadn't been fully fit for the last eighteen months, and although the cortisone injections had dulled the pain, they merely staved off the inevitable surgery. After the operation I saw the surgeon twice, to hear encouraging reports, and I worked hard in the gym all winter to regain full strength and fitness.

There were many consolations for me during that time, when cricket did seem inconsequential. Lynn and I spent our tenth wedding anniversary in Venice, we took the kids to Lapland just before Christmas, and the big day at home with all the family was as special as I knew it would be. I did the school run consistently for the first time as a father, and I loved it. Andrew would come with me to Stamford Bridge to watch Chelsea, and I enjoyed our bonding. I wouldn't change a thing about that winter, and my only regret remains that the England management weren't as understanding as they could have been.

I watched England playing on the television, but I didn't regret not being with them because I wasn't fit. In any case, I'd taken the decision to stay home before the elbows operation became a necessity. The ambition to continue playing for England burned inside me – that wouldn't leave me until I'd played my last match, scored my last runs and taken my last catch – but I could be detached about watching the cricket. Of course, I desperately wanted England to win every match on all their tours, and I made a point of saying that whenever I knew I was being quoted by the media during those months. With James Foster struggling early on, he didn't need any knocking comments from me, and he wasn't going to get any. A young keeper who is also expected to get runs needs support, especially when he's made the massive leap from university cricket to the international arena in the space of a few months.

During the one-day series in Zimbabwe at the end of September, James missed a skier and it didn't look very good. I was summarizing in the Sky Sports TV studio and I knew I'd be expected to criticize the lad. I said that the ball would have been coming out of a clear blue sky, that there was probably a swirling wind to contend with, and to remember that he had already taken one good catch. More Trevor Brooking than Alan Hansen, I suppose, but he deserved a chance. We've all missed those in our time.

On the eve of his Test debut in India, I sent Fozzie a 'good luck' e-mail. I did the same to Nasser and Duncan. Fozzie and Duncan replied gratefully. Nasser's e-mailing skills have always been poor! I genuinely wanted James to perform well, and I got no pleasure from the fact that he had a poor match in England's defeat in that first Test. He would have been very down about that debut and I thought he showed a lot of character to come back strongly for the next two Tests.

But how Fozzie did wasn't really part of the equation for me. I knew that I was still the best wicketkeeper-batsman, but would my time off affect my international future? Six months is a long period to be off the pace in modern cricket – would I still have that crucial sharpness? The other imponderable was the attitude of Nasser Hussain and Duncan Fletcher towards me. Word was filtering back to me that they were very keen on Fozzie and that they were going to give him every chance to nail down the position that had been mine for some years. I picked up on a quote from Nasser – 'Foster is our number one keeper now' – and wondered whether he really meant that, or was just trying to boost the lad's confidence on a difficult tour.

I wanted to pressurize the England selectors into picking me again the following summer, but I didn't know how level the playing field would be. Part of a successful international sportsman's make-up, however, is competitiveness, and I was determined to go out there and prove that I was still the best. I made sure I was my usual diplomatic self whenever I had to make any public comments about England's performances that winter. Nothing I said was going to be twisted and later get back to Nasser and Fletch that might be construed as bitching by me.

Yet I did feel that my time might well have passed. Nasser's regular column in the *Sunday Telegraph* during the tour gave a few hints about the way he and the coach were thinking, and he was very complimentary about Fozzie and his character under pressure. Nasser made occasional references to the future and Fozzie's part in that, and I could read between the lines. Several correspondents were filing positive reports about the young keeper, with the inevitable rider that the curtain had come down on my England career. That was just the spark I needed to make me even more intent on trying to prove them wrong. A lot of my career has been spent battling against adversity, and I was going to make sure that when I turned up at Surrey at the start of the season, I had given myself every chance of performing at my best. My preparation would be 100 per cent, and then we'd see who was the best man for the job.

When Fozzie was handed a central contract as soon as England came home from New Zealand, the writing was on the wall for me. Centrally contracted players are on the inside track, as long as they stay fit, and it's become harder to break through when you're on the outside. I had no problem with that. Fozzie deserved his central contract, while I had done nothing in the previous six months to justify one. I was also 39 now. Would that tell against me, or would my frank exchange of words last August spell the end of my England career? Were we good enough to persevere with a talented youngster, full of promise and guts, when our best eleven for the summer of 2002 would have included me as wicketkeeper-batsman? I felt the omens weren't good for me.

At least I was 100 per cent fit at the start of the season, and absolutely raring to go. At the beginning of March I had my first indoor net since the elbows operation. My Dad and Geoff Arnold supervised the bowling machine and they worked me very hard. They both know my game inside out, and it was invaluable to have them on hand for encouragement and technical advice. The physical demands were the first worry. How were the elbows? After twenty minutes on day one, all my muscles around the elbow joints were tired and I had to stop. Eventually I built up to one hour against the machine, which is equivalent to four hours out in the middle when you consider the amount of deliveries you face from the machine. I felt marvellous, rejuvenated and relieved that there was no pain in my elbows.

We had a fantastic pre-season at Surrey. The weather was fine, the wickets at the Oval were superb, and confidence oozed out of us. I felt on top of the world. Normally, I don't do a full pre-season with Surrey, because I have usually needed a rest after getting back from an England tour. This was the first pre-season I'd really looked forward to in the last thirteen years – since I became an England player – and it couldn't have gone any better. I knew a big month lay ahead for me that would decide just how long I had left as a professional cricketer, and at least I was physically prepared and mentally refreshed.

Inevitably, in all the early-season media gatherings, I

was asked about Fozzie's winter and my England prospects. All the platitudes came out – that he'd done well, played some valuable innings, showed a lot of pluck, and don't forget he's still just a kid – and I meant all that. I also added that I was after my England place and that James would expect a fight from me, just as I had faced challenges from other contenders during my time as England's keeper. Of course, I had watched Fozzie closely during the winter and knew he wasn't the finished product at such a young age, but I wasn't going to say that. It was definitely time for me to be remain diplomatic as I wondered if the door had been slammed shut in my face for good.

The first couple of weeks of the season went excellently for me. I kept wicket to a very high standard and I batted very satisfactorily. I got 99 in the first championship match at the Oval against Sussex, nicking a half-volley to be caught behind, and then I played very well on an indifferent wicket up at Headingley to make 96. This time I was done by extra bounce to be caught in the gully, and I was really disappointed not to have converted those two innings into centuries. I knew how well I had batted, but centuries would have got me extra publicity to – in the old cliché – 'nudge the selectors'. I needed all the help I could get to regain my England place. Within a week, I was to get it from an unusual quarter.

If there are any sad, misguided souls who have a deep knowledge of my career, I would set them this essay question – 'Discuss the Role of Andy Clarke in the Career of Alec Stewart'. Now that might lead to a few bouts of head-scratching. As far as I'm concerned, Andy Clarke got me back in the England team, and he did it on Saturday, 4 May 2002. Andy Clarke, a 27-year-old bowler of medium pace who had appeared in a few one-day games for Essex the previous season, was in the nets at Chelmsford that Saturday morning. James Foster was facing up to him, without an armguard. Clarke bowled one short, and Fozzie had a go at it, missed, and took a whack on the arm. It was broken. Another imponderable: what if James Foster had remembered to put on an armguard before he went into the nets that day? Would I have ever played for England again?

I heard the news about Fozzie's injury at the Oval after I came out of the indoor nets. Three press reporters were waiting for me with the news, seeking my reaction. My reply was, 'That's not good news for Fozzie – I wonder if it's good news for me?' I wouldn't have been human if I hadn't thought that this was my chance to get back, even though I was disappointed for Foster. At least I would now get the answer to the question that had been bugging me since last August. Had my frank words to Nasser, Fletch and Grav finished me with England? I believed that if I wasn't picked again now, it would be for that reason. I was still the best in my opinion, and my form and fitness were now excellent.

I had had no contact with Nasser and Duncan all winter, apart from Duncan's polite acknowledgement of my e-mail to him in India. I had talked a couple of times to David Graveney – once by chance when I rang the Professional Cricketers' Association office, and he happened to be there and came on the line for a pleasant chat. We were still a little distant with each other, but he did tell me to get myself fit – 'because you never know'. But I imagine he would say that to everybody who had dropped out of contention in the last year – that's the sort of encouragement you'd expect from the chairman of selectors.

I also shared a platform with Grav during one of Martyn Ball's benefit lunches. Grav, a former Gloucestershire captain, was master of ceremonies for the current Gloucestershire beneficiary, and one of the questions to me from the audience was about my England prospects. I said, 'Well, you'd better ask the man alongside me. I'm biased, but if they're going to pick their best side, then I should be in it.' I saw no point in false modesty. Grav said, 'Well, the door's not shut – don't be surprised to see him back.' But he'd have to say that in the context of the occasion and, in any case, I knew that the most significant people in all this were the captain and the coach.

Three months after that benefit evening, the captain, the coach and the other selectors had to make a decision. The England squad for the first Test was due to be announced the week after Fozzie's accident and I was keyed up, aware what a significant moment this would be in my career. I've never been one of those who could happily drift along in county cricket, because I have always had the ambition to improve myself, then be tested against the best. A challenge is vital to me, and without the stimulus of playing for England, I was facing up to the fact that this might be my last season with Surrey. So the selectors' decision would determine how much longer I would stay in the game.

The day before the squad was due to be announced, Duncan Fletcher came to the Oval, where we were playing Lancashire in a championship match. After a private chat with recent tourists Mark Butcher and Graham Thorpe, he asked to see me in the physio's room. Following an exchange of pleasantries, Duncan said, 'Look, I hate doing this, because the squad's not due to be announced till tomorrow, but I'm letting you know now – you're in.' I thanked him and a huge smile appeared on my face. He then said, 'Anything said in that hotel room is now forgotten.' My reply was forthright: 'I agree, but I still stand by what I said. But I have a lot of respect for you and I like to think you have for me.' Duncan suggested we shake hands and carry on as professionals, working together. No disagreement from me: 'Mate, that's fine by me, what's done is done. It's great to be back and I'll give you and England all that I've given in the past.'

I was absolutely thrilled. It was almost as exciting as getting picked for my first Test, twelve years earlier. There had been a lot of speculation in the media that Foster's injury would let me back in, but none of those reporters was aware of the words exchanged between me and three of the selectors back in August.

It was a special pleasure to make my comeback at my favourite ground, Lord's. Sri Lanka were lacking the injured Muralitheran, it was a very flat wicket, and I fancied my chances of making a healthy contribution on my return. Sadly, John Crawley ran me out in the first innings, taking three steps down the pitch before he shouted, 'Yes!' I responded, but was run out by yards. It was disappointing for me, and John was honest enough to be very apologetic to me as soon as he came back to the dressing-room. These things happen.

I was definitely more nervous than usual on that first morning. I knew that I had to make a good impression right from the start, because Fozzie was the contracted player, not me, and the word was that he would soon be fit again. When I returned to the England dressing-room, two days before the Test started, I was set on being unassuming and quiet, to ease myself gently back into the surroundings, aware that I wouldn't be able to share memories of the recent tours with the lads. That lasted only three days before I returned to my usual brash, noisy ways! I enjoyed the mickey-taking. 'Oh sorry, Stewie, I forgot, you weren't there, were you? 'No, I was watching Chelsea, on holiday in Venice and in Lapland with my kids!' When we had our first team meeting, I piped up, 'Oh, is that just for those who've got contracts? Shall I wait outside and wait to be told what you've decided?' All very juvenile, I suppose, but it broke the ice, while Nasser and Fletch were very welcoming to me, as if I'd never been away.

Although I felt so fresh and rejuvenated, I was disappointed not to have taken a chance from Aravinda De Silva down the leg side on that first day. But apart from that, I believe I kept wicket well. I did all the media interviews with my tongue in my cheek, trying to hide my excitement at this new challenge. Some of those interviewing me had written me off just a few months earlier, but I didn't take it personally. It was just another thing to spur me on to prove people wrong. I do read the papers, and so do the majority of the England players, even though some of them won't admit it. There's nothing wrong with reading other people's opinions, even if you don't agree with them. I find it can be an extra motivation.

That was certainly the case in the build-up to the third Test, at Old Trafford. This match would see me drawing level with Graham Gooch as England's most-capped player, so I was inevitably put up to talk to the media two days before the start. Not a problem. Except that Graham Otway, of the *Daily Mail*, had clearly decided to write me off before a ball had been bowled. Early in the press conference, he asked, 'Do you think this will be your last Test?' He followed up by asking if I felt under particular pressure. I was slightly taken aback, but said that it was a little early to bin me when I had kept wicket well, and had only had three innings in the series so far – run out for 7 through no fault of my own, 26 not out, then out for 7 at Edgbaston to a good ball from Muralitheran. Next morning, Otway wrote in the *Daily Mail* that I would not beat Gooch's record because James Foster was due to return for the next Test, against India at Lord's. So Old Trafford was to be my swansong.

Now I am perfectly happy for people to write or broadcast anything they like about my cricketing abilities and whether I should be in the side or not – but you've got to be able to take it as well as give it out. On Saturday night, it was Otway's turn to take the stick from me. On that third day I made 123, playing with a fluency and control that gave me great pleasure. So I was ready for the press conference. I looked Otway straight in the eye and said to him, 'I read what you wrote before the Test started, and I'll be very interested to see what you write in your paper on Monday. I think you'll have to contradict yourself.' When I did the TV and radio interviews, I repeated how much I was looking forward to reading Monday's *Daily Mail.* I just felt that it was silly to be so dogmatic about what's going to happen in the course of a game before a ball has been bowled. No one needed to tell me that Foster was on the way back to full fitness, but it was up to me to keep him out of the side. You tend to stay in the England team if you've scored a hundred, or kept wicket well.

I had a small piece of luck off my first ball at Old Trafford, although if Mahele Jayawardene had caught me in the gully off an absolute screamer, that would have been the best catch that ever dismissed me. But the hundred pleased me because I needed to get some runs and I did that by playing my natural, attacking game. I love batting at Old Trafford. The ball doesn't go off the straight for the seamers, the bounce is good, and you don't need a great deal of foot movement. You just transfer your weight forward or back and hit through the line of the ball. If you're a good timer of the ball, Old Trafford is the place to bat. So when they pitched it up, I drove it, and when they dropped it short, I hooked, pulled and cut. I raced to my hundred with four boundaries in a row and felt a sense of relief and pride when I got there. It was my fifteenth Test hundred and just as important as the fourteen that had preceded it. It also consolidated my place in the England team for a while longer and brought nearer the possibility that I might get on the tour to Australia later that year, for the fourth time – another goal I had set myself some months ago.

That Saturday was a very happy day for me, because while I was batting, England were beating Denmark at football in the World Cup. Anyone who knows my fondness for football and my patriotism will appreciate how pleased I was, setting that alongside the significance of my hundred. I was able to watch some of the action while at the non-striker's end during my innings. There was a huge screen in the car park and I managed to switch off my concentration when not on strike to enjoy our 3-0 victory. When Chaminda Vaas went around the wicket, though, I couldn't see the screen, so I had to rely on the cheers from the England supporters out there in the car park. With our ten-wicket victory nailed down in exciting fashion a couple of days later, that Test match will always be a special one for me.

So to Lord's and a new record for me. I became the most-capped English Test cricketer, with 119 appearances, one ahead of Graham Gooch. In the build-up to the Test, I played the record down as much as possible, largely out of respect for Graham Gooch, the England team-mate I have admired above anyone else. His dedication, his attitude to fitness, his achievements over such a long period and his fierce pride in representing his country have all inspired me. He was the captain who handed me my first cap, who never stinted in giving me advice and encouragement. Graham was a great cricketer and remains a good friend.

I was very touched when he took me and Mike Atherton out to dinner after we played our hundredth Tests for England at Old Trafford in the summer of 2000, and he was equally kind when I broke his record at Lord's. He rang to congratulate me, then sent a lovely photo album commemorating my first Test in Jamaica, complete with photographs of the players involved – all of them signed – plus the scorecard of that Test. There was a handwritten letter from Graham and a cricket print. I was very moved by that and I like to think that I shall do something similar when someone breaks my record. They are there to be broken and shouldn't be the preserve of any one player. We are just custodians for the traditions of a great game.

The media were very kind to me about surpassing Goochy's record. I had to smile. Having been one of 'Dad's Army' at the start of the international summer, along with John Crawley and Dominic Cork, I was now an institution. That's why it's best not to get too fussed about your press coverage, unless you can use it for extra motivation when it's been unfavourable. My age was an easy line for the journos to trot out, but I feel it's better to look at how people perform on the field of play, rather than at their birth certificates. For example, Mike Atherton was an old 33-year-old when he packed up, owing to his chronic back problems, while Nasser Hussain's 34-year-old bones were creaking in the summer of 2002, by his own admission. I had come back into the England team feeling fitter and fresher than at any time in the previous two years and I knew I could take on team-mates who were ten years younger than me in the fitness tests.

After my first game of that season, against Sussex, I was tired because I lacked match fitness, even though my pre-season training in the gym had gone very well. You do around six hundred squats when you keep wicket for the whole day, so I was bound to feel stiff. By the next match, I had the necessary match fitness in my legs and felt as good as gold. The age thing has been hanging over me since Raymond Illingworth wanted to phase me out in the summer of 1996, when I was 33, but I've kept bouncing back. I just love to prove wrong people who have written me off, and that helps to spur me on in my fitness regime. If a player is fit enough and good enough, why weaken the side by leaving him out? I know it's important to build for the future, but England haven't been successful enough to enable us to manage that transition easily. We're not like the Australians, who change their team from a position of strength. They could replace Ian Healy with Adam Gilchrist while still winning, so that the great Healy was barely missed. The same applied to Allan Border, David Boon and Mark Waugh. With Australia, you can get a player in when he's not quite ready, but full of potential. With England, it's a case of 'we've got to win this Test'. We've thrown in lots of young players in recent years, but there's been a lack of long-term strategy and most have fallen by the wayside. Only Marcus Trescothick and Michael Vaughan have become automatic selections. Perhaps the injury to James Foster may prove to be a blessing in disguise for him, because he went away to Australia as number two to me, willing to learn, and hopefully will be stronger for the experience, ready to take over from me.

So I opted for a low-key approach to my 119th Test, feeling more pleased about the fact that I'd stayed at the top of my profession for the past thirteen years than about setting the new record. My England team-mates are hardly sentimental types, but they were very complimentary to me. One of them said, 'I've played about twenty Tests and I'm knackered. How have you managed it?' Ashley Giles told me that when he was sitting his 'A' levels, he'd switch on the television to watch the Tests and there I was. That made me feel old! Nasser Hussain made a point of congratulating me in his team talk on that first morning and everybody applauded. My Dad wrote me a nice letter, congratulating me. When I told him that he needn't have bothered, he replied: 'I don't see why not – if it had been Athers or Nasser, I'd have written. I was your coach, after all.'

That first morning, I was very proud to be presented with a full-size cricket bat in a glass case, detailing all the times I had played Tests against particular countries. Lord MacLaurin, the chairman of the ECB, did the honours and it was only after I'd posed for the photographers that I noticed that the inscribers of the plaque had got me down as 'Alec Stewart OBE' when in fact I was an MBE. That means something to me, so it had to go back to be altered, I'm afraid. Perhaps the engraver knew then that in 2003 I'd be honoured with the OBE!

When I went out to bat later on that first day, I was amazed at the reception I received. The members clapped me all the way through the Long Room and down the Pavilion steps. The applause kept going all the way to the middle, and after I had acknowledged it, I thought, 'What am I going to do now?' Luckily, it was a drinks interval and after shaking hands with Nasser Hussain, who had scored a hundred, I started to worry about getting a first-baller! I had been very moved by the great reception. A few Indian players congratulated me as they walked past, which was appreciated, but I soon settled down to batting for England, rather than worrying about thanking the crowd. I played well that night, finishing on 19 not out, and I got a lot of messages overnight, many saying that it would be typical of me to score a hundred on such an auspicious occasion. That would have been wonderful on my favourite ground, but next morning I got a good one from Zaheer Khan and was plumb out lbw without adding to my overnight score. I thumped a few in the second innings to make a rapid 33 to help set up our declaration, and our victory by 170 runs, after I'd played very well, felt much more important than my record-breaking appearance. That's how it should always be.

Better to be remembered as someone who kept going for a long time and continued to perform well. That's why I admire so much players like Graham Gooch, Allan Border and Steve Waugh, great cricketers who never knew when they were beaten. They wouldn't put the pursuit of records ahead of the side's interests, and neither would I. For me it was just great to be back in the England side again, after thinking that I was gone for good. Nasser and Duncan were fantastic to me all summer, and I was very grateful that we had wiped the slate clean after the emotional exchanges at the Oval. At the end of a Test summer that saw me average almost 56 and keep wicket to the standards I had set myself, I was also delighted to be able to look forward to my seventh series against Australia. What a difference a year makes, to coin a phrase. Something to talk about with James Foster as we travelled around Australia. And I made a mental note to enquire about the welfare of one Andy Clarke!

CHAPTER FIFTEEN

my final ashes failure

As I sat in the dressing-room in Perth, I felt a wave of intense disappointment wash over me. It didn't leave me for several weeks. We'd failed to win back the Ashes – again. It would be my last attempt as a player, at the end of a period stretching back twelve years and seven series. We'd lost this one in just eleven days of play, and the current three-nil scoreline could easily turn into five-nil within the next month. Outside, the Australian supporters were crowing all around the WACA stadium, while the England players could only sit in numb despair. I'd ended up 66 not out as we were blown away, but that meant little to me as I sat slumped, with my kit still on and a towel over my head. I didn't move for at least five minutes, trying to come to terms with this all-too-familiar scenario. Winning back the Ashes would now remain an unfulfilled ambition for me, and I could only hope that in time the empty feeling would pass. We'd won only three sessions in those three Tests and that also hurt. We hadn't done ourselves justice, the Australians ought to have been pushed harder, but various factors had conspired against us. They just kept pulling away from us when the pressure was on, but it was still no consolation to be beaten by such a fantastic side.

I'd gone out there genuinely believing that we could win back the Ashes this time. You have to show such optimism, otherwise there's no point in competing. For me, the chance to overturn history was a bonus. I'd set myself the goal of one last tour to Australia after our series at home against them in

2001. I'd thoroughly enjoyed being home for the previous eighteen months, and it was hard to say goodbye to my family for five months in October 2002. Emily saw me packing, but didn't say anything – her face told the story – while it was even harder for her elder brother. Nine-year-old Andrew and I had got used to going to watch Chelsea and doing other father-and-son things together, and he was very upset when I went to the airport to meet up with the England squad. He wasn't the only one. I'd thought this would be my last tour, so there was extra incentive to justify my going to the other side of the world for so many months. Regaining the Ashes and then winning the World Cup in South Africa before returning home at the end of March were my aims, and I had every reason to expect that double ambition to be shared by the rest of the lads. If I was going to be parted from my family for so long – apart from Christmas and New Year – I wanted it to be worth the sacrifice.

I faced the press at the airport and they asked me why I thought this Ashes series would be different from the previous six I'd played in and lost. I acknowledged how good they were, but said that in the past we'd just aimed to compete and stay in the game. This time we had to be more positive, back our own ability and take the game to them. For me, the aim was to win every match out there. I then threw the question back at the reporters, 'You tell me: do you think we're going to win?' Not one did so, and I said, 'Remember that when you write about us on tour. I'm going out there knowing it'll be tough, but determined to do all I can to make sure we win. Any player with a different attitude may as well stay at home.'

As soon as we got to Australia, it started to fall apart on the injury front. The squad of sixteen turned into one of just twelve, and the same side played two warm-up games in a row, which had been designed in the itinerary to give everyone the chance to play. The two most worrying injuries were to Darren Gough and Andrew Flintoff. Goughy's knee had troubled him for months and it had been a gamble to take him. I thought it was justifiable as he was a key player and our spearhead as a strike bowler, with a good record against Australia, whose players respected him. In his month with us, Goughy was up and down in his moods, and it must have been desperately hard for him to deal with the various setbacks. He finally conceded defeat and went home. I must admit I felt he might never bowl another ball for England after that, but he went to see a knee specialist in Colorado and has bounced back with his usual bravado and optimism. But if only he'd been fit for Australia…

Freddie Flintoff's hernia injury baffled me. A few recriminations were flying around about his slow rate of recovery, and some people suggested that he hadn't done his rehabilitation properly, which Freddie hotly denied. The fact is that our main bowling all-rounder wasn't fit for the next five months after his hernia operation, while the Aston Villa footballer Steve Staunton was playing again inside four weeks after his. Now I know that a big lad like Freddie may put more pressure on his body by bowling fast than a footballer does, but that's a hell of a time difference. The England management had to take a chance in delaying Freddie's operation. If England had beaten India at Trent Bridge at the start of August, he'd have missed the last two Tests, but it was a draw, and the desire for victory in the series played an important part in the Flintoff saga. He did outstandingly well to bowl as he did when he was in such pain, but it was clear that he needed surgery as soon as possible.

Then we lost Simon Jones to that horrific knee injury on the first day of the series, in Brisbane. He'd impressed me with his fast bowling from the time of his first Test at Lord's in July through to the warm-up matches in Perth, and I believed he would take the Aussies by surprise. A tough, athletic lad with great natural ability to bowl fast, Simon was an unknown quantity to the opposition and he'd already put in a promising first spell in Brisbane when the ball went past him at mid-on. He turned to chase after it. He then went for a sliding pick-up near the boundary, but his knee crumpled horribly and he lay there in agony. Some moron in the crowd shouted, 'Get up, you soft Pommy bastard!' but it was obvious that this was serious, because Simon isn't the sort to lie down if he's not in great pain. His cruciate ligaments were shattered and he faced up to a year out of the game. That just about summed up our tour so far. With his pace and his big heart he'd looked a good shout to stand in for Goughy, and now they were both out of it.

Then Ashley Giles had his wrist broken in the nets by a short ball from Steve Harmison as we prepared for the second Test in Adelaide. He played in only one of the Tests and also went home. On top of that, Michael Vaughan struggled from time to time with his dodgy knee. This had troubled him for months and never seemed to get any better. At no stage was he 100 per cent fit in that Ashes series, which makes it all the more remarkable that he batted so brilliantly.

I mention the injuries not to excuse our performances for most of the Ashes series, but to underline the pressure that built up on Nasser Hussain. It was a very hard tour for him, made worse by his intense desire to beat the Australians. Nasser gets aggravated by their air of superiority, and the comments about English domestic cricket made by the likes of Steve Waugh, and he too has got frustrated by our losing cycle against them. He didn't believe in socializing with the Australian players in either dressing-room at any stage of the series because he was so driven in his determination to beat them. Nasser felt the heat more than any of us at this time, and it was no surprise that the old familiar passion that he displayed when younger often came bubbling to the surface. I'm sure he'd now admit that occasionally he went over the top at his players during this series. It was understandable, considering all that was crowding in on him, but sometimes we were surprised by the severity of his rollickings. I've always said that the captain feels the hurt of failure more than any other player, and pulling up short in the biggest challenge of his England captaincy disappointed Nasser deeply.

He'd always enjoyed a good relationship with the media since taking on the job in 1999, but once the results kept going against him in Australia, he found it hard to remain the same Nasser Hussain who had impressed us all. Some of the flak he took was ridiculous, however. Mike Gatting had a pop at him in a paper early on the tour because Nasser hadn't travelled out with the squad, but had left for Perth earlier. This was because Nasser's wife Karen was heavily pregnant and needed to travel early, otherwise she wouldn't have been allowed to fly. Why should she stay home and have the child without Nasser at the bedside? So Nasser based Karen and their eldest child with his sister in Perth and he took a couple of days out from the tour, at a quiet time, to be with her as the baby was induced. That was totally understandable, in my view, and no one in the tour party disagreed. Gatt felt that the England captain should have been on the plane with the team – but what for? To listen to me bend his ear about Chelsea being superior to his team, Leeds? To watch an inflight movie alongside Matthew Hoggard? He was in the hotel foyer to greet us when we arrived in Perth and that was all he needed to do in his capacity as tour captain. I was surprised at Gatt for making those comments.

Nasser copped some rather more relevant stick from the media on the first day of the Ashes series at Brisbane, when he won the toss and put Australia in. At the end of the first day, they were just two down, with more than 300 on the board. That set the tone for the rest of the series, and Nasser was in the firing line. I admit that I was surprised when Nasser stuck them in. There was a bit of grass on the wicket, but it's always like that, and although it can help the fast bowlers early on, it's good to bat on. You certainly wouldn't want to bat last on it, especially against Shane Warne, who enjoys bowling there. But the hardest thing for a captain to do is make the right decision when he's won the toss and it was big of Nasser to admit that he got it wrong. It happens. In any case, Steve Waugh hit the nail on the head when he said on TV just before the start, 'It doesn't matter who wins the toss, it's how you play.' And we didn't play well enough. That's why we lost.

At the close on the first day, it would have been easy to think those 'here we go again' thoughts as I sat in our dressing-room. We were all very down, aware that after putting them in we were looking to bowl them out cheaply rather than be chasing the ball around the park. So I changed into my shorts and went for a run around the ground. I needed a stretch after keeping wicket for ninety overs and I wasn't going to sit there in the dressing-room with my head down, resigned to another hammering. Once the captain has made his decision, everyone has to be fully behind him – and off we go. No way do I blame Nasser for sticking them in; I know what it's like to be the captain and carry the can. I was a little surprised, though, when he said later that our bowlers needed all the help they could get and that something around 300 for 5 at the close would have been satisfactory. If you put a side in, you're looking to bowl them out for around 250 or less, so

I thought that Nasser's comment was a little negative and didn't boost the bowlers' confidence.

Nasser wasn't the only one who'd rather forget Brisbane. I got two noughts, the first 'pair' of my Test career, which was hardly the ideal way to start my last Ashes series. You could say luck was against me both times. In the first innings I shouldered arms to Jason Gillespie, but I didn't get the bat high enough or out of the way quick enough and the ball cannoned off it into the stumps. Then, in the second innings, I got a rare long hop from Shane Warne's second ball and cut it firmly, only to see the ball hit Matt Hayden in the gully. He was two yards away from me and turned his back as the ball hit him – and then he took the rebound. That just about summed up Hayden's match – he'd hit a big hundred – and mine. When I walked into the dressing-room, I said, 'You can't do much about that!' and Nasser smiled ruefully, telling me to forget it. He had other things on his mind, as we slid to a damaging defeat.

In the next Test, at Adelaide, I took ten balls to get off the mark, and thus avoid getting three ducks in a row. I had my mate Adam Gilchrist in my ear behind the stumps, well aware that we'd bantered about that possibility the night before. We'd done a piece for local TV when Adam talked about how he'd avoided two noughts at Brisbane. In the second innings he smashed a straight six to avoid the dreaded 'pair', and I told the TV reporter that I hoped I'd do the same in Adelaide. I must admit it was a relief when I moved off nought. I made 29 and 57 at Adelaide, the second-innings effort being a case of staving off the inevitable as we slid to another defeat.

In our second innings at Perth, by contrast, I decided to go down with all guns blazing. Before the start, Steve Waugh had warned that it would be a rapid wicket and that some blood would be spilt. He was dead right. Alex Tudor was hit above the eye by Brett Lee while batting with me in the second innings, and it wasn't a pleasant sight. He ducked into one, and as he lay on the ground he had a panic attack. Darren Lehmann and I got to him quickly and I told him he'd be all right – if a little uglier! – while waiting for medical attention, but it was a worrying time for Tudes. I've always relished the challenge of playing fast bowling, as it gets the adrenalin going, and it tests your skill and courage. Brett Lee was seriously quick that day – reminiscent of Wasim and Waqar at Old Trafford in '92 and Allan Donald at Johannesburg in '95, who were the fastest during my time with England. He had the Freemantle Doctor behind him as he roared in. It was the quickest, bounciest wicket I had batted on. I played every shot in the book, finishing with 66 not out, and although it was hardly textbook batting, I didn't back down against Lee's assault. But we lost – again – and my runs were no consolation at all. We had been here before, too many times.

By now the knives were out for Nasser and for me. Derek Pringle, the cricket correspondent of the *Daily Telegraph*, seemed to take particular exception to my place in the England side. Since the England players had been given laptops to enable them to send e-mails home, I'd got into the habit of going on-line at night to check out the sports news on the BBC website and read the British newspapers. I've always read the papers and never denied it, unlike some of my colleagues who seem very well-informed considering that they maintain they can't be bothered with the press! I'm interested in the opinions expressed and have no problems with what they write about me, as long as it's factually accurate and fair. When Stephen Brenkley wrote a constructive piece about me early in the tour for the *Independent on Sunday*, I made a point of thanking him, so I don't just look out for someone who's had a go at me. But Derek Pringle's stuff got more and more biased. He described my 29 in the first innings at Adelaide as an effort typical of someone playing for a new contract and the sort that you'd expect from someone growing up in the Surrey dressing-room of the 1980s. There I was, doing my best against the best team in the world, and he was going on about Surrey all those years ago. I didn't know what he was on about, and I suspect the *Daily Telegraph* readers were equally baffled. According to Mark Nicholas, who also wrote for the *Telegraph* on that tour, there were a lot of complaints about Pringle's attitude to me in print, and Mark made it clear to me that he disapproved as well.

I wasn't aware of any history between us when we played for England, or against each other in county cricket. We were different types, that's for sure. He was a public schoolboy, educated at Cambridge University with an opinion on everything and a more relaxed attitude to his career than I had. A good one-day player, who bowled superbly in the '92 World Cup Final, he was an average Test cricketer. During this last Ashes tour, I happened to see television highlights of the Headingley Test of 1989 against Australia. In that game Pringle got out to two shocking shots, dropped a catch and had his bowling smacked all round the park. The day after watching that, I read more hostile stuff from him, as he continued slagging me off. I know that every journalist or commentator has a job to do, but Pringle was abusing his position on a respected paper like the *Telegraph*. It was almost trial by tabloid. I wondered about his agenda. As a former Essex player, was he pushing for the Essex keeper James Foster to take my place? Had he been disappointed that I'd come back from my time off and replaced James in the England team? I'll never know. I'd had dinner with Pringle, along with Gus

Fraser and Mike Atherton, earlier in the tour at Hobart, but he never broached the subject with me then. We seemed to get along fine that night. Perhaps it was easier to keep knocking me in his column, rather than face to face.

James Foster got his chance for the Melbourne Test and did very well, both with the gloves and the bat. I liked working with James and I could see what Nasser and Duncan saw in him. He's not short of bottle, and seems to have a sound, competitive temperament. We worked well together all tour. Although some of the media felt I ought to be dropped anyway, I couldn't see what that would do for the balance of the team as long as my recently sustained injury allowed me to play. Craig White wasn't fit, so who would bat at number six if I missed out? And if I were dropped, would it be because of the clamour for youth now that we'd again lost the Ashes, or because it would actually strengthen the side? At the age of 39, I was an easy target, but there was no Ian Botham available as an all-rounder who could win you Tests with bat and ball.

However, I was struggling with my right hand after the one-dayer in Perth just before Christmas. I had an X-ray when we got to Melbourne and fortunately there was no fracture, but I knew deep down that I wouldn't be fit for the Test, due to start on Boxing Day. It was an easy decision after trying to take a few catches at eight-thirty on that first morning at the MCG. When he heard I was out, David Lloyd, who was there commentating for Sky, said to me, 'I've just lost my mortgage – I was sure that you'd make it.' Not this time, I'm afraid, and now the question was whether I'd be fit for Sydney. I honestly didn't believe I'd played my last Test, although some had already written it up in the papers. That Melbourne Test saw me doing twelfth-man duties throughout, in between sticking my hand in a bucket of ice for ten minutes, three times an hour, in an attempt to reduce the swelling and inflammation.

Nasser and Fletch kept faith in me once I'd declared myself fit, and I was delighted to go out on a high note in my Ashes career with a good individual performance and a fine victory for us. That Sydney Test was a terrific occasion, as it invariably is when we play at that marvellous, atmospheric ground. The first day was amazing. All through the series Steve Waugh had been the subject of intense debate in the media concerning his form, fitness and whether or not he should retire. He'd said he would make a decision when the series was over, but many had already written his cricketing obituary when he came out to bat at the SCG, his home ground. What happened over the next few hours was pure theatre.

In this innings, Waugh reverted to his earlier aggressive style, taking on the bowlers, and pressurizing the fielders with quick singles. At the start of the last over, he was closing in on his hundred and I said, 'You write your scripts well, mate.' He turned around, grinned and replied, 'Mate, you're right, but I've had a pretty tough twelve months!' We had a good laugh and then we tried our best to deny him his century that night. At one point he lost the strike, but Adam Gilchrist did very well to steer a single and get it back for him. He needed a boundary off the last ball, and the noise was amazing. Chants of 'Waugh! Waugh!' swept around the ground and when he cut the ball for four, the place just erupted. Even though I had wanted Waugh to get out off every one of the previous balls he had faced, I admit that I wasn't overly upset that he had got the four he needed off the last ball. It was dramatic, exciting and a great effort from a top cricketer.

Every England player shook his hand as soon as he got to his hundred, and we walked over to his area and clapped him into the Australian dressing-room. That was genuine respect for a batsman who may lack the sheer natural ability of a Lara or a Tendulkar but is the best at making the most of what he's got. His mental strength has been remarkable, and I was very happy for him because of the flak he's taken over his age and the criticism that he's hung around too long. I could relate to all that. It was a feather in the cap for us elder statesmen of international cricket. Steve Waugh has been an outstanding player in a crisis for years, and that's why I respect him so much.

At the end of this Test, Steve and I chatted about our remaining ambitions and what spurs us on. We both agreed that enjoyment and pride in performance were fundamentals. He told me he was undecided about going to the West Indies in a few months' time but that he was tempted. Australia had drawn 2-2 on their previous visit to the Caribbean, when the genius of Brian Lara won two games for the West Indies. Steve said that if the challenge wasn't there, then he saw no point in playing on. He was keeping an eye on his three young children as we spoke, and I could tell that he didn't want to spend much more time away from them. I told him this was probably my last tour for the same set of reasons, and we both accepted that we'd miss the banter of the dressing-room, the buzz of a full house at Lord's, the SCG or the MCG, and the challenge in trying to better yourself, whatever your age. In the end, Steve did go to the Caribbean, where he scored runs and led his team to yet another crushing series win. So he'd achieved a further ambition by winning over there. I was very pleased for him – he's a good man and he's been a tremendous cricketer.

It would have been fantastic if I'd matched Steve Waugh by getting a hundred in my last Ashes Test, and I should have done so. I played at my best in making 71 and then got bowled off my pads when the ball was deflected on to my off-stump. I'd played as well as I could, going in the night before to fire off three boundaries in the final over, then continuing to bat with the same freedom next morning, when I suddenly missed a ball that nine times out of ten would have been stroked past wide mid-on for another boundary. The ball was missing another two stumps down the leg side, and I couldn't believe I'd missed out. That was a big personal disappointment. It still rankles that I scored only one Test century against Australia.

That night I did the media duties. Our media liaison officer, David Clarke, told me, 'I want you to do it, even though they don't want to hear from you, because so many of them had written you off.' So, reluctantly, I did the TV and radio, then went into the press conference. I sat there for twenty seconds before anyone asked me a question. I was wondering how long I'd have to sit there before the first question was asked. When one came it was about a rash that I had picked up, that had been suspected chickenpox, a few days earlier. Not exactly probing stuff. I knew what was on the minds of all those in the room. Steve Waugh was mentioned and I praised him highly, pointing out that he'd also scored 70-odd in the previous Test at Melbourne. The important thing was how good you are, not how old you are. I then pointed out Derek Pringle and said that he'd been writing me off for the past six weeks, yet I'd played all those Tests because I was a good player and was still performing at the required standard. They asked me about passing Geoffrey Boycott's Test aggregate, and I replied that the way I had just played surely proved I had something to offer. Normally, it would have been water off a duck's back to me, but I felt I wanted to get these things off my chest. When the press conference broke up, I walked past Pringle looking straight at him. He kept looking at the floor as I tried to catch his eye, and he didn't respond. It would have been impressive if he'd said, 'Well played,' because that would have been true – but it would also have contradicted the bias he had shown against me for the previous six weeks.

One of the English tabloid correspondents said to David Clarke afterwards, 'Doesn't he know that he'll never win if he takes the press on?' but I didn't see it that way. Was it OK for the press to keep hammering me, and for me to be expected to just shrug it off? Not this time. I had batted as well as ever, proving that my age was irrelevant. Yet it had suddenly become open season on me. Stephen Brenkley, the writer of that excellent piece on me two months earlier, now suggested in his column that Buzz Lightyear, a cartoon character, had more chance than me of playing in the first Test against Zimbabwe the following May at Lord's. I thought of that forecast as I sat in the home dressing-room at my favourite ground on Thursday 22 May 2003. Perhaps a slice of humble pie now and again might be in order? I have no problem with criticism as long as it is constructive and is justified.

However, all that mutual hostility was just a sideshow in Sydney. The most important aspect was our victory, with Andy Caddick bowling magnificently in their second innings. They crumbled against his accuracy and the steep bounce of Steve Harmison and it was some consolation to get one back in front of thousands of noisy England supporters. And don't buy into that theory about Australia getting complacent when they've won a series, then taking their foot off the gas. If so, why were Matt Hayden and Adam Gilchrist hauled before the match referee for dissent over decisions that went against them? Australians don't know how to coast along in sport; it's just not in their nature. The truth is that, without the injured Shane Warne and Glenn McGrath, they were vulnerable, and we outplayed them when they were under pressure. Warne and McGrath are not just big wicket-takers, they are also very economical, and that's a huge bonus for a captain. It means that Brett Lee can attack at the other end, trading wickets for runs, knowing that pressure will be exerted by either McGrath or Warne. When they're missing, it makes such a difference. Andy Bichel is a good seam bowler, but no world-beater, while Stuart MacGill can be pulled and cut much more easily than Warne. If Shane Warne had played for us rather than the Australians over the past decade, the Ashes might not have stayed with them all that time. With his tactical brain and massive ability, he has been a fantastic bowler, one of the most influential in the game's history.

If we had lost the Test series 5-0, I think Nasser would have resigned as England captain. He would have stayed on for the World Cup, but after that he'd have probably given it away, because he's a proud man. He would not have wanted to to go on after becoming only the second England captain in history to lose all five Tests to Australia. All that fronting up to the media with platitudes after defeats was taking its toll. It all comes with the territory, as I know only too well, and my sympathies were with Nasser. He did excellently to maintain his form with the bat, and his fielding remained very good – but he got more and more frayed in his temper.

Basically, Nasser batted and bowled every ball in his mind in Australia, and at times his fierce, proud, competitive nature boiled over into frustration. It was the timing of his outbursts that sometimes surprised me. In the past, he seemed to have it spot-on when he chose to hand out a few home truths. But the chemistry between captain and players wasn't always right in Australia, compared with other tours I've been on under Nasser's captaincy. However, as I know from experience, things that seem minor to some aren't to the skipper when he's under pressure, trying to cope with desperate disappointment. That's why the job of England cricket captain is so hard, and I did feel for Nasser in Australia, even though he did rub a few of his players up the wrong way. There's no hiding place out there. Their players and public are in your face all the time. Cricket is almost as big in Australia as soccer is in Britain and, wherever you go, the locals do remind you in their charming way that they're better than you. That may have wound Nasser up, and at times he took it out on his players.

The major factor in our defeat was that Australia had simply got even better than the last time we'd played them, in the summer of 2001. They are the best unit I've ever played against. When all their top players are fit, they are tremendous. The opening partnership of Matt Hayden and Justin Langer is more solid than the previous one of Hayden and Michael Slater, and Ricky Ponting has got better and better at number three. That also applies to Jason Gillespie, while Adam Gilchrist is a genius as wicketkeeper-batsman and Brett Lee is very fast and dangerous. He and Gillespie can also hold a bat, while Warne's ambition is to score a Test century, which he could easily do. They could even afford to drop Mark Waugh, who I believe has been a fantastic Test cricketer: a wonderful catcher, the best slipper I've ever seen, and an elegant batsman with a great record against England. At the start of the series we all thought they were weakened by playing Darren Lehmann and Martin Love instead of Waugh.

Australia have made cricket a more attractive game. The rate at which they score and the speed with which they bowl sides out mean they've taken Test cricket to a different level. They look to win Tests inside four days now, rather than five, and boring draws seem to be a thing of the past.

They take chances and sometimes fail when they bat so positively, but aiming for a minimum of four runs per over is a great attitude. Allan Border's hard, dogged approach was built on by Mark Taylor, and then Steve Waugh added an extra dimension. Ian Healy was a magnificent, tough wicketkeeper who chipped in with useful runs, but now Adam Gilchrist is in a different league. He is a great talent; he sees the ball very early, and he has a solid technique that enables him to whop the ball around whatever the state of the match. He'll come in at 100 for 5 or 420 for 5 and still play in the same free manner. That is a great luxury but Gilchrist has the talent to capitalize on this positive approach by the whole team. In our team talks, we'd have plans for Gilly. Don't let him swing his arms by bowling wide of the off-stump. Try to trap him on the crease, bring him forward, bowl at his off-stump, pack the gully and backward point areas, get him playing the ball in the air. Then you look at the scoreboard and he's made a hundred off the same number of balls! He's a remarkable cricketer, the most dangerous in the world.

Their bowlers have the skill and discipline to carry out a line of attack effectively. Look at the way Gillespie lined up Marcus Trescothick, bowling across him at around off-stump and forcing him to nick it. McGrath has the ability to put the ball in the right place, ball after ball. Then there's Shane Warne...

There will come a time when we beat them and regain the Ashes. Warne and McGrath aren't going to be around for much longer, and although Darren Gough and Andy Caddick almost certainly won't operate again as an opening pair against Australia, I'm convinced that we have the pace bowling talent to compete with them. Steve Harmison's bounce is a great asset; James Anderson has a high, bouncy action and can move the ball away at good pace; Matthew Hoggard is a class swing bowler with a great heart; Simon Jones will hopefully recover, and trouble Test batsmen with his speed and his ability to reverse-swing the ball, while Alex Tudor has all the ingredients if he can establish his place in the side. The biggest problem for our lads is the domestic wickets. It's too easy for them to put the ball in the right areas and rely on the surface to get wickets, whereas on a proper Test match surface you're looking for something extra. Gillespie and McGrath have accuracy and a sharp mental attitude, Lee has extra pace, while New Zealand's Shane Bond has speed and the ability to swing the ball late. We need to develop our young guys to that standard, which I believe we are doing successfully.

Flat wickets in Tests also expose our spinners. Regulation finger spinners don't win many in Tests these days. Our crying need is for someone like Saqlain Mushtaq, or India's Harbajhan Singh, who can do unorthodox things with the ball and add some mystery to their bowling. Again, our wickets at home don't encourage bowlers like them. I have a bee in my bonnet about our practice wickets. In Australia, the groundsmen take pride in producing excellent practice facilities, so that the bowlers can come in off their full run, armed with a brand new ball, and try to dismiss a batsman who isn't worried about getting his head knocked off because of an under-prepared wicket. A lot of the time in England, it's deemed a chore to produce a good practice wicket. It's only for one or two days, so why bother? But outstanding practice facilities help to produce outstanding cricketers. The Australian climate obviously does help, but in England, even on Test grounds, you can't always practise away from the actual playing area while the Test is going on. For worthwhile practice, you need to be able to simulate match conditions.

Our structure is improving at last. I think the Academy

is a great idea and long overdue, although I would still like to see England 'A' matches home and away. There's nothing wrong with pinching ideas from Australia, as long as they are good ones. The whole set-up for cricket over there is very good, from the Under-10s upwards. It is structured in such a way that only the best players play with and against each other. They also have this intense desire to do well, and the financial incentives are sensibly arranged. No state player can earn more than one who is on a central contract with Australia, whereas in England a county cricketer who's got a good deal can in fact earn more than the basic wage that an England player gets. That's wrong. The financial rewards from playing for your country should be higher than for any other pro. You need incentives for players to keep improving and aim high – reward success, not mediocrity.

It's not a matter of whether we can regain the Ashes, but when. These things come in cycles and we're on the road back. When Lord MacLaurin was the ECB chairman a few years ago he issued a mission statement in which he said that England's target was to be the best in the world by the year 2007. I see nothing unrealistic about that ambition. Once we have achieved the position of number one, we must then make sure we give ourselves the best chance of staying there for as long as possible. Ambition and dreams are great; realizing and achieving them are even better.

CHAPTER SIXTEEN

the zimbabwe affair

I was looking forward so much to the 2003 World Cup. It would be my fourth and last and, after the shambles of 1996 and 1999, I genuinely felt that that we were well-prepared and a good bet to reach at least the semi-finals. After that, it was game on, and even the Aussies could be knocked out in a one-off. But it was not to be, and the traumatic events over one weekend in Cape Town just before the tournament started brought home to us that we were no longer involved in simple contests between bat and ball. Politics became inextricably linked with the World Cup and we, the naïve England players, got dragged into it. It was not a pleasant experience, and none of us in the squad will ever forget the emotional, draining strain of it all.

When the World Cup draw came out more than a year earlier, the England players didn't take much notice of the fact that we were scheduled to play one game in Zimbabwe, on 13 February, in Harare. Some may even have thought that the entire tournament was to be held in South Africa, but clearly the ICC believed that the game of cricket needed to be popularized in other parts of Africa, so games were also scheduled for Zimbabwe and Kenya. These were countries that had had more than their share of political tension and upheavals – but as many involved in sport down the years have said, why can't we keep politics out of sport? We were eventually to realize that such an idea just wasn't possible in the modern world.

We left England in the middle of October for the Ashes series, after which we'd be taking part in a triangular one-day series in Australia, and then going on to the World Cup. If all went according to plan, we wouldn't be back home till the end of March. As usual, I went into cricket mode, concentrating on doing my very best as a sportsman, aware that it would be a very hard tour. I'm sure that was the mindset of the other guys as well. This is just how it is on a modern cricket tour, when you're shooting around a vast country like Australia, dealing with the constant shuttling between airport, hotel and cricket ground. There's hardly any time to step back and think about issues other than your family back home and what you're out there for. So it wasn't surprising that we took some time to get to grips with the Zimbabwe situation. We weren't aware until the end of the Ashes series early in January that this was becoming such a serious matter, with opinions divided back home on whether we should go to Harare the following month.

We weren't so stupid as to be totally ignorant of the deteriorating situation in Zimbabwe. Most of us had been on England tours out there in recent years, and some of their top players had played either club or county cricket in our country, and they'd told a few of us how it was under the dictatorship of Robert Mugabe. For instance, Nasser Hussain and Ronnie Irani had Andy Flower with them at Essex in the summer of 2002, and I know that Andy had marked their cards about how difficult life was getting in Zimbabwe. So we didn't have our heads in the sand, but it was demanding enough trying to compete in the Ashes series while at the same time looking forward to the arrival of our families over the Christmas and New Year period. We also believed that, if the issue was now that serious, then our employers at Lord's and the British Government would sort it out, leaving us to get on with our job of playing for our country wherever we were sent. That was the first of many naïve assumptions over the next few weeks.

After the final Test ended in Sydney on 6 January, Nasser said a few significant things to us. He said that the situation over Zimbabwe was now very complex, that we were going to get dragged into it, and that some hard thinking lay ahead of us. 'Make sure you take your grown-up pills,' and although that seemed a harsh statement at the time, it certainly made me sit up and take notice. How right he proved to be. It turned out to be a huge burden on our captain, as he tried to work out the World Cup strategy, to settle on our best eleven, and to win a triangular series in January, while being asked all the time by the media about Zimbabwe. It was far too much for one cricketer to take on.

Some of our families who turned up for the holiday period had told us that Zimbabwe was now a hot topic at home, that the politicians were wriggling, expecting the ECB to make the decision about going there, while keeping their own hands clean. The ECB were pointing out that many British countries traded in and with Zimbabwe without getting any stick, so why pick on English cricketers? Lord's wanted Tony Blair to make the final decision, but the Government just tut-tutted and stayed on the boundary edge. This summary was confirmed by the guys in the one-day squad who joined us in Sydney. They said the issue was now leading the TV news bulletins, occupying the newspapers and generating a lot of opinion polls. The British public appeared to be split, which wasn't the best news for us. Whatever we decided to do, we'd get hammered by a large section of the British public. No wonder Nasser wanted us to get thinking hard about Zimbabwe. Politics was mixing with sport, whether we liked it or not.

Let me make it clear that we were genuinely concerned about the moral issues. The more we read about the situation in Zimbabwe when we were in Australia during the month of January, the more we worried about the effect a game of cricket would have. Every day I logged on to the internet and read four English national newspapers, grateful for the balanced coverage. We weren't getting that from the Australian press, which didn't seem particularly interested. Strange, considering that Australia were due to play one game there as well. A TV programme that was filmed undercover in Zimbabwe was seen by Nasser on the CNN channel when we were in Sydney. That made a big impression on him – and on us, especially when he reminded us that we had played golf on the same course where opponents of Mugabe were dumped in bunkers after being tortured to death. On that programme, the Mayor of Harare said that the English cricketers wouldn't be welcome next month, while his counterpart in Bulawayo – where the Aussies were due to play – took a different stance. How were we going to take the right decision when there were contrasting opinions about our trip in Zimbabwe itself?

During our team meetings in Australia, we all agreed that we hated what was going on in Zimbabwe and that we now had to step outside our usual mind-set as professional cricketers and look at the wider issues. But would one game of cricket make any difference? Would President Mugabe soften his attitude to opposition if we took a moral stand? All the information that was coming our way suggested not.

I found it very hard to make a concrete decision and stick to it during January. I felt that the British Government ought to have taken the decision away from us, but the fact that I've bothered to vote only twice at elections underlines my general lack of political knowledge. We were going to be on our own on this one, and likely to get serious stick whatever we decided. It was argued that we shouldn't go because that one game of ours could lead to a peaceful demonstrator being killed or seriously injured. I'd read about the death of an activist who had been arrested and tortured because he handed out anti-Mugabe leaflets during the Test against Pakistan in November. Meanwhile the ECB kept telling us the match would go ahead, provided our safety was guaranteed. The possibility of forfeiting four points was another factor mentioned by the ECB chairman, David Morgan, when he came out to advise us in Australia. That was important to us, of course, but we could still get through the qualifying stages even if we did forfeit those points. All we had to do was play well against the other sides in our group and win. That was the cricket perspective – but what about the moral one? Everybody in the squad, from twenty-year-old James Anderson to 39-year-old Alec Stewart, was grappling with the dilemma a month before we were due to go to Zimbabwe. Anyone who criticized us for sticking our heads in the sand ought to remember that. From the start of January, we were asking all sorts of questions. Too late, perhaps, but no one should doubt our sincerity and anguish over a dilemma that was to leave us isolated for a time when we got to South Africa.

Before we left Australia, something else was put into the mix. Every member of the squad at the Sydney cricket ground received an envelope containing a document outlining the current situation. This came from a protest group that urgently requested us to stay away from Zimbabwe. There were four pages in which strong views were expressed but – contrary to some press reports – no death threats were made. In fact there was no hint at all of physical violence if we did play in Harare. The documents included clearly expressed opinions and important, up-to-date information about what it was like to live in Zimbabwe under Mugabe. It was propaganda, of course, but we didn't doubt the sincerity of the views and the conviction that there might be serious disorder if we went there. We were asked to think about our responsibilities as human beings rather than just as international cricketers.

Those envelopes were a big talking point over the next few days as the Professional Cricketers' Association representative, Richard Bevan, started putting pressure on the ECB and the ICC on our behalf. Richard had various conference calls from London with Nasser, confirming that the situation in Zimbabwe was extremely volatile and needed to be monitored closely every day. With a fortnight to go before we were due to fly to Harare, we were still going – provided the safety and security issues were satisfactorily addressed – but we were unsure about it and getting concerned that we were being pushed out on a limb. We had signed contracts to play in the World Cup for our country, including going to Zimbabwe, but had the position fundamentally altered since putting pen to paper?

On Monday 27 January, just one day before we were due to fly to South Africa to prepare for the World Cup, we came out against playing in Harare. In a statement delivered on our behalf in London by Richard Bevan, we called for the match to be moved to South Africa for moral, safety and security reasons. We'd talked it over and over and had come to the conclusion that the new information gathered by Richard suggested that it was less safe to go to Zimbabwe than it had appeared a week or so earlier. The Mayor of Harare could no longer guarantee security, and we understood that the police would put down any protests in brutal fashion. We didn't want our presence there to be a reason for anyone being hurt as they made legitimate, peaceful demonstrations. Our statement deplored the lack of involvement by our own government and also expressed sympathy for the ECB's position – but we didn't want to go.

Before we flew out, Nasser told us all to say absolutely nothing in public, as Richard Bevan and the PCA were doing a fine job for us back home. We just had to sit tight, and hope our appeal would be granted and that we'd have no more meetings to endure, with people talking round and round the subject. By then I was convinced that we wouldn't be going to Zimbabwe, whatever the ICC's security experts offered to ease our worries. I was fairly optimistic that the ICC would move all the Zimbawe games to South Africa when they had their board meeting later in the week. There was still time to re-locate the matches, starting with ours on 13 February, and any compensation to the Zimbabwe Cricket Union could surely be met out of the fat profits that were going to be made out of the World Cup. Which just shows how naïve we cricketers can be...

After a few days in South Africa, I understood that England's standing in world cricket's corridors of power wasn't very high. We were seen as whingeing Poms, too precious about our own welfare. Other countries were going to Zimbabwe, so why were we so special? Also it became clear that Dr Ali Bacher, who was in charge of the whole thing, saw this as a World Cup for Africa, not just his own country. So both Kenya and Zimbabwe would stage their matches, whatever we said. It was politically too sensitive to pull out altogether. We were isolated. There was another consideration that dawned on us as we surfed the internet, gathering facts and opinions. South Africa desperately wanted to stage the football World Cup in 2010, having missed out on previous ones. Votes from the other African nations were vital in the next round of wheeler-dealing, so it made sense to spread the cricket around other African countries. They didn't want anything to go wrong in the 44 days of the cricket World Cup, so if England had strong reservations about playing in Zimbabwe, we would be left out on a limb. The stakes were too high to bother about what England cricketers thought.

I wasn't surprised that the ICC World Cup technical committee turned down our request to move the Harare fixture, nor that our appeal was rejected the following day. Nelson Mandela had just voiced his disapproval of England's attitude and when a man of his great stature and integrity comes out on the other side, you have a problem. We were in a corner, aware of the financial damage we'd be doing to English domestic cricket by the proposed boycott, concerned about forfeiting four points and anxious about how it looked to the British public. Were we being over-cautious about our safety, or should we take a stand over the morality issue? They were to be the discussion points during an agonizing, traumatic weekend that nobody in that England squad will ever forget. It would leave us very angry, and convinced that we'd been hung out to dry by people following their own selfish agenda.

On the evening of Friday 7 February, the players met with Tim Lamb, the ECB's chief executive, and David Morgan, its chairman. We then had to digest a letter that had been sent to the ECB offices at Lord's and was, to say the least, a bombshell. Dated 6 January and sent from Harare, it came from an organization called Sons and Daughters of Zimbabwe. The message was frightening. It said that if we went to Zimbabwe, we'd be scoring propaganda points for Robert Mugabe and that there would be deaths as a result.

The third paragraph contained this sentence, typed in capital letters: COME TO ZIMBABWE AND YOU WILL GO BACK IN WOODEN COFFINS! We were then told that people who oppose President Mugabe end up in a pool of sulphuric acid in a place called Goromonzi, a few miles outside Harare. The bodies are dissolved, leaving no trace. The letter compared such treatment to what took place in the concentration camps of Nazi Germany.

The threats then came closer to home. 'Anyway, we know your team. Come to Harare and you will die. And how safe are your families back there in the UK? Even if you survive, there are foreign groups who are prepared to hunt you and your families down for as long as it takes, and they will do that in your very own country. Our advice is this: DON'T COME TO ZIMBABWE OR YOUR PLAYERS WILL BE LIVING IN FEAR FOR THE REST OF THEIR LIVES.'

Now I know many have criticized that group of England cricketers for staying away, but I wonder how any reasonable person would have reacted at the first sight of that letter. It certainly frightened the life out of me. Thousands of miles from home, we were being asked to make a decision that would possibly have a major impact on our families' lives, never mind our own personal safety. And we had to reach that decision very soon.

Tim Lamb was bombarded with hostile questions. He said he felt sure it was a hoax letter, and that it had been passed on to the Metropolitan Police. When did the ECB get the letter? Lamb said they'd thought it best to check out its authenticity before worrying us unduly. We wanted to know why, if it was the work of a crank, and therefore harmless, we weren't told about it when we were in

Australia, agonizing about whether to go to Zimbabwe. Lamb replied that he didn't want to panic us, because we were playing in the triangular VB series, and he wanted us to concentrate on our cricket. That evening he totally downplayed the significance of that letter. Yet, as David Morgan would confirm, we were talking about the Harare issue during that series – in great detail. Even to the extent of getting briefed by Morgan himself. And now, 72 hours before we were scheduled to fly to Harare, we were scared. All Morgan could so was stress to us that our safety was of paramount importance to the ECB.

We asked Tim Lamb and David Morgan to support our call for a boycott on the grounds of personal safety, on behalf of ourselves, our families and any demonstrators at the match. They asked for more time. Clearly it was going to be a fraught weekend in the Cullinan Hotel.

Our next meeting that evening was with Malcolm Speed, the chief executive of the ICC. He began by saying he only had a few minutes, which didn't impress us as we tried to come to terms with that frightening letter. Nasser fronted him up straight away about it, and Speed said it would be dealt with in a security briefing with us shortly. He was evasive and very unimpressive. He kept saying that everything would be dealt with later by someone else. We felt he was fobbing us off and Nasser was very forthright. A week later, it was suggested that Nasser swore at Speed in that meeting and that ECB executives had to apologise to him for our captain's rude behaviour. That was nonsense. At no stage did Nasser or anyone swear in that short meeting with Malcolm Speed. Voices were raised and quite right too because we were getting nowhere with him. In ten minutes, he didn't give us one satisfactory answer. He must have understood our concerns, but he showed no sign of it.

It got worse. We now went into a meeting with three

security experts who had come along to try to reassure us and get us on that plane to Harare. There was Patrick Ronan, the head of the World Cup security directorate, Andre Pruiss, the number two of South Africa's police who was also in charge of policing the competition, and Peter Richer, who was employed by Kroll Associates. This was an independent risk-analysis company which had checked out the security and safety aspects in Zimbabwe and come to the conclusion that there would be no worries about staging any of the World Cup matches there. All three of them were to prove unimpressive. They were exposed and humiliated by our representatives, Richard Bevan, who had now flown out to join us in his PCA capacity, and Gerrard Tyrrell, our lawyer. Another lawyer, Mark Roper-Drimie, was there to represent the ECB.

First we had to sit through a slide show. I'm not joking! We were told it wouldn't take long. It did – an hour and a quarter. All it offered was assurances that security and safety would be guaranteed and that the World Cup was going to be a huge success. Nothing about the issues which were worrying us. We had to sit through all that, wondering when the big picture was going to start? It was insulting. We didn't need to be told about the competence of our security guards in South Africa – we were all used to that. We wanted to know about that letter and the safety of our families at home. Thet letter had come to our attention only two hours earlier, but they took no notice of how much it had wound us up.

Patrick Ronan told us he'd never heard of the Sons and Daughters of Zimbabwe, while Andre Pruiss was dismissive, saying he probably got about twenty similar letters every day. He would know about the organization if it was a serious one – but he operated out of South Africa, someone pointed out, so why would he know about a

Zimbabwean group? He said he worked closely with his counterpart in Zimbabwe. We weren't convinced at all. The discussions started to get heated because we felt we weren't being treated seriously. They gave off the feeling that they were the professionals in this area, and they wouldn't tell us how to play cricket, and that meant that serious safety matters should be left to them, without any questions being asked.

Peter Richer, the Kroll man, was particularly patronizing and arrogant. His attitude was that his company was one of the biggest surveillance units in the world and that they knew best. He was pulled up by Gerrard Tyrrell, who was outstanding in his cool, clinical way. Gerrard had seen the Kroll report, which had rubber-stamped the security measures for the World Cup games in Kenya and Zimbabwe. He asked Richer to confirm that five intelligence items had been omitted from his final report for security reasons, and could he tell us why? If the letter was just a hoax, then why leave it out of his report? Why not come clean and show confidence, rather than appear to be covering something up?

Richer just waffled. He wouldn't be drawn by Gerrard Tyrrell, other than to confirm that the five items had been reported orally to the World Cup security directorate. He gave no credible reason why they weren't down in black and white in his report. For the next 45 minutes, he was on the back foot, deflecting all questions and panicking. Finally, Mark Roper-Drimie, who had also seen the Kroll report, asked him if he would like to take further instructions on the matter – legalese for 'can I see you outside?'. We were about to learn that Richer had in fact addressed the ICC on the letter earlier and that this had been kept from us. Roper-Drimie had been at the same meeting and had taken Richer outside to remind him of that fact. When they returned to our meeting Richer then blurted out that someone had been arrested three days earlier in connection with the letter but had since been released. Yet, an hour earlier, he had told us the whole thing was just a hoax! He wouldn't go into details about the arrest, pleading security reasons, but he was just digging a bigger hole for himself. With the stakes so very high, Richer's company had been paid a lot of money to do this report, but he was very unconvincing on the central issue – safety and security.

By now it was dawning on us that we were just pawns in a far bigger game. The World Cup was about to start, with the opening ceremony to take place the following night, here in Cape Town. The ICC, the World Cup Organizing Committee and all their security back-up people just wanted the tournament to go ahead without a hitch for the next 44 days and everything else to be swept under the carpet. Including death threats to England cricketers and their families. Whatever happened subsequently could be dealt with, even though it might be highly relevant to the World Cup. South Africa must be shown in its most favourable light.

Our mood was very hostile as all that sank in. Questions were thrown at the three security experts and voices were raised. Understandably so. We were being patronized and misled, and the full picture was being dragged out of them unwillingly. Pruiss told us, 'We can't say anything about the letter, but there's a long story behind it. We're not prepared to identify the person behind the Sons and Daughters of Zimbabwe.' Amazingly, as the questions rained down on him, he then blurted out, 'Don't worry, boys, if anything goes wrong, we've got the South African SAS to pick you up and take you out.' How reassuring was that? When he said that, the players all just switched off, amazed at how hopeless these people were. David Morgan just sat there, shaking his head in disbelief. We were very angry now; we felt our time had been totally wasted. When the security blokes left, the players took a vote. It was a secret ballot, with fifteen pieces of paper passed around the room. It came out fifteen to none against going to Zimbabwe. That was the only vote taken by us all throughout that weekend, and although some later wavered and changed their minds, the majority remained against going.

So, after seven hours of anguished wrangling, we broke up. At no stage did any of our tour management attempt to influence us, the only advice and guidance we received coming from Richard Bevan, with legal input from Gerrard Tyrrell. I know that many outsiders have questioned Duncan Fletcher's role in all these discussions because of his Zimbabwean connections, but he didn't get involved at any stage. Duncan was admirable, refusing to offer any opinion, because he realized that he mustn't be seen to influence the players one way or the other. He could have talked for hours about the drastic changes in his homeland since he had captained Zimbabwe twenty years earlier, but he correctly said it was the players' decision and only theirs. We respected his judgement on that, and at no stage was he pressurized to give his views. Duncan's integrity was never in doubt during the whole saga.

But it was clear that we fifteen England players were on our own. In our meeting I had said to the other players, 'I hope everyone in this room is asking himself hard questions, rather than just taking the easy option by simply saying, "I won't go." We've got to make an honest, adult decision.' Easier said than done, however. We were in and out of each other's rooms in the early hours of that Saturday morning, tossing around the options and sharing impressions from the various meetings we'd just endured. I didn't get to bed until after two o'clock after talking to Lynn and my parents. I didn't want to panic Lynn, so I didn't tell her a great deal about the contents of that disturbing letter. As far as I was concerned, at that stage I wasn't going. I assumed from the contents of the letter that my family and I would be safe if I stayed away from Zimbabwe in a few days' time. No contest, then. I was torn on the morality issue. It would have been terrible if demonstrators got hurt because we were there, so on that basis too the game shouldn't go ahead. Then I played Devil's Advocate – would that game of cricket really be a huge propaganda boost for President Mugabe? Didn't a lot of Zimbaweans want us to go there to boost their morale? What about making some sort of gesture of support for Mugabe's critics when we arrived at the ground?

I asked Dad his opinion. He felt that the issue was bigger than a game of cricket, and that if any Zimbabwean people were going to be hurt or killed because of our presence there, then I shouldn't go. That was also my gut instinct, but it was good to have it confirmed by someone whose judgement I totally trusted and who had been around the world a lot in the course of a long cricketing career. This was unlike anything he had ever undergone, but at least he could visualize from first-hand experience how cricketers were having to make major decisions, even though out of our depth. The central issue was that letter. It wasn't being taken seriously enough by the security executives, and we had been very disappointed and angry at our shambolic meeting with them.

On the Saturday morning, our unanimous vote against going to Zimbabwe was conveyed to the ECB executives, after which the chairman, David Morgan, had one-to-one discussions with all of us over the next 24 hours. I had been impressed by David over the past month as he tried to steer a path through all the complicated procedures. He was at all times calm, reasonable and sympathetic to the anguish that the players were suffering. I spent half an hour with him and, although he had his ECB hat on, I felt he was very impressive. David pointed out the ramifications to English domestic cricket if we didn't play in Harare – the loss could be up to £10 million; a lot of county cricketers could lose their jobs; and Zimbabwe might play tit-for-tat and boycott their tour of England, which was scheduled for May and June. I took all that on board. It was a good, constructive chat, and I know from talking to the younger players that they were all impressed by David, and the absence of arm-twisting. All he did was set out the scenarios in an intelligent, sensible manner.

But I still wasn't budging in my decision. That letter remained the central issue for me. On that Saturday afternoon, we had another meeting with Tim Lamb and David Morgan that lasted three hours. I noticed a change of emphasis in their approach. Tim was particularly keen to stress the financial implications for the game in England if we boycotted Zimbabwe. It appeared to us that he was now focusing too much on money, rather than the genuine fears for our safety or the moral issues that troubled us. He had seen the impact that letter had on us the night before, but it didn't seem so vital to him. I got the impression that he was convinced it was a hoax and that, given time, it would all blow over, removing a crucial objection to the match. He had more faith in the security experts than we did! We also thought it strange that after Tim Lamb had spent the last week trying to convince the ICC it was unsafe for us to go to Zimbabwe he now had turned it around and was asking us to go there after all. This was no time for inconsistency. It was a frustrating, disappointing meeting.

Then, just as a reminder of why we were in South Africa, we rushed to Newlands for the opening ceremony. It was a fantastic occasion, superbly staged, but in its own way it only confused us further. As Nasser led us around the packed stadium, carrying the flag of St George, I felt very proud to be English and thrilled to be taking part in a wonderful sporting event that seemed to be generating such joy among the people of South Africa. That ceremony brought home to me just how special this World Cup was going to be. My earlier thought kept coming back to me – 'make sure you're asking yourself all the right questions.' This was the sort of occasion you work and live for as an international sportsman, and we were relishing the fantastic atmosphere in Newlands, yet we were being pulled all over the place emotionally. We could handle representing our country at the highest level but not meeting after meeting in the Cullinan Hotel.

I barely managed an hour of sleep that Saturday night as I tossed all sorts of arguments around in my head. Late on Sunday morning we had another players' meeting, which proved to be the most emotional of all. Nasser had clearly been affected by the opening ceremony and he began by saying, 'I want everybody in this room to give his reasons for going or not going.' This had to be the time when the issue was sorted out once and for all. The match was to be played in four days' time, and we needed to travel and prepare for it if the vote came out in favour of going. We'd had enough meetings, and Nasser made it clear that the time for decisive action was now. He'd been under a lot of strain, having had to fend off media enquiries for the past six weeks. He'd also been trying to keep the players switched on to cricket, while at the same time asking them to read up on political issues. It was too much for anyone, and it was understandable that he was fraying around the edges.

Ronnie Irani spoke first. An emotional man, passionate about his cricket, Ronnie had been deeply troubled. He'd been in my room the night before, telling me that until he had found out about the letter, he had been prepared to go. Now, he said, the opening ceremony had inspired and moved him. Ronnie spoke to the players from the heart and he was heard with respect. This was his last chance of winning the World Cup, and he was concerned that we were in danger of early elimination if we sacrificed four points by staying away from Harare. He wondered if we were over-dramatizing the safety issue. Perhaps that letter really was a hoax? Ronnie said he'd spoken to a number of people in sport that he really respected, including Keith Fletcher, his Essex coach, Frank Dick, the athletics coach, and Andy Flower, the Zimbabwean batsman who'd become close to him the previous summer at Essex. He said he'd worked all his life to play in the World Cup. It was an impressive, emotional and honest speech from someone big enough to admit that he'd had second thoughts.

Then it was my turn. For once in the presence of my team-mates I too was emotional. I told them I couldn't vote because I was now too confused. Too many contradictory factors were cramming in on my mind, and I couldn't be 100 per cent sure I would be making the correct decision. I said, 'I just can't come up with a definite answer. I hope everyone else in this room has thought about it as deeply, because it's easy just to say no. I'm not sitting on the fence, I'm just too confused.' They seemed to take my feelings in the right spirit, and then the others all spoke in turn. Some spoke for just a minute, others for five minutes. Ashley Giles was particularly well-informed and articulate, saying that the welfare of his family was paramount, so he wouldn't be going. The atmosphere was one of total mutual respect: nobody was shouted down, and no one simply said, 'I agree with what he's just said.' Everyone – from youngster to the veteran Stewart – contributed constructively and in an adult manner.

As one of the players was speaking, the door opened and in walked the ECB's Director of Legal Affairs, Mark Roper-Drimie. He seemed rather agitated, saying he had some vitally important news that he must share with us. Nasser dealt with him rather abruptly, giving the impression that he'd had enough of outside advice and that he wanted this to be solely between his players. Roper-Drimie was sent out of the room with his tail between his legs, and told to wait until we had finished our meeting. When it was over, no vote was taken.

Then it was time to hear Mark Roper-Drimie's news. He came back in with Tim Lamb and David Morgan. Roper-Drimie said that the ECB had made the decision for us. We were shown an e-mail from Interpol confirming that the Sons and Daughters of Zimbabwe was a genuine organization and was active in that country. So much for the letter being a hoax. I'm afraid the ECB trio then bore the brunt of the frustrations that been boiling up in us all weekend. Because of the emotional nature of the speeches we had just heard, and all the bearing of souls, some of us were already close to tears. That e-mail put the closure on everything. We were demanding to know, 'How come you've just found out about this when you've had the letter for nearly a month?' Tim Lamb repeated that he hadn't wanted us to be distracted from playing cricket in January, and that it had been important to check out the organization using the proper police channels. But that cut no ice with us.

We had wasted the last 48 hours in meeting after meeting. We'd been palmed off with assurances that the letter was a hoax, that the organization didn't exist. All that agonizing over whether or not to risk going to Harare, all those phone calls back home, trying to reassure our families that we'd do the right thing eventually – those honest, open speeches from the lads, as we shared our fears and our confusion…Why should international cricketers have to cope with that, just before the start of the World Cup? We should have been treated with more honesty and respect. We weren't just cricketers, we were human beings with the same doubts and fears as anyone else. Matthew Hoggard, who spends a lot of time on the Internet, looked up the Sons and Daughters organization as soon as we had been told about it, and reams of stuff then churned out of the printer. The players gathered round, reading up about them. How come the ECB and the ICC security experts were less curious than Hoggy about the group that was threatening us? Why were we being treated so dismissively?

There was no need to take a vote after that dramatic news from Interpol. None of us would be going to Zimbabwe, whatever our employers said. We felt we had been lied to and patronized, and that those in the know had been evasive when asked direct questions by us. Anything I felt about my last World Cup and the wonderful opening ceremony went straight out the window. The safety of my family was the most important thing. None of us was now concerned about the financial implications to English domestic cricket or the loss of four points in the tournament. We had been dodging the huge media scrum gathered in our hotel for the past 48 hours, and had been cooped up in a room, tossing alternatives around, hardly getting any sleep – those reporters downstairs would have had a field day if they'd known just how big a shambles it had become. Anger poured out of us. We were the fall-guys, the ones getting the stick for appearing to be hesitant and faint-hearted, when in fact we had been the victims of evasiveness and lies.

At least Tim Lamb and his two colleagues realized the force of our anger. He said that we wouldn't be going to Zimbabwe in view of the contents of the Interpol e-mail. The ECB had a duty of care to its cricketers and wouldn't put us at risk. The meeting broke up, the players had lunch, and then, two hours later, the meeting was reconvened. We were told that the ECB would be going back again to the ICC with a new appeal, on the grounds that fresh and vital information about security issues had emerged. That would take up the next couple of days.

I never thought we had a chance of winning that appeal, and the events of the next few days proved me right. Our best chance was a 'no result', with the four points shared between us and Zimbabwe. England's board wasn't the most popular within the ICC. Other boards were playing catch-up, particularly those from Asia who had the perception that we were part of the old guard who had run the game worldwide for too long. The power base had shifted, and there was no doubt that England's influence had been reduced. Also Dr Ali Bacher was determined that this World Cup would go ahead without any hitches, with an eye on his country's credibility and the possibility of South Africa staging other prestigious sporting events. In that wider context we weren't important.

We eventually ran out of time the following Saturday, when our last appeal failed. We lost all four points by not fulfilling the Harare fixture, so the next day, when we took the field in East London, against Holland, our World Cup campaign finally started from scratch. It had been a long, emotionally draining week, and it was a relief to be shot of meetings to do with things other than cricket. Trying to get runs on a slow pitch at Buffalo Park was a far more familiar challenge than attempting to cut through the bluff and bluster of Peter Richer and Andre Pruiss.

If the whole issue had been dealt with earlier and with more professionalism, the England players needn't even have been involved. I appreciate that our critics, who felt that we had been naïve, blinkered and ill-prepared, had little sympathy for us, and it's true that we'd had a massive reality check from the start of January. However, more sophisticated minds than ours ought to have been homing in on the Zimbabwe question since the election there in March 2002. Clearly the country had huge social and political problems, so why didn't our Government get more involved? I understand that, when we were out in Australia, a few Government ministers kept giving nods and winks to the media, saying that the trip to Harare shouldn't go ahead – but then they'd shy away from direct involvement. The ECB could have seen this one coming months earlier and thrashed it out with the Government. It was too important to leave to the judgement of fifteen England cricketers. We should have turned up in South Africa at the start of February, knowing exactly where we would be on the 13th, rather than having to search our consciences and grapple with complicated matters over that awful weekend in Cape Town. As soon as we got to South Africa, we knew this was about politics and not sport.

We all appreciated the ECB's position, but for a while we felt that they were more concerned about the financial implications than about the welfare and morale of their employees, the players. And our families. The division between the ECB and the players lasted for only a day, before the emergence of that crucial e-mail from Interpol, and the stick that Tim Lamb and the others got from us was due to frustration. After that, once they confirmed that we weren't going to Zimbabwe, relations improved, and I certainly had no hard feelings towards the ECB officials who were in Cape Town. But there was a vacuum of leadership from both the ECB and our Government over the preceding months. I agreed with the suggestion Nasser made when it was all over – that there should be a committee set up between sporting administrators and the Government to pick their way through issues like the Zimbabwe one. Matters such as the desirability of going to a country with a dodgy human rights record, compensation and safety should all be thrashed out by this committee. It should be the job of experts to sort these things out, not the people playing the sport. Otherwise, when similar situations arise in the future – as I'm sure they will – the ones who represent our country with pride and dedication will once again get dragged into an area where they're out of their depth.

There were a couple of positive aspects to emerge from it all. Because we had been through so much before we bowled a ball in the World Cup, our team spirit became even stronger. Everyone respected the views expressed in our meetings, no one was shouted down and the subject was considered with as much intelligence and sincerity as possible. There was a gap of nineteen years between the oldest and youngest in our squad, and at no stage did anyone play the old pro with the most inexperienced youngster. We may have been unimpressive as we failed to qualify for the later stages in the World Cup, but that had nothing to do with our morale. After what we'd gone through in Cape Town we were as close as any squad can be.

Nasser Hussain also emerged with great credit for his powers of leadership through all the talking. He had created the environment where every player could talk openly, without any recriminations whatsoever. On a smaller scale I had been under pressure as captain during our pay dispute with the ECB before the 1999 World Cup, so I knew how he must have felt as it all crowded in on him since the start of January. Duncan Fletcher felt that, with his Zimbabwean connections, he couldn't be seen to have a public or private opinion, and we all respected that – but it just meant that Nasser was the sole official face and voice of our stance. He coped very well indeed with his media duties, saying just enough to hint at the players' frustrations while being careful not to reveal privileged information. There were a few times during the Ashes series when I felt that Nasser's anger at our failures and his desperate desire to succeed led him to make some harsh remarks, but he was first-class throughout the Zimbabwe discussions. At the end of it all he said to us, 'Look, I know I was a bit aggressive when I said that you'd got to take your grown-up pills, but you did take them and I'm proud of you all for acting in such an adult manner.'

I think the Professional Cricketers' Association grew in stature and influence during those six weeks. The ECB did finally wake up to the significance of it all when we were in Australia, but this was largely because Richard Bevan was there, prodding them on our behalf, and keeping Nasser up to speed with developments. When he came out to South Africa, he and our lawyer Gerrard Tyrrell were absolutely outstanding, asking questions that wouldn't have occurred to us, and letting nobody off the hook. It's been said that Richard has carved out a name for himself as a result of the Zimbabwe episode, and that he is now a very important figure in English cricket, but that's fine by the players who were in Cape Town. We were greatly reassured to have him there and I wish he'd been at my side during the World Cup pay wrangles in 1999. The ECB and the county chairmen will just have to get along with Richard Bevan and the PCA, because the players have complete confidence in him.

Two Zimbabwean cricketers were absolute heroes in our minds. When Henry Olonga and Andy Flower wore black armbands during their first World Cup match, we thought that was a fantastically brave gesture. Their long statement about 'the death of democracy' in their country was hugely impressive. Our decision not to go had been made by then, but their stance would have definitely swayed any of us who might have been wavering. Those two guys will always be regarded with great respect by us. Nasser Hussain and Ronnie Irani had spent some time with Andy, their county colleague, just before the opening ceremony on that Saturday, and they'd reported back that Andy appreciated what a terribly difficult decision it was for us to make. He was very sympathetic, but clearly he wasn't happy about the events in Zimbabwe. That black armband was a brave, symbolic gesture that sent exactly the right message around the world. Later that week, in his press conference, Nasser described Olonga and Flower as 'great men' and we all agreed with the tribute.

One of our former team-mates wasn't exactly flavour of the week around that time. Mike Atherton, in his Sunday newspaper column, was rather dismissive about our motives during that long weekend in Cape Town. He wrote that we were only concerned with the public relations aspects, rather than the rights and wrongs of going to a country like Zimbabwe. His implication was that we were just looking at a way out of it all, that we were typical hard-nosed international sportsmen who couldn't see past our own noses and were not concerned with the humanitarian issues. That didn't go down at all well with us, because we'd been grappling with the moral issues for the past six weeks. In Sydney, a month earlier, we had told David Morgan that we wanted as much information as possible, including press cuttings from England. Richard

Bevan also e-mailed stacks of relevant news from Zimbabwe about the risk of disorder and how things were deteriorating out there. At the end of it all, we could honestly say that we'd paid as much attention to all the aspects as possible. Athers didn't give enough credit to the players' intelligence and sincerity. He didn't know all the facts or what we were going through and should have known better than to write something like that.

We never lost sight of the danger to Zimbabwean people if we'd gone there. We would have been in and out in the space of about 48 hours, but what would happen to those who demonstrated in Harare? We knew about the tortures and mysterious disappearances of those who dared to challenge Mugabe, and we felt all along that a cricket match was not worth one death or serious injury. A few months later, in the official magazine of the Professional Cricketers' Association, an article by a Zimbabwean journalist and broadcaster confirmed our fears. Georgina Goodwin praised us for not going and revealed that an average of fifteen people were arrested for each World Cup game played there. They weren't allowed to see their families or lawyers, some were beaten up by the police, and had electric shock treatment to their tongues and genitals. The Zimbabwean police had assured the ICC that peaceful demonstrations would be tolerated. In the event some people were arrested just for wearing black armbands or for carrying one particular newspaper that didn't publish Mugabe's propaganda. They were thrown into jail for at least a week.

Georgina Goodwin's article didn't surprise me, for I'd read about how the situation was deteriorating in the build-up to the World Cup in January. It was very nice of her to praise us for not going to Zimbabwe, but that's just her opinion and we all knew how complicated the whole issue was. It brought the topic of politics mixing with sport right into my front room, and it's not an experience I ever want again.

We are scheduled to go to Zimbabwe for a Test and one-day series towards the end of 2004. All I can say is that a lot has to change there for England to justify making the trip. Zimbabwe wanted to come to us in May/June 2003 because they needed the money and I had no problems about them playing here from a moral point of view. But going there is a different matter unless the social and political circumstances have drastically improved, quite separately from the safety and security of the England team. You won't find many of the England cricketers who'd been holed up in the Cullinan Hotel all that willing to go. I hope that the Government and the ECB will be thrashing this one out long before the players get sucked into it all. I wouldn't wish any of what we experienced on any cricketer.

It's been said that dipping out of the Harare match lost us the chance of qualifying for the latter stages of the World Cup. I disagree. That game may have looked like a banker four points for us, with Zimbabwe short of quality players, but it wasn't a guaranteed four points. In sport, you can't take such things for granted. Look at Kenya beating Sri Lanka. All the wranglings over Zimbabwe certainly didn't affect the way we played. Anyone who saw us on the field in that tournament, or in practice or around our hotels, could tell you what a close-knit unit we had become. Morale in the squad was never a problem once we started to play.

We went out early because we failed to beat Australia in Port Elizabeth. They needed 70 more to beat us, with just two wickets left, on a poor pitch that inhibited stroke-makers. You really needed to graft on that wicket and I thought our score of 204 for 8 was par. We then got stuck into them and looked home, but you never write off

Australia, especially with Michael Bevan still there. He played wonderfully, Andy Bichel was sound and sensible, and the game ran away from us. Nasser got some stick for preferring young James Anderson to Andy Caddick for the penultimate over, but I can't criticize him for that. We shouldn't have still been out there, Anderson had bowled splendidly in the tournament, and if he'd got a wicket, Nasser would have been hailed as a tactical genius. You've got to back your captain when he has such a difficult call to make. Nasser was always struggling against our inability to take wickets with the old ball in the World Cup. We lacked the variety and the match-winning bowlers in the middle and end of an innings that top sides enjoy. Darren Gough would have made a great difference if he'd been fit.

In winning that match, Australia showed their mental strength. In three out of our last four games against them in 2003 – at Hobart, Melbourne and Port Elizabeth – we should have beaten them in close contests. Successful sides are quick to recognize the key moments when you can win a tight contest, and Australia have the confidence to take it away from you before you realize it. It's the art of winning, and that's why they are a great side.

The day after that huge disappointment in Port Elizabeth, I made up my mind to retire from one-day internationals once the World Cup was over. I knew we were relying on Pakistan to beat Zimbabwe the next day, even to get through to the next stage, but the rain in Bulawayo put a stop to that. So my one-day England career ended in Mauro's restaurant, across the road from the team hotel, when Nick Knight and I got the phone call over lunch. Match abandoned in Bulawayo. England out of the World Cup.

I talked my retirement over with Dad, and he advised me just to let the dust settle, to think it over before I made any decision, but in my mind I knew it was time to go. Duncan Fletcher also advised me to give it some thought, but I've always set myself realistic, achievable targets, and the World Cup in 2007 was out of my reach. I've always played for a purpose, but this time I was also looking at the bigger picture and what was best for England. The selectors needed to start planning for the future. It was time to go.

Nasser Hussain had the same idea. He announced his retirement from one-day international cricket before we left Port Elizabeth for basically the same reasons as me. It would have been preferable if the squad had been told about it before we saw it on satellite television, but that's Nasser's way. I felt Athers handled it better in 1998, telling us about his resignation in the dressing-room in Antigua before going to the press conference. The players should be in the know before the media, in my opinion.

So Nasser and I ended our one-day England careers at the same time, more than thirteen years after they had started, in India during the 1989 Nehru Cup. We had been through a great deal together, and it was a sad way to bow out. It was an anti-climax, but we couldn't use Zimbabwe as an excuse. When it came to the crunch, we didn't do it on the field, and that's where it counts.

CHAPTER SEVENTEEN

still going strong

When the new season began in England after our disappointing early exit from the World Cup, the call was for new, younger blood in the national side. I could understand that – and I was fully aware that my name could come up as a possible casualty. I was forty in April, just a month before the Test action was due to start, and many media pundits and former players felt it was time for a change of wicketkeeper, with Chris Read being the favourite to take over following some rave reviews from the former Australian wicketkeeper and now England selector, Rod Marsh. I had no problems with that, because it's all a matter of opinion. Some are obviously better informed than others, but there was nothing I could do about the speculation. All I could do and all I've ever done is to maintain the standards I had set myself, which had been high enough to enable me to perform at the highest level for the previous thirteen years. If the selectors were to make changes, as far as I was concerned it would be a policy decision on the side of youth rather than a signal that I was no longer the best man for the job.

Fortunately the opinions that really mattered were those of Duncan Fletcher, Nasser Hussain and David Graveney. I very much appreciated a phone call from Grav early in the season, in which he stated his support of me and my position in the team. As the announcement of the team drew closer, in the run-up to the first Test, speculation in the newspapers increased. My form with

Surrey early in the season had been very good – I had passed 50 on each of my three visits to the crease, including an excellent 98 against Nottinghamshire before the Lord's Test, on a difficult Trent Bridge wicket. My desire to continue playing Test cricket was as strong as ever. I had announced my retirement from one-day international cricket at the start of the season, as I believed the time was right to start planning for the 2007 World Cup – a tournament for which I would not be around. I could easily have continued playing, but my decision to stand aside would mean that the selectors could consider new, younger players and give them vital experience of high-pressure games over the next few years, thus maximizing England's chances of winning in the Caribbean in 2007. I believe this is the right strategy to follow in one-day cricket, but Test cricket is different. Test series are there to be won and therefore the best side should be picked. By all means have one eye on the future, but don't weaken the strength and balance of the team just for the sake of it.

Being written off as too old or not good enough in some sections of the media has never really bothered me – people are always entitled to their opinions. However, I have to admit that an article written by Scyld Berry, the cricket correspondent for the *Sunday Telegraph*, did amaze me. His opinions on the game are not well respected in the England dressing-room, and his article about the number of games I had lost as an England player, and why, on that basis, I should not be playing any more, was particularly poor. I received a huge number of letters from cricket supporters around the country, all expressing their disgust that such an article should have appeared in a well-respected newspaper – this would suggest that Mr Berry's thoughts on the game are not always appreciated by the readers. Nasser, who writes a column for the same newspaper, told me that he had received a call from Scyld Berry, who informed him that he was writing this piece. Nasser had rightly told Berry to write what he wanted but stressed that he didn't agree with it.

I know that you can use statistics selectively to prove almost anything, but in the past two years on Test duty – starting with the home series against Pakistan in 2001 – I averaged almost fifty. So I don't believe I'm in decline in terms of my worth to the side and certainly not in terms of my fitness and reactions as a wicketkeeper. The scepticism in some quarters is just another small motivation for me as I remind myself that you're a long time retired. I'm sure David Seaman has the same mind-set. Why else would he move from Arsenal to Manchester City? Because he's a proud professional, still believes he's good enough to be England's first-choice goalkeeper, and wants to play every first-team game he can so that he can prove it. I can relate to all of that.

Personal goals have never driven me, but naturally I was interested that I passed David Gower's tally of Test runs when I scored 68 in the Durham Test against Zimbabwe. The innings pleased me more than that milestone, because it was a slow, low wicket, not at all conducive to stroke-making, and it was great to turn the innings around with Anthony McGrath. Even better to win by an innings with two days to spare, as we did at Lord's. I don't buy into this feeling that those two crushing victories were devalued because Zimbabwe were so weak. A win is a win in professional sport. Throughout the history of Test cricket, some sides have been rolled over comprehensively and we should be glad that we did the job comprehensively. I'm sure we would have copped a lot of stick if we'd struggled to beat Zimbabwe.

As for beating David's aggregate – it didn't mean all

that much, to be honest. He was a top player, and a pleasure to bat with in my early England days, but I'll appreciate such things more when I've packed it in and can mull over my career at leisure. It was nice to be interviewed by David on TV that night and to reminisce, but winning games is more important to me by a long way. The fact that I need only a few hundred runs to pass Graham Gooch to be England's record Test run scorer is also neither here nor there. If that's why you play, then you're there for the wrong reasons. You play for your country, do your best to perform well and, most importantly, hope you do well – but above all you want the team to excel. If you break records along the way, it's an added bonus.

By the end of June, I'd batted five times in the 2003 season. I'd scored four fifties and felt in great nick, but it also seemed very strange not to have played more by this time of year. In years gone by we used to talk about reaching a thousand runs by the end of May, but now I hadn't even batted for a thousand minutes, let alone a thousand deliveries! Surrey had taken the decision that, as England-contracted players, neither Mark Butcher nor myself would play any one-day domestic cricket for them unless injuries occurred and we were needed to fill in. I took this decision in the right spirit but I was frustrated and disappointed, as I've always enjoyed playing for Surrey when not with England. I personally think that we should pick our best available side in the major competitions to give ourselves the best chance of being successful, and to keep our members, supporters and sponsors happy. We at Surrey are very fortunate to have such a strong and talented squad of players at our disposal and I firmly believe that when England players are available to play, they should be selected. My relationships with Keith Medlycott, the coach, and Adam Hollioake, the captain, did not suffer, although they were both aware that I desperately wanted to play. Another downside of the decision was that I had to wait a whole fortnight after the Durham Test before I could get some meaningful practice on grass – and then only because I was able to make use of the net bowlers provided for the England one-day squad at the Oval before the game against Pakistan. Just a few months earlier I had been an important member of England's World Cup squad; now I was struggling to get a net! It was proving to be an odd kind of season…

There were many high points, however. Being awarded the OBE in the Queen's Birthday Honours List was a proud moment for me and my family. Six weeks before the announcement, I received the usual letter from the Prime Minister's office, asking whether I would accept the honour – a bit unnecessary for a proud Englishman like me! I had also drawn level with Dad, who, in his familiar competitive way, had often reminded me that his OBE was one up on the MBE that I had been awarded in 1998!

I was also surprised and delighted to be the subject of *This Is Your Life*, screened by the BBC in June. Michael Aspel and his production team had stitched me up well and truly, with the willing assistance of my family and friends and the main instigator, Richard Thompson, my testimonial committee chairman. I had no suspicions about Richard's suggestion of a pleasant round of golf with him, Ali Brown and Graham Thorpe at the RAC Club in Epsom, followed by a quiet lunch. How wrong I was – as I left the eighteenth green I was greeted by TV cameras and Michael Aspel with the big, red book. For once in my life I was almost lost for words!

On the way to the studios in Teddington, I wondered who the special guests would be, and I was hoping that Kevin and June Gartrell would have made it from Perth in

Western Australia. They had indeed been flown over, and it meant a lot to me to have them there – they had done so much for me during my time playing club cricket in Australia in the eighties. Kevin's contribution lasted about twenty minutes – fortunately the editors did a skilful job and cut him down in the finished product! I was also very pleased that Geoffrey Boycott was able to come down from Barnsley to pay tribute. That was his first public appearance since contracting throat cancer the previous summer, and it was a fantastic effort by a man who has helped me so much with my cricket since my early days of playing for England. Many others who have helped shape my career were there too, as well as my Surrey team-mates and the likes of Graham Gooch, Nick Knight, Angus Fraser, Graeme Hick, Mike Gatting, Tom Moody, Duncan Fletcher and my first Surrey room-mate, Graham Monkhouse. John Hollins, my hero at Chelsea when I was a boy, was present, and current Chelsea players such as Gianfranco Zola, Marcel Desailly, Graeme Le Saux and Frank Lampard paid tribute to me in a video from the training ground. Brian Lara and Sir Bobby Robson also sent video messages to help make the day a very special one for me and my family.

When you're the subject of *This Is Your Life*, it usually means that you've done something worthwhile in your chosen profession, and there's also a hint that you might be nearing the end of your career. Two months after that programme was recorded, I took the decision to retire from Test cricket at the end of the summer. It was something I had been considering since the start of the season and once I had made my mind up I felt very comfortable with my decision.

Believe it or not, I finally sorted it out on my own as I was driving up the M6 motorway. You have a long time to think these days on Britain's motorway system! I was on my way to Birmingham on the Sunday night before the Edgbaston Test and things simply slotted into place for me. When I checked into my hotel, I rang Lynn and my parents to tell them my decision. The response in both cases was: 'Are you one hundred per cent certain?' and no pressure was put on me at all. That's always been the case with Lynn throughout our marriage and Dad knew me well enough to know that I needed to make the decision on my own. He might have tried to talk me out of it, so it was best to work it all out by myself.

On the Tuesday morning before we left for the nets at Edgbaston, I informed Duncan Fletcher, David Graveney and Nasser Hussain. I told Duncan first and I know that he was surprised. He was excellent about my decision, very supportive. He said, 'I won't talk you out of it, you always have to make four or five crucial decisions in life and this is one of them.' I'd talked to Grav at Edgbaston a fortnight earlier during a county match for Surrey and said that I'd tell him about my plans as soon as I knew what I wanted to do. He didn't put any pressure at all on me – just reminded me that the selectors needed to know my intentions some time in August. Of course, I understood that and felt relieved when I'd finally sifted through all the permutations.

I still believed I could play at the highest level, and my innings in the second Test against Zimbabwe in a tricky situation confirmed that. The challenge of a Test series against South Africa would certainly motivate me – after Australia, they have consistently been the toughest competitors in the four series I'd played against them – so there would be no problem about motivation for me for the rest of the summer. But the thought of touring again was the main issue that made up my mind.

At that time, England were scheduled to tour Bangladesh and Sri Lanka before Christmas 2003, then the Caribbean from the following February onwards – just too long a haul for me. There was the lure to tour the West Indies again, because I love playing out there, but it would have meant a ridiculous amount of time away from home. I had made up my mind up and was 100 per cent happy with my decision.

The time I had taken off in the winter of 2001–2 had been an eye-opener. I'd thoroughly enjoyed leading a normal life. There's life outside of cricket and that six months I spent away from the England team made my eventual decision an easy one. Mind you, Lynn is aware of the new deal – every other Saturday spent at Stamford Bridge and then into Europe with Chelsea as long as they stay in the Champions' League!

That Edgbaston Test was the end of an era in two ways, with Nasser Hussain announcing his resignation as England captain at the end of the match. I completely respect his decision and the reasons for it. I could relate to how he felt when he walked back into the England dressing-room after being away for the one-dayers, when Michael Vaughan had been in charge instead. I had a taste of it for a time when returning at Lord's for the Sri Lanka Test in 2002, after missing out on the tours to India and New Zealand. The boys would chatter about things that had happened when you weren't there and you just had to keep quiet and make no contribution to the banter. That's hard for the likes of me and Nasser!

On that first day at Edgbaston, when we took a hammering in the field, his captaincy was slightly different, not as animated, particularly compared to the previous Ashes series a few months earlier. Nasser wasn't stamping his style in the field as he normally did. He had given everything to the job and clearly felt he had nothing more to give. Losing in Australia had taken its toll, he'd been left out on a limb over the Zimbabawe issue and he knew that some commentators in the press were favouring Michael Vaughan to take over, rather than staying with the familiar face.

Players always know that something's up, so we weren't all that surprised when the announcement was made. All the selectors were at Edgbaston, gathered in one room and I just sensed that Nasser was going to make an announcement. When he came off the field, not out after a rain break in that final session, I had a private word with him. I'd been there when Graham Gooch and Mike Atherton had resigned and recognized the vibes, so I told him, 'I'm not going to persuade you to stay on, but just be clear in your own mind what you want to do. Don't get talked into anything that you don't want to do.'

When the game drifted to a draw, the South Africans came in, shook hands and left our dressing-room. Nasser did what he usually does in such situations: he talked us through the game, pointing out that South Africa had had the better of the draw and stressing the need for us to improve for the rest of the series. Then he calmly announced he would no longer be captain and that Michael Vaughan would take over – but he'd still be available as a player. We all applauded Nasser – out of respect – and then Duncan stood up, saying some very complimentary and justified things about Nasser. After more sincere applause from the players Nasser went off to the press conference and the familiar dressing-room joking kicked in. Anthony McGrath, a funny man and close team-mate of Vaughan, said to him, 'Does that mean I don't have to do short-leg any more, because I'm your mate?' I then piped up, 'Don't forget that Goochy did that job in his first Test after handing it over to Athers. So I reckon Nass is the prime candidate!' Then Ashley Giles, a huge mate of the new captain, offered to carry Vaughany's kit to his car. Dressing-room humour can certainly be cruel to be kind!

Beneath all the banter, I felt sad. It's never a happy moment when an England captain stands down and this was the third time I'd experienced it. I'd seen what it had taken out of Nasser in his four years in the job and I knew what I'd gone through in just one year as captain. We have got to know each other pretty well down the years and I admire the way he has given so much of himself to the job and the pride he has displayed at the honour. His passion and dedication shine through and that's why he occasionally went too far in his rollickings on the field, especially on that last tour to Australia. Some people say he's selfish about his cricket, but I disagree. I prefer to describe him as single-minded. Why shouldn't he want to have extra throw-downs in the nets, keeping the bowlers there for a session that he feels he needs? Nasser wanted to do well for himself and the team and his strong work ethic was something to be admired.

I hope that Nasser will now go out and express himself as a batsman, without the cares of captaincy. In my time, former England captains have been easily re-assimilated into the chemistry of the side when they are just players, and there's no reason why Nasser can't be the same as Gooch, Gatting, Stewart and Atherton. It was important that Nasser didn't throw away his England career at Edgbaston, no matter how tired he was feeling. He's still one of England's top six batsmen and I hope he goes on. His most important legacy is that he, along with Duncan Fletcher, improved England as a unit and also laid the foundations for continued success. No one could have given more of himself to the job than Nasser Hussain.

CHAPTER EIGHTEEN

the final curtain

Two days before my final Test match, I had decided that I would retire from all cricket immediately afterwards. I would never play another game. So my final England appearance would be the last time I appeared on a cricket field, playing the sport I loved so much.

My reasons were perfectly straightforward. I had changed my mind about ending my career where it had all begun, with a farewell season with Surrey. I told Paul Sheldon, Surrey's chief executive officer, and Richard Thompson, chairman of cricket, that I was now questioning what I'd still be playing for. The motivation of proving myself at the highest level would have been no more, so I'd just be playing for the sake of it and to me, if you can't strive to reach the top then it's time to move on.

My contract was up and I question whether Surrey would have given me another one anyway for just one more season. The club was feeling the pinch, with all the ambitious redevelopment plans for the Oval meaning a lot of expenditure. Our fine batsman Ian Ward had been a casualty of the belt-tightening, with no new contract offered to him, and he left to join Sussex. So I was perhaps helping Surrey out of a dilemma by packing it in.

I was flattered that several other counties were after me but there's no way I could have played for anyone else. It will always be 'Surrey's Alec Stewart' and I'm proud of my long association with a great club, sharing in its many successes. So I'd be going out, hopefully on a high note, in less than a week's time, on 8 September.

In the weeks between my retirement announcement at Edgbaston and the Oval Test, there was a lot of press speculation that the selectors were possibly being soft about keeping me in the side, and that younger, fresh blood was needed. After all, Chris Read had impressed in the one-day series before we played South Africa in the Tests and I was the obvious target again for those who clamoured for youth. Nasser Hussain was also rumoured to be vulnerable, especially after his indifferent start in the series.

I didn't take any notice of the discussions in the press, because I had gladly learned to trust the selectors in their desire for consistency and continuity. I trusted in my own ability, and believed my experience and skills were still required during the transitional period between Nasser handing over the captaincy and Michael Vaughan bedding down in the job. At no stage did I ever feel I was putting the selectors on the spot about my continued presence in the side. All I had said at Edgbaston was that I would no longer be touring and that the South African series would be my last. I never said that my last Test would be on my home ground at the Oval, I just hoped to be good enough to stay in the team for the whole of the series.

It would have been a disappointment if I hadn't stayed the course, because I felt I was still worth my place. I had a poor Test at Lord's, both with the bat and the gloves. The ball swung and wobbled all over the place when we bowled, but that's no excuse. I wasn't up to my usual standard and because I was now forty years of age, one bad game was deemed to be relevant in some quarters. But the opinions of those who matter the most prevailed and the selectors kept faith in me for the next Test at Trent Bridge. That was a good match for the two veterans, with Nasser

Hussain's gutsy hundred showing the importance of character and an intense competitive spirit, while I made 72, batting well with the tail. On a poor pitch, where I had to stand much closer to the stumps, I felt I'd kept wicket very well, back to my best. More importantly, we made the best of the difficult pitch and won, to square the series.

Then we threw away the fourth Test, at Leeds. That was a game we should have won. We played good cricket for seventy per cent of that match, yet they won the key sessions. Marcus Trescothick and Mark Butcher admitted they got it wrong in going off for bad light when we were hammering the South African bowlers on the second day. They thought we'd be off for some time, but the South Africans regrouped in the dressing room, bowled much better at the resumption of play, and we then lost key wickets and the momentum. Hindsight's a wonderful thing, though.

So when we came to the Oval, 2-1 down in the series, my last Test was of secondary importance, I'm glad to say. I did all the necessary media stuff two days before, and was glad to get it out of the way to concentrate on the game. I can honestly say that I treated it like any other Test match, with the incentive of squaring the series against a top South African side very strong.

I was very touched by all the messages of goodwill, from the likes of Steve Waugh and the Australian Prime Minister, John Howard, to England supporters whom I didn't know. They all meant a great deal to me. Surrey presented me with a bat that had all my England career details inscribed on the front. Unfortunately, someone spelled 'dismissals' wrong, so it had to go back to be corrected! Can't get the staff these days...

At the England team meeting on the eve of the Test, the lads had a good laugh at my expense. Malcolm Ashton, our excellent analyst, put together a video of good individual performances from us during the series, then Duncan Fletcher said some kind things about me. I thought that was it until Malcolm said, 'Oh, just one last video, Stewie', and proceeded to show a catalogue of all my cock-ups behind the stumps and poor shots with the bat. Typical Malcolm, a very funny, dry wit and just the right way to get the boys in the right, relaxed mood. As a perennial winder-up of everyone in the dressing-room, I was more than happy to grin and bear it.

I couldn't have asked for more from that Oval Test. The crowd reception when I went out to bat on the Saturday was outstanding. The state of the game – a high-scoring one – meant that I'd almost certainly bat just the once and I wanted to avoid a nought at the very least and perform well. This was the only time in that Test when the occasion and its significance got to me. I knew my family was there, along with so many friends, and as I walked down the steps to bat for the last time, it hit me. The applause was fantastic and I had to take three or four deep breaths as soon as I got onto the outfield. It was important to me to clear my mind, despite all the emotion, and do my best for the team.

As I got close to the square, Graeme Smith, South Africa's impressively mature young captain, had called his players together to perform a guard of honour and to applaud me to the crease. We had done the same three years earlier at the Oval for Curtly Ambrose and Courtney Walsh and I'm sure they appreciated that gesture as much as I did. Shaun Pollock, who I've always got on well with, didn't miss the chance to throw a little curved ball at me, making me laugh when he joked, 'Don't forget, Stewie, if you get nought here, you're in good company – Bradman did it as well!'

It took me sixteen deliveries to get off the mark and the

cheer from the crowd was deafening. I then played as well as I could, stroking the ball fluently, until Pollock got me lbw for 38. It should've been 138; I was batting so confidently on an excellent pitch. Polly got the last laugh two days later, when we exchanged shirts and he wrote on his, 'This is the shirt I wore to finish off your career!' Many thought the South Africans were a dour lot, but I disagree. They've been excellent opponents in the last decade, playing it hard but enjoying a drink with us afterwards. Guys like Polly, Gary Kirsten, Herschelle Gibbs and Jacques Kallis are top blokes and Graeme Smith is the most impressive 22-year-old I've met in sport. He carries himself very well indeed and he'll be an outstanding representative for South Africa over the next few years.

That Oval Test will always be a special game for me. To win by nine wickets when they were 345 for 2 on the first day was a fantastic effort by England. A key dismissal was that of Gibbs near the close for 183. He was playing so brilliantly that he could easily have reached 300, but he had a dip at Ashley Giles and was bowled. Gibbs got some stick over that dismissal, but that's the way he plays. If that one had gone for six, everyone would have praised a wonderful shot, but this time he chose the wrong option. It happens – as I know only too well!

Dismissing Neil McKenzie off the last ball of that first day gave us hope for the morning session and we bowled brilliantly to dismiss them for 484. A huge stand by Marcus Trescothick and Graham Thorpe brought us close to their total; Freddie Flintoff batted very maturely to get 95 and they then folded in the second innings. It was one of the best fightbacks by England I could recall. The South Africans had been desperate to make up for the disappointment of losing the Test series over here in 1998 and the pressure was on them. That must have been a very quiet dressing room at the end, after they had enjoyed such a great first day, but to their credit they were as good as gold when they came into our rooms for a drink. That's how the game should be played.

So, just after lunch on a lovely sunny afternoon, my cricket career ended in the way I would have wanted: England winning, a flag draped around me, being carried around the ground by Freddie Flintoff and Steve Harmison, and the England supporters cheering themselves hoarse at our great victory. The perfect way to bow out; I couldn't have asked for more.

It was a great boost for our new captain, who had impressed me as he took over under difficult circumstances. Michael Vaughan had just two days to get his head around the job as we went from Edgbaston to Lord's, where we played badly and lost by an innings. I still believe it was a brave decision by Nasser to hand over the captaincy at that stage of the series. Some have suggested that his timing was poor, but I believe he made an honest decision for the good of English cricket; his critics don't know how much the job meant to Nass. He wouldn't have resigned without giving it a great deal of thought and doing what he believed was the best thing for the game.

When reduced to the ranks, Nass handled it all very well, giving advice when asked for it and supporting the new captain to the hilt. That transition period has always been handled well in England sides of my experience – from Graham Gooch onwards – and this was no different.

Michael Vaughan is different in personality to Nass and that's no bad thing. He's a quiet achiever, a good thinker on the game, thorough in his preparation in all aspects of his cricket and already has a good relationship with the coach, Duncan Fletcher. They are both very keen on physical fitness and from what I gather from the lads who were on tour with England over the winter, the fitness levels are now higher than they have ever been. It's important that captain and coach are on the same wavelength.

From his very first Test in charge, at Lord's, Vaughany was good in team meetings. He stressed he wanted advice from Stewart to Anderson, from Hussain to Flintoff and he gave us some deserved stick on the Sunday, after we had lost heavily. He told us that this performance was not good enough, and that we should each of us go away and think about our individual game. It was precise, firm and just what was necessary. He continued to impress me for the rest of the series.

So how will England fare under Michael Vaughan in the long term? I think it's vital that our key players stay fit. Our fast-bowling unit is very promising, with Simon Jones, Steve Harmison, James Anderson, Matthew Hoggard, Freddie Flintoff and Alex Tudor all competing for places. But they need to get on the park consistently. Freddie is improving all the time as our all-rounder and I liked the mature way he built that innings of 95 in the Oval Test. He must keep working on his fitness, because he will bat at number six and bowl a fair number of overs. His bowling is a must for the balance of the side and I hope to see him getting a lot of wickets. He hits the seam and the pitch hard. Freddie also bowls well at left-handers. It's about time he got some luck with the ball, because he has bowled superbly in the past couple of years with not much to show for it.

If we could unearth from somewhere a mystery spin bowler, then we really would be in business. Other countries have them but we possess only regulation finger spinners and they don't win many Tests, with all respect to them. We need to find someone special soon.

Our batting is fine, in my opinion. We'll lose Nasser Hussain soon due to his retirement, but Mark Butcher goes from strength to strength, consistently improving; Marcus Trescothick is a class destroyer; and Graham Thorpe proved with his Oval century that he can stay in the team for as long as he wants. Thorpey is that good. His main asset is his mental strength and now that he's settled and content in his private life, that is good news for England. We have some fine young batsmen around; I've got my eye particularly on Ian Bell, Mark Wagh and Michael Lumb, with older ones like Ian Ward, Robert Key and Ed Smith not out of contention. At least the selectors will give these guys a chance when they get into the side. The days are gone when you were playing for your place in your third innings for England.

Australia are due here in 2005 and they'll still be the ultimate test. Steve Waugh may have gone, but the two top bowlers, Glenn McGrath and Shane Warne, will surely be on the trip. They have been fantastic performers, giving the captain control and great professionalism. But they can't go on forever. Let's see how we go against the Aussies in their back yard in 2007. The ECB's mission statement is for England to be the best in the world by 2007 and I think we can regain the Ashes that year, if not before. The wheel will start to turn in our direction, I'm certain. Fitness, confidence from the selectors and a 'mystery' spinner could easily do the trick for England.

So what will I be doing during all that time? Working for Surrey for some of the period as their Ambassador and Director of New Business. Nice to have a title! My brief is a PR/corporate role as well as trying to attract new sponsors and members to the Oval. It's a job that will see me there for the big international and domestic games, aiming to help Surrey pay for the new ground development, which will make the Oval an excellent new stadium.

I'll be keeping tabs with what goes on out in the middle

as well. We were disappointed to lose the championship last season to Sussex and that's taking nothing away from Chris Adams' excellent team. We failed to win key matches that we would have won in the past; Saqlain Mushtaq was tired after perhaps being over-bowled. We still won two trophies, but Surrey have set the standard and we were annoyed at losing the big one. The team's focus on winning the championship wasn't what it should or could have been.

I was surprised and disappointed that Ian Ward was allowed to leave. The club said they couldn't afford him, but he'd been one of the lowest-paid capped players at our place and his new contract would merely have taken him up to parity. Ian was gutted at leaving and his departure weakened us and strengthened Sussex. He's an absolute banker for 1,200 championship runs per season and he's just as valuable in one-day cricket, as well as being natural captaincy material.

Keith Medlycott also left as our cricket manager. Under his leadership we had won so many trophies, but once Adam announced he was standing down as captain, that meant an excellent working relationship was at an end. The club felt they needed a fresh start in both areas and I was delighted that we got the Australian Steve Rixon as coach. He took New Zealand forward a few years ago and has done excellently with New South Wales. He'll be top drawer for us and it'll be interesting to see how our new captain works with him. Jon Batty has a lot on his plate as opening batsman/wicketkeeper/captain, something I know a little about. I spoke to him about the pros and cons of doing all three jobs, but he wants to do it – and that's a major plus. He's one of the most popular blokes in our dressing room, but he knows that he now has to manage his time very intelligently – a tough task but I hope he succeeds.

I hope Alan Butcher's role is expanded to use his expert

coaching skills with all Surrey teams, from the first eleven down to the various youth teams. Alan will be invaluable for Jon Batty as he learns the ropes and develops his new understanding with Steve Rixon.

Along with my Surrey role, I'll also be working for a sport and entertainment management company called Merlin Elite. There are top-class sports people on the books and I'm enjoying the job from the other side of the fence. But NO, I'm not an agent!

For the next couple of years, I'll look to broaden my outlook in the real working world, rather than go straight into cricket coaching or the media, which can be a little insular. If I'm missing the game a great deal, I could always go back to it full-time, but I feel it's important to see how I can operate in different areas. Hopefully, the jobs at the Oval and at Merlin Elite will help me in man-management and how to organise my time. That can only be beneficial as my new career unfolds.

I didn't miss playing for England at all in the winter. The choice was Bangladesh or watching Chelsea put five past Lazio in Rome – now which one would you go for when you've turned forty? I was sure I'd miss cricket on the day that Surrey were due to report back for training, having enjoyed that day for more than twenty years at the Oval. I'll also have a twinge or two on the first day of the Lord's Test, my favourite ground.

But with the jobs I'm involved in, this is an enjoyable transition. After doing no training at all for three months after the Oval Test, I went back to the gym and I now train three times a week. Can't afford to buy clothes in a larger size, so I must keep the weight down! Golf is my new sporting challenge – but not in the winter – plus some football with Corinthian Casuals. Life after cricket carries on and it's one that I'm enjoying.

statistics

All statistics were supplied by Wendy Wimbush and cover Alec Stewart's career up to and including the Test series against South Africa in summer 2003.

Key
M	matches
I	innings
NO	not out
HS	highest score
Av	average
Ct	catches
St	stumpings
PS	partnerships
HP	highest partnership
BB	best bowling
rh	retired hurt
Dis	dismissals
MM	Man of the Match
Sun	Sunday League
BH	Benson & Hedges Cup
NL	National League
NW	NatWest Trophy
C&G	Cheltenham & Gloucester Trophy
WC	World Cup

test match career

	M	I	NO	HS	Runs	Av	100	50	Ct	St
1989–90 WI	4	8	1	45	170	24.28	-	-	2	-
1990 NZ	3	5	0	54	147	29.40	-	1	5	-
1990–1 Aus	5	10	0	91	224	22.40	-	2	8	-
1991 WI	1	2	1	38*	69	69.00	-	-	4	-
1991 SL	1	2	1	113*	156	156.00	1	-	-	-
1991–2 NZ	3	5	0	148	330	66.00	2	1	3	-
1992 Pak	5	8	1	190	397	56.71	1	2	5	1
1992–3 Ind	3	6	0	74	146	24.33	-	1	-	1
1992–93 SL	1	2	0	63	66	33.00	-	1	5	2
1993 Aus	6	12	0	78	378	31.50	-	3	14	-
1993–4 WI	5	9	0	143	477	53.00	2	2	2	-
1994 NZ	3	4	0	119	196	49.00	1	-	3	-
1994 SA	3	5	1	89	226	56.50	-	2	2	-
1994–5 Aus	2	4	1	33	73	24.33	-	-	2	-

		M	I	NO	HS	Runs	Av	100	50	Ct	St
1995	WI	3	5	0	37	113	22.60	-	-	9	-
1995–96	SA	5	8	0	81	235	29.37	-	1	1	-
1996	Ind	2	3	0	66	136	45.33	-	2	3	-
1996	Pak	3	5	0	170	396	79.20	1	2	2	1
1996–7	Zim	2	4	1	101*	241	80.33	1	1	5	-
1996–7	NZ	3	4	0	173	257	64.25	1	1	14	2
1997	Aus	6	12	1	87	268	24.36	-	1	23	-
1997–8	WI	6	11	1	83	452	45.20	-	4	6	-
1998	SA	5	10	1	164	465	51.66	1	1	23	-
1998	SL	1	2	0	32	34	17.00	-	-	3	-
1998–9	Aus	5	10	1	107	316	35.11	1	2	11	-
1999	NZ	4	8	1	83*	215	30.71	-	2	4	-
1999–2000	SA	5	8	0	95	342	42.75	-	3	13	1
2000	Zim	2	3	1	124*	148	74.00	1	-	4	-
2000	WI	5	8	0	105	195	24.37	1	-	13	1
2000–1	Pak	3	6	1	29	99	19.80	-	-	4	1

test match career (contd)

		M	I	NO	HS	Runs	Av	100	50	Ct	St
2000–1	SL	3	6	1	54	117	23.40	-	1	4	1
2001	Pak	2	3	1	44	102	51.00	-	-	10	-
2001	Aus	5	9	1	76*	283	35.37	-	2	13	-
2002	SL	3	4	1	123	163	54.33	1	-	9	1
2002	Ind	4	6	1	87	287	57.40	-	2	7	1
2002–3	Aus	4	8	2	71	268	44.66	-	3	11	-
2003	Zim	2	2	0	68	94	47.00	-	1	2	-
2003	SA	5	8	0	72	182	22.75	-	1	14	1
		133	235	21	190	8463	39.54	15	45	263	14

Bowling 3.2-0-13-0 England v. West Indies 1993–4

	M	I	NO	HS	Runs	Av	100	50	Ct	St
West Indies	24	43	3	143	1476	36.90	3	6	36	1
New Zealand	16	26	1	173	1145	45.80	4	5	29	2
Australia	33	65	6	107	1810	30.67	1	13	82	2
Sri Lanka	9	16	3	123	536	41.23	2	2	21	3
Pakistan	13	22	3	190	994	52.31	2	4	21	2
India	9	15	1	87	569	40.64	-	5	10	2
South Africa	23	39	2	164	1450	39.18	1	8	53	2
Zimbabwe	6	9	2	124*	483	69.00	2	2	11	-
	133	235	21	190	8463	39.54	15	45	263	14

Debut West Indies, Kingston 1989–90
HS 190, Pakistan, Edgbaston 1992

test match hundred partnerships

Wkt	Runs				Partner	
2	148	New Zealand	Lord's	1990	GA Gooch	
5	122	Australia	MCG	1990–1	DI Gower	
2	+139	Sri Lanka	Lord's	1991	GA Gooch	
3	179	New Zealand	Christchurch	1991–2	RA Smith	
3	227	Pakistan	Edgbaston	1992	RA Smith	
1	123	Pakistan	Lord's	1992	GA Gooch	
2	111	India	Madras	1992–3	GA Hick	
4	122	Sri Lanka	Colombo, SSC	1992–3	RA Smith	
1	121	West Indies	Kingston	1993–4	MA Atherton	
1	171	West Indies	Bridgetown	1993–4	MA Atherton	
4	+115	West Indies	Bridgetown	1993–4	GA Hick	
5	+150	West Indies	Bridgetown	1993–4	GP Thorpe	R
5	115	South Africa	Headingley	1994	JP Crawley	
1	130	India	Trent Bridge	1996	MA Atherton	
2	+154	Pakistan	Lord's	1996	MA Atherton	

374

Wkt	Runs			Partner	
3	107	Pakistan	Headingley	N Hussain	1996
5	108	Pakistan	Headingley	NV Knight	1996
2	+137	Zimbabwe	Bulawayo	NV Knight	1996–7
4	+106*	Zimbabwe	Harare	GP Thorpe	1996–7 R
2	182	New Zealand	Auckland	MA Atherton	1996–7
1	106	Australia	Trent Bridge	MA Atherton	1997
1	+129	West Indies	Port-of-Spain (2)	MA Atherton	1997–8
1	+101	West Indies	Bridgetown	MA Atherton	1997–8
4	+116	South Africa	Lord's	N Hussain	1998
3	+226	South Africa	Old Trafford	MA Atherton	1998
4	119	Australia	MCG	MR Ramprakash	1998–9
4	+104	South Africa	Johannesburg	MA Butcher	1999–2000
4	156	South Africa	Durban	N Hussain	1999–2000
5	+125	South Africa	Centurion	MP Vaughan	1999–2000
4	149	Zimbabwe	Lord's	GA Hick	2000
5	114	Zimbabwe	Lord's	NV Knight	2000 R
4	179	West Indies	Old Trafford	ME Trescothick	2000
10	103	Australia	Edgbaston	AR Caddick	2001

test match hundred partnerships (contd)

Wkt	Runs			Partner	
8	102	Sri Lanka	Old Trafford	2002	AF Giles	R
5	+117	India	Headingley	2002	N Hussain	
6	149	Zimbabwe	Chester-le-Street	2003	A McGrath	R

R = Record for England against the other country

test match opening partners

	Partner		PS	Runs	HP		
1989–90	W Larkins	WI	4	60	42	St John's	1989–90
1991–2/92–3	GA Gooch	Pak	15	528	123	Lord's	1992
1992–3	RA Smith	Ind	2	56	46	Madras	1992–3
1993–4/97–8	MA Atherton	WI	50	1930	171	Bridgetown	1993–4
1998–9/1999	MA Butcher	Aus	6	173	57	SCG +	1998–9
			77	2747	171	Bridgetown	1993–4

hundred opening partnerships

1	123	GA Gooch	Pak	Lord's	1992
2	121	MA Atherton	WI	Kingston	1993–4
3	171	MA Atherton	WI	Bridgetown	1993–4
4	130	MA Atherton	Ind	Trent Bridge	1996
5	106	MA Atherton	Aus	Trent Bridge	1997
6	+129	MA Atherton	WI	Port-of-Spain (2)	1997–8
7	+101	MA Atherton	WI	Bridgetown	1997–8

test matches as wicketkeeper

	M	I	NO	HS	Runs	Av	100	50	Ct	St
1990–1 Aus (5)	2	4	0	11	29	14.50	-	-	6	-
1991 WI (5)	1	2	1	38*	69	69.00	-	-	4	-
1992 Pak (5)	2	4	0	31	49	12.25	-	-	4	-
1992–3 Ind (3)	1	2	0	49	49	24.50	-	-	-	1

test matches as wicketkeeper (contd)

		M	I	NO	HS	Runs	Av	100	50	Ct	St
1992–3	SL (1)	1	2	0	63	66	33.00	-	1	5	1
1993	Aus (6)	6	12	0	78	378	31.50	-	3	14	2
1995	WI (6)	3	5	0	37	113	22.60	-	-	9	-
1996	Pak (3)	1	2	0	54	98	49.00	-	1	1	1
1996–7	Zim (2)	2	4	1	101*	241	80.33	1	1	5	-
1996–7	NZ (3)	3	4	0	173	257	64.25	1	1	14	2
1997	Aus (6)	6	12	1	87	268	24.36	-	1	23	-
1997–8	WI (6)	1	1	1	9*	9	-	-	-	-	-
1998	SA (5)	5	10	1	164	465	51.66	1	1	23	-
1998	SL (1)	1	2	0	32	34	17.00	-	-	3	-
1998–9	Aus (5)	3	6	1	63*	112	22.40	-	1	9	-
1999	NZ (4)	1	2	0	12	23	11.50	-	-	3	-
1999–2000	SA (5)	5	8	0	95	342	42.75	-	3	13	1
2000	Zim (2)	2	3	1	124*	148	74.00	1	-	4	-
2000	WI (5)	5	8	0	105	195	24.37	1	-	13	1

		M	I	NO	HS	Runs	Av	100	50	Ct	St
2000–1	Pak (3)	3	6	1	29	99	19.80	-	-	4	1
2000–1	SL (3)	3	6	1	54	117	23.40	-	1	4	1
2001	Pak (2)	2	3	1	44	102	51.00	-	-	10	-
2001	Aus (5)	5	9	1	76*	283	35.37	-	2	13	-
2002	SL (3)	3	4	1	123	163	54.33	1	-	9	1
2002	Ind (4)	4	6	1	87	287	57.40	-	2	7	1
2002–3	Aus (5)	4	8	2	71	268	44.66	-	3	11	-
2003	Zim (2)	2	2	0	68	94	47.00	-	1	2	-
2003	SA (5)	5	8	0	72	182	22.75	-	1	14	1
Tests as WK		82	145	15	173	4540	34.92	6	23	227	14
Tests not WK		51	90	6	190	3923	46.70	9	22	36	-
TOTALS		133	235	21	190	8463	39.54	15	45	263	14

379

limited-overs international career

	M	I	NO	HS	Runs	Av	100	50	Ct	St
Sri Lanka	22	22	1	88	683	32.52	-	7	24	1
Australia	30	29	1	79	737	26.32	-	4	23	2
Pakistan	22	21	0	103	551	26.23	1	2	24	2
India	20	18	3	116	487	32.46	1	2	14	3
West Indies	25	23	3	100*	659	32.95	1	6	17	3
New Zealand	20	19	2	81	522	30.70	-	1	18	2
South Africa	15	15	2	77	441	33.92	-	3	14	-
Zimbabwe	10	10	1	101	399	44.33	1	1	23	1
UAE	1	1	0	23	23	23.00	-	-	-	-
Holland	2	1	0	5	5	5.00	-	-	1	1
Kenya	1	1	0	23	23	23.00	-	-	1	-
Bangladesh	1	1	1	87*	87	-	-	1	-	-
Namibia	1	1	0	60	60	60.00	-	1	-	-
In England	56	54	7	103	1816	38.63	3	11	63	6

	M	I	NO	HS	Runs	Av	100	50	Ct	St
Overseas	114	108	7	116	2861	28.32	1	17	96	9
TOTALS	170	162	14	116	4677	31.60	4	28	159	15

		Sri Lanka	Delhi	15.10.1989
Debut		Sri Lanka	Delhi	15.10.1989
HS in Eng	103	Pakistan	Oval	22.5.1992
HS overseas	116	India	Sharjah	11.12.1997

test matches – batting positions

No	Inns	NO	HS	Runs	Av	100	50
1	4	0	45	117	29.25	-	-
2	73	2	190	3231	45.50	8	17
3	35	5	173	1307	43.56	3	5
4	24	1	164	650	28.26	1	2
5	43	5	164	1299	34.18	2	7
6	44	3	123	1421	34.65	1	11
7	12	5	76*	438	62.57	-	3
	235	**21**	**190**	**8463**	**39.54**	**15**	**45**

man of the match awards

1	New Zealand	Perth	7.12.1990	29*	–
2	South Africa	MCG	12.3.1992 WC	77	–
3	Pakistan	Oval	22.5.1992	103	–
4	West Indies	Port-of-Spain	6.3.1994	53	2ct
5	India	Sharjah	11.12.1997	116	1st
6	Sri Lanka	Lord's	14.5.1999	88	3ct
7	Zimbabwe	Edgbaston	18.7.2000	101	4ct
8	Zimbabwe	Lord's	22.7.2000	97	1ct
9	Bangladesh	Nairobi	5.10.2000	87*	–
10	Sri Lanka	Brisbane	17.12.2002	64	2ct

first class career

		M	I	NO	HS	Runs	Av	100	50	Ct	St
1981	Sy	1	2	0	8	10	5.00	-	-	3	-
1982	Sy	1	2	0	16	25	12.25	-	-	4	-
1983	Sy	10	17	4	118*	525	40.38	1	2	4	1
1984	Sy	15	21	3	73	570	31.66	-	4	26	-
1985	Sy	23	36	4	158	1009	31.53	1	5	28	1
1986	Sy	25	39	3	166	1665	46.25	3	14	15	-
1987	Sy	22	34	2	132	1219	38.09	3	8	20	-
1988	Sy	22	32	3	133	1006	34.68	2	6	25	1
1989	Sy	23	42	5	206*	1637	44.24	4	5	55	3
1989–90	Eng/WI	9	18	1	125	516	30.35	1	1	5	-
1990	Sy/Eng	17	29	6	100*	984	42.78	1	9	24	-
1990–1	Eng/Aus	9	17	0	95	497	29.23	-	4	10	-
1991	Sy/Eng	19	34	8	113*	1161	44.65	2	6	24	-
1991–2	Eng/NZ	7	10	2	148	550	68.75	3	2	8	-

		M	I	NO	HS	Runs	Av	100	50	Ct	St
1992	Sy/Eng	19	33	4	190	1234	42.55	2	8	22	-
1992–3	Eng/Ind	7	13	1	74	230	19.16	-	1	4	3
1992–3	Eng/SL	1	2	0	63	66	33.00	-	1	5	1
1993	Sy/Eng	16	28	1	127	1094	40.51	2	8	34	2
1993–4	Eng/WI	7	12	0	143	590	49.16	2	3	5	-
1994	Sy/Eng	16	23	3	142	936	46.80	3	4	20	1
1994–5	Eng/Aus	5	9	4	101*	291	58.20	1	1	3	-
1995	Sy/Eng	10	18	1	151	647	38.05	2	2	23	-
1995–6	Eng/SA	11	16	2	110	769	54.92	2	4	5	-
1996	Sy/Eng	14	24	1	170	966	42.00	1	7	15	1
1996–7	Eng/Zim	4	8	1	101*	324	46.28	1	1	8	-
1996–7	Eng/NZ	5	6	1	173	450	90.00	2	1	22	3
1997	Sy/Eng	15	26	2	271*	994	41.41	2	3	39	-
1997–8	Eng/WI	9	15	1	83	538	38.42	-	5	10	-
1998	Sy/Eng	14	24	2	164	963	43.77	1	5	41	-
1998–9	Eng/Aus	8	16	1	126	530	35.33	2	3	14	-

first class career (contd)

		M	I	NO	HS	Runs	Av	100	50	Ct	St
1999	Sy/Eng	12	20	2	95	511	28.38	-	3	15	2
1999–2000	Eng/SA	9	13	1	95	399	33.25	-	3	21	1
2000	Sy/Eng	10	15	1	124*	451	32.21	2	-	24	1
2000–1	Eng/Pak	5	8	1	59	205	29.28	-	1	9	3
2000–1	Eng/SL	5	9	1	54	191	23.87	-	1	9	2
2001	Sy/Eng	12	18	3	106	581	38.73	1	2	36	1
2002	Sy/Eng	11	16	2	123	751	53.64	1	5	34	4
2002–3	Eng/Aus	6	11	3	71	353	44.23	-	3	16	-
2003	Sy/Eng	13	18	1	98	727	42.76	-	7	36	1
		447	734	81	271*	26,165	40.06	48	148	721	32

Debut		Surrey v. Gloucestershire	Cheltenham	1981
HS	271*	Surrey v. Yorkshire	Oval	1997
BB	1-7	Surrey v. Lancashire	Old Trafford	+1989

Bowling   83.4 over, 446 runs, 3 wickets, Average 148.66, BB: 1-7

Three first-class wickets

1	MP Speight (Sussex)	hit wicket	0	Hove	+1988
2	RF Pienaar (Kent)	lbw	16	Canterbury	+1989
3	WK Hegg (Lancashire)	c Boiling	11	Old Trafford	+1989

first class hundreds

	+ 2nd innings				
1	118*	Surrey	Oxford University	Oxford	1983
2	158	Surrey	Kent	Canterbury	1985
3	132	Surrey	Yorkshire	Oval (1)	1986
4	127	Surrey	Middlesex	Oval (2)	1986
5	105	Surrey	Somerset	Oval (3)	1986
6	132	Surrey	Yorkshire (2)	Oval (4)	1987
7	127	Surrey	Middlesex (2)	Oval (5)	1987
8	105	Surrey	Somerset (2)	Oval (6)	1987
9	133	Surrey	Essex	Oval (7)	1988
10	119	Surrey	Sussex	Hove	1988
11	206*	Surrey	Essex (2)	Oval (8)	1989
12	+148*	Surrey	Middlesex (3)	Oval (9)	1989
13	120	Surrey	Essex (3)	Chelmsford	1989
14	199*	Surrey	Sussex (2)	Oval (10)	1989
15	125	England XI	Leeward Islands	St Kitts	1989–90

16	100*	Surrey	Hampshire	Oval (11)	1990
17	109	Surrey	Gloucestershire	Guildford	1991
18	113*	England	Sri Lanka	Lord's	1991
19	148	England	New Zealand	Christchurch	1991–2
20	101*	England XI	Central Districts	New Plymouth	1991–2
21	107	England	New Zealand	Wellington	1991–2
22	140	Surrey	Sussex (3)	Oval (12)	1992
23	190	England	Pakistan	Edgbaston	1992
24	109	Surrey	Leicestershire	Leicester	1993
25	127	Surrey	Sussex (4)	Hove (2)	1993
26	118	England	West Indies	Bridgetown	1993–4
27	+143	England	West Indies	Bridgetown (2)	1993–4
28	126	Surrey	Lancashire	Old Trafford	1994
29	+119	England	New Zealand	Lord's (2)	1994
30	142	Surrey	Leicestershire (2)	Oval (13)	1994
31	+101*	England XI	Australian XI	Hobart	1994–5
32	151	Surrey	Durham	Oval (14)	1995
33	+150	Surrey	Sussex (5)	Horsham	1995

first class hundreds (contd)

34	+101*	England XI	SA Invitation XI	Soweto	1995–6
35	110	England XI	Orange Free State	Bloemfontein	1995–6
36	170	England	Pakistan	Headingley	1996
37	+101*	England	Zimbabwe	Harare	1996–7
38	153rh	England XI	NZ Select XI	Palmerston North	1996–7
39	173	England	New Zealand	Auckland	1996–7
40	271*	Surrey	Yorkshire (3)	Oval (15)	1997
41	+170	Surrey	Kent (2)	Canterbury (2)	1997
42	+164	England	South Africa	Old Trafford (2)	1998
43	126	England XI	Victoria	MCG	1998–9
44	107	England	Australia	MCG (2)	1998–9
45	124*	England	Zimbabwe	Lord's (3)	2000
46	105	England	West Indies	Old Trafford (3)	2000
47	106	Surrey	Essex (4)	Oval (16)	2001
48	123	England	Sri Lanka	Old Trafford (4)	2002

five dismissals in a first-class innings

1	6ct	Surrey	Lancashire	Southport	1988
2	6ct	Surrey	Leicestershire	Leicester	1989*
3	+5ct	Surrey	Leicestershire	Leicester	1989*
4	6ct	Surrey	Glamorgan	Oval	1993
5	6ct	England	Australia	Old Trafford	1997
6	5ct	England	South Africa	Lord's	1998
7	+5ct	England	South Africa	Trent Bridge	1998
8	5ct	England XI	Combined XI	Centurion	1999–2000
9	+3ct/2st	England XI	Governor's XI	Peshawar	2000–1
10	5ct	England	Australia	Lord's	2001
11	4ct/1st	Surrey	Lancashire	Oval	2002
12	5ct	Surrey	Lancashire	Oval	2002

* Equalled world record for number of catches in a first-class match

eight dismissals in a first-class match

1	8ct	England	Australia	Old Trafford	1997
2	8ct	England	South Africa	Trent Bridge	1998
3	8ct	England	South Africa	Durban	1999–2000
4	9ct,1st	Surrey	Lancashire	Oval	2002

	M	I	NO	HS	Runs	Av	100	50	Ct	St	MM
Sun/NL	186	170	17	125	4652	30.40	7	26	146	14	
BH	80	80	12	167*	3134	46.08	4	24	64	11	
NW/C&G	50	46	8	125*	1842	48.47	3	13	57	5	
	316	296	37	167*	9628	37.17	14	63	267	30	11

Bowling 3 balls, 4 runs v. Somerset (Weston-super-Mare) 5.8.1984
1 ball, 4 runs v. Nottinghamshire (Trent Bridge) 20.5.1990

Debut		Surrey *v.* Gloucestershire	Cheltenham	9.8.1981 (Sun)
HS	167*	Surrey *v.* Somerset	Oval	26.4.1994 (BH)
5 Dis/Inns	7ct	Surrey *v.* Glamorgan	Swansea	27.7.1994 (NW)
	6ct	Surrey *v.* Berkshire	Oval	27.6.1995 (NW)
	5ct	Surrey *v.* Lancashire	Oval	12.5.2002 (NL)

hundreds: 14

1	107*	Middlesex	Oval	10.8.1988	NW
2	100*	Sussex	Oval	16.7.1989	Sun
3	119	Glamorgan	Oval	6.8.1989	Sun
4	125	Lancashire	Oval	6.5.1990	Sun
5	110*	Somerset	Taunton	4.5.1991	BH
6	105*	Leicestershire	Oval	16.8.1992	Sun
7	103*	Middlesex	Oval	30.8.1992	Sun
8	104*	Dorset	Oval	22.6.1993	NW
9	167*	Somerset	Oval	26.4.1994	BH
10	160	Hampshire	Oval	28.4.1996	BH
11	101	Somerset	Taunton	5.5.1996	Sun
12	112*	Derbyshire	Oval	2.6.1996	Sun
13	125*	Essex	Oval	14.8.1996	NW
14	108	Somerset	Oval	8.5.1998	BH

index